# The Party's Primary

Primary elections were supposed to limit the influence of party bosses on the nomination process. The decision to run for House or Senate and a candidate's success in securing the party's nomination for these offices have been considered to be largely candidate-centered. In *The Party's Primary*, Hans J.G. Hassell shows that parties have a strong influence on the options available to voters and shape the outcomes of the nomination process. Drawing on interviews with party insiders and candidates, Hassell highlights the resources parties have at their disposal that are not readily available outside of the party network and the process by which party elites coordinate in support of preferred candidates. Using data from almost 3,000 nomination contests for House and Senate in the past decade, this book shows that parties use these tools to clear the field for their preferred candidate and exert a strong influence on the outcomes of primary elections.

**Hans J.G. Hassell** is Assistant Professor of American Politics at Cornell College. He received his PhD in Political Science from the University of California, San Diego and his BA from Pomona College. Prior to attending graduate school he worked as a campaign and party staffer.

# The Party's Primary

*Control of Congressional Nominations*

**HANS J.G. HASSELL**
*Cornell College*

# CAMBRIDGE
UNIVERSITY PRESS

University Printing House, Cambridge CB2 8BS, United Kingdom

One Liberty Plaza, 20th Floor, New York, NY 10006, USA

477 Williamstown Road, Port Melbourne, VIC 3207, Australia

314–321, 3rd Floor, Plot 3, Splendor Forum, Jasola District Centre, New Delhi – 110025, India

79 Anson Road, #06-04/06, Singapore 079906

Cambridge University Press is part of the University of Cambridge.

It furthers the University's mission by disseminating knowledge in the pursuit of education, learning, and research at the highest international levels of excellence.

www.cambridge.org
Information on this title: www.cambridge.org/9781108420990
DOI: 10.1017/9781108355803

© Hans J.G. Hassell 2018

First published 2018

Printed in the United States of America by Sheridan Books, Inc.

A catalogue record for this publication is available from the British Library.

ISBN 978-1-108-42099-0 Hardback
ISBN 978-1-108-41310-7 Paperback

*To Amy, whose support and encouragement*
*I am grateful to have*

# Contents

# Figures

# Tables

# Acknowledgments

This book is about the role of parties and party elites in primary elections for the US House and Senate. For the last few decades academics have largely considered candidate emergence and primary elections to be candidate-centered affairs. This book challenges that assumption and provides evidence that parties and party elites play a big role in shaping the field of candidates who run in the primaries and in shaping the outcomes of those primary elections.

This book has a long personal history. As a result, there are countless individuals whose input has been crucial in helping develop the ideas found within it. Portions of this project originated as an undergraduate independent study on primary elections, with David Menefee-Libey at Pomona College. David's enthusiasm for teaching and his willingness to take on a little extra work in meeting with me on a weekly basis in the spring of my junior year, to discuss the unique nature of primary elections with an overeager undergraduate, was what began this whole process.

My interest in elections was further enabled by a summer undergraduate research project, funded by Pomona, which opened up the opportunity to work on a campaign in Minnesota that summer. This was further facilitated by the invitation of a political operative working in Minnesota who had worked previously with me in Maine, in the summer of a previous election cycle. This individual, whom I now consider a friend, encouraged me not just to work there through the summer but to take an entire semester off and work as a field staffer for the party through the fall campaign. Working directly for the state party organization and with the network of party elites that cycled through and around the party apparatus allowed me to start to see how the party was involved in the process long before the primary election was held late in the summer. Working as a party staffer allowed me to see firsthand some of the processes described in this book and to talk with countless others who were much more involved in party politics than I was. In short, while the words on the pages are mine, the experiences and insights do not uniquely originate with me and I am grateful for the countless informal conversations that I have had with individuals working in politics, many of whom I am happy to call friends. While there are too many to single out every one, I am specifically grateful for the discussions and banter I had with Bryan Humphreys. Bryan graciously agreed to have a roommate that fall and provided me with hours of conversation and insights throughout that fall campaign. Although he would never admit it, I have found him to be one of the smartest, savviest, and hardest working in the business.

I am also grateful to the many individuals involved in politics who have taken the time to converse with me while I was formally working on this project. In addition, many of the interviews reported in this book would not have been possible without the assistance of friends who leveraged their political connections within both political parties. I am grateful to Paul Waelchli, David Andrews, Joe Andrews, and Adam Dynes for their help. Specific thanks are owed to my cousins, Bill and Ruth Hassell, for their kindness in allowing me to stay with them while conducting interviews in Minnesota.

The actual manuscript has benefited from the comments and feedback of a number of colleagues. Many individuals have read this manuscript, or portions of it, provided feedback, and/or offered support and encouragement throughout the process. For that I am grateful to Craig Allin, Brian Arbour, Andrew Dowdle, James Fowler, Sam Garrett, Boris Heersink, Patrick Hickey, Sam Kernell, Vlad Kogan, Thad Kousser, Gary Jacobson, Eddy Malesky, Seth Masket, David Menefee-Libey, Matt Miles, Hans Noel, Sam Popkin, James Rauch, Brian Schaffner, Jaime Settle, and Neil Visalvanich. I am also thankful for several conversations with Kathy Bawn and John Zaller – when the project was in its later stages – that helped further develop some of the ideas presented here. In the same way, I am indebted to Sam Kernell and Sam Popkin, who made comments early on in the process which forced me to think more rigorously about what evidence was needed to show that parties were not merely jumping on the bandwagons of already successful candidates.

I am also thankful to Caroline Tolbert and her colleagues at the University of Iowa for inviting me to present my work there and for the comments they provided. I am also grateful to David Karol for the invitation to participate in the Hewlett Conference on "Parties, Polarization and Policy Demanders" and the participants at that conference who provided good conversation on the topics of parties and party networks. The paper has also benefited from comments from individuals at presentations at Cornell College, Vanderbilt University, and Virginia Tech, and at the Midwest and American Political Science Association (MPSA and APSA) conferences. I am grateful to a number of individuals who came to those presentations and offered their thoughtful comments, including my father, Lewis Hassell, who showed up and sat in the back of one MPSA presentation. His laughter at one of the quotes that is now in this book helped me know I had something worth sharing.

My grandfather, Norris Finlayson, was willing to read the entire manuscript (twice) and take on the painstaking job of editing the manuscript for clarity and grammar. Despite his best efforts, my own shortcomings as a writer dictate that there may still be passages that are awkwardly phrased in the chapters that follow. However, he saved me (and my readers) on several occasions from particularly painful prose and has helped me to better craft sections of the text to make them more easily comprehended by a nonpolitical scientist.

Sara Doskow at Cambridge University Press has been very helpful in her encouragement and support of the project from the beginning. I am incredibly grateful to the anonymous reviewers who were quick in their response, but more importantly, thorough and insightful. I was blown away by the detail and care given to the manuscript in its initial form.

As an academic, I have been blessed with a number of mentors and colleagues who have been kind enough to guide me and to help me understand what good research looks like. I am especially grateful for the mentorship and kindness of Gary Jacobson and Sam Kernell. Their patience with me and their encouragement have made a big difference in my academic career. I am similarly grateful for the support of Zoli Hajnal and Marisa Abrajano, who have been both gracious and encouraging. I am also thankful to the group of graduate students in the department of Political Science at the University of California, San Diego, while I was there, including Jaime Settle, Lydia Lundgren, Matt Kearney, Vlad Kogan, Justin Leavitt, Dan Maliniak, Chris O'Keefe, Nicole Bonoff, Rob Bond, Michael Rivera, Neil Visalvanich, Devesh Tiwari, Lindsay Nielson, Michael Plouffe, Brad LeVeck, Matt Childers, Dan Smith, and Yon Lupu.

Gathering information on tens of thousands of candidates was a large undertaking. While I did most of the work myself, at junctions when I was too exhausted from searching the Web and NewsBank for dropout dates of obscure congressional candidates, I was able to call on the support of the research assistance of Katy Banks, Ellie Burshtyn, Sandra Gomez, Ryan Kelly, Nick Marn, Alex McGee, Kelly Oeltjenbruns, and Ashley Uphoff, who all provided help in spurts.

I am specifically grateful to my colleagues at Cornell College (the original Cornell), where academic pursuits are interdisciplinary and where teaching and mentoring are a priority. In the Department of Politics I am grateful to my colleagues David Yamanishi, Aparna Thomas, Rob Sutherland, and Craig Allin for the support and encouragement that they gave me, and for the times when they were willing to shoulder my responsibilities of advising new students during New Student Orientation while I was attending poorly timed APSA conferences to present portions of this work. Craig and Rob's ninety-six combined years of service at Cornell also helped a lot in navigating the teaching load and the other aspects of the job. I am thankful to the Cornell College Dean of Faculty, Joe Dieker, for providing funding at timely moments to help in the completion of the manuscript. The manuscript also benefited from a Cornell College Emil and Rosa Massier Award for the Social Sciences and several McConnell Travel Fund Grants that enabled me to present this work in various venues.

I am also indebted to Aaron Hagler, Johanna Schuster-Craig, and Rebecca Wines, who formed the core of a group of junior faculty from a wide range of fields in my first years at Cornell, and who were willing to meet together, read each other's work, and provide comments. In addition to the valuable interdisciplinary feedback that they provided, the deadlines they set helped me keep my research on track amidst the busy one-course-at-a-time schedule.

Lastly, and above all, I am grateful to my family. I am thankful to my parents, Lewis and Mary Bliss, whose praise and encouragement I value immensely. I am especially thankful to my wife, Amy, and to our children, Johannes, Acadia, and Finnegan. Their smiles, their encouragement, the sweet notes they wrote me, and the hugs and smooches they give me when I arrived home make writing a book a much less daunting task.

# The Primary

## *Of Political Operatives and Academics*

*The people can vote for whom they please if they let me do the nominating.*
—Boss Twead[1]

The 2006 Minnesota Senate Republican primary race promised to be a good one. Although he had lost his reelection campaign in 2000 by about five percentage points, former Republican senator Rod Grams saw an opportunity to regain his seat again in 2006 from the man to whom he had lost it in the previous election cycle. Infamously dubbed "The Blunderer" by *Time* magazine, many of Democratic Senator Mark Dayton's failures and bumblings were clearly visible to the public (*Time* 2006), and by early 2005 his approval ratings had sunk into the low 40s (*New York Times* 2005).[2]

The perceived electoral vulnerability of incumbent Senator Mark Dayton was also evident by the quality and quantity of the potential challengers

---

[1] This quote and a number of variants of it have been attributed to Boss Twead. The earliest source I could find was this version of it, cited in a speech given at the City Club of Los Angeles by Francis J. Heney, who was an Assistant Prosecuting Attorney of San Francisco. Heney's speech was covered in the *Los Angeles Herald*. 1908. "Great Welcome Is Given Heney" (May 3) Pg. 3.

[2] Dayton, like a smart politician, recognized that he would face an uphill reelection battle and ultimately decided to pause his political career and not seek reelection to the Senate. It was not clear whether he enjoyed being in the Senate either. Just hours before his term ended, he mused that he would be a better fit for a more "proactive" political job, rather than the deliberative position of US Senator, which he considered too focused on political gamesmanship and procedural maneuvering (Diaz and Doyle 2010). The more "proactive" job he had in mind was the office of Governor, which he would run for and win in 2010 after winning a close primary and then a tougher general election and would then win re-election in 2014 (Grow 2011).

who expressed interest in running for the seat. By early 2005, in addition to Grams, two of the three sitting Republican Congressmen from Minnesota, Gil Gutknecht (R–MN1) and Mark Kennedy (R–MN6), had expressed interest in running, as well as Minnesota Secretary of State Mary Kiffmeyer, former Republican gubernatorial candidate and successful businessman Brian Sullivan, and an up-and-coming conservative State Senator by the name of Michele Bachmann (Black 2005; Hotakainen et al. 2005).[3] Yet the contested, expensive, and divisive primary that many in the Democratic–Farmer–Labor (DFL) Party eagerly anticipated never happened.[4]

While the former Senator and other potential candidates were originally optimistic about their chances, these aspirants to the Senate quickly found that there were serious obstacles to their candidacy. For Grams, those obstacles were neither the challenge of persuading voters nor the problem of rallying grassroots conservative financial support, which he generally enjoyed. Instead, Grams found that, despite the media coverage of his early campaign, the support among grassroots activists, and his previous tenure as US Senator, he struggled to garner the support of the political elites within the party. Grams discovered that party leaders had coalesced their support around another candidate, Congressman Mark Kennedy, who announced his candidacy a short time after Grams (Black 2005). With tacit support from the Bush White House, party leaders, including Governor Tim Pawlenty, moved quickly to support Kennedy. Only days after Kennedy announced his candidacy, state Republican Party Chair Ron Ebensteiner, referring to Kennedy, remarked, "I think we are going to know very shortly who will be the obvious choice" (Hotakainen et al. 2005; Stassen-Berger 2005a). Other candidates felt similar pressure from the party. When fellow Congressman Gil Gutknecht announced in March of 2005 that he was not going to run for the Senate and instead would seek reelection to the House, breaking his previous pledge to limit himself to six terms, he explained that he would not be endorsing Kennedy, stating, "I don't really believe in some of the king-maker stuff that has been going on here in the last three or four weeks"

---

[3] The third member of the Republican congressional delegation, John Kline (R–MN3), might also have expressed interest; however, he had only recently won election to the US House of Representatives during the previous election, after his third attempt in three consecutive election cycles, and was not inclined to run for higher office at that early point in his political career (von Sternberg 2002).

[4] In Minnesota, the Democratic party is known as the Democratic–Farmer–Labor Party formed as a result of the merger of the Minnesota Democratic Party and the Minnesota Farmer–Labor Party in 1944 (Haynes 1984).

(Diaz 2005).[5] This statement came as a surprise to many party leaders, including state party chair Ron Eibensteiner, who explained, "As I heard it, that was the plan (to endorse Kennedy)" (Diaz 2005).

It was Eibensteiner who would draw Grams' wrath only a few days later. When asked by reporters, more than a year before the party convention and primary, about the state of the nomination contest, Eibensteiner remarked that with so many key party leaders supporting Kennedy, "it appears right now that the Republican endorsement is a fait accompli. There is no race" (Diaz 2005). Grams took offense at Eibensteiner's comments and responded forcefully, objecting to what he perceived as heavy-handed attempts to clear the field. "It's an attempt to sabotage the process. He's trying to pick the slate," remarked Grams when asked about Eibensteiner's take on the race. "What kind of third world politics does he want to impose on the Republican Party? The delegates won't be elected for another year. The convention is 18 or 17 months away and Eibensteiner wants to have a single name on a slate. That's kingmaking. I thought the role of the party … was to encourage all good candidates to run" (Homans 2005; Stassen-Berger and Salisbury 2005). In response, almost ironically, the Minnesota GOP issued a statement clarifying Eibensteiner's remarks and explaining that "Chairman Eibensteiner and the Republican Party of Minnesota are currently, and have always been, neutral in the race for the Senate" (Forliti 2005). While the Minnesota Republican Party maintained a façade of neutrality in the primary, behind the scenes the party and party leaders were unmistakably working to clear the field for their preferred candidate.[6]

---

[5] Gutknecht's announcement that he would not be running for the US Senate also coincided with his announcement that he would be running for his House seat again, breaking his original pledge that he would seek to serve no more than 12 years. He did not, however, get a chance to serve his seventh term because he lost a tough reelection campaign to DFLer Tim Walz. After that loss, in a difficult cycle for Republicans, he was asked if he had any future political aspirations. To this inquiry he retorted, "That's a little like asking a woman who's just come out of a 38-hour labor and delivered a 12-pound baby, 'Well, don't you want to get pregnant again?' Not today" (Frommer 2006).

[6] Party involvement can have negative side effects (Herrnson 1988). The clear visibility of the party's machinations in Minnesota would not be costless for those involved. It was Minnesota Republican Party Chairman Ron Eibensteiner's perceived lack of neutrality that would play a significant part in his inability to win reelection as party chair that summer. Challenged by a number of candidates who decried the involvement of the official party in the nomination process prior to the official party endorsement process, Eibensteiner was defeated after several ballots at the meetings of the Party's State Central Committee in 2005 by businessman Ron Carey who, as part of his platform, promised to maintain the party's neutrality until the party's official endorsement process had occurred (Shaw 2005; Smith 2005).

Yet, in spite of his rants, Grams soon realized that without party support he had little chance of winning. Just a month after he had accused the party of engaging in kingmaking, Grams dropped out of the race for the Senate nomination, citing a desire not to "tear the party apart" with a divisive primary that would hurt the eventual nominee's chances. In dropping out of the race, Grams vowed to support the party's nominee and turned his sights to the race for the House in Minnesota's 8th congressional district (Forliti 2005).[7]

Such insider political maneuvers are not uncommon in electoral politics, nor are they unique to the Republican Party. At the same time that the Republican Party of Minnesota was uniting behind a single candidate and dissuading viable alternatives from competing for the nomination, the DFL in Minnesota was doing almost the exact same thing in the exact same election cycle for the exact same seat. Even though DFL chair Mike Erlandson had denounced the fact that viable Republican candidates were "forced out of the Senate race by ... party kingmakers" (Stassen-Berger 2005b), many of the same tactics were used to unite Democrats around Hennepin County Attorney Amy Klobuchar and to convince nationally recognized child advocate Patty Wetterling to pursue a congressional seat in the 6th congressional district instead (Stassen-Berger 2006b). As one individual within the party indicated "There's been pressure on [Wetterling] to get out [of the Senate race] from the start" (Lopez 2006a). Another party insider interviewed in the aftermath of the 2006 election reported that

When [Patty Wetterling] went to talk to [party] leaders and other party officials, she found that most of them were already supporting Klobuchar. I think she dropped out because she realized that ... without the support of party leaders she had no chance at winning. (Hassell 2007)

DFL party elites also worked hard to convince businessman Ford Bell to drop out and to convince wealthy attorney Mike Ciresi not to run against Klobuchar (Smith 2006; Stassen-Berger 2006a).[8] The pressure

---

7  Grams would win the party's endorsement and the nomination for Congress in the 8th congressional district, but was unsuccessful in his attempts to return to Washington, as he lost the general election to Congressman Jim Oberstar in a tough year for Republicans.

8  Some in Minnesota politics suspected that Ciresi, who had come in second to Dayton in the primary in 2000, after having spent close to $3 million of his own money on the primary (McCallum 2000), and who had well-known ambitions to be Senator, had been promised an easier road to the DFL nomination for US Senate in 2008, when Republican Senator Norm Coleman would be up for reelection (North Star Politics 2006; Republican Minnesota 2006). As expected, Ciresi would run for Senate in 2008, but would drop out

Democrats brought to bear on these individuals was clearly evident. At one point during the primary race, Ford Bell decried actions taken by national Democrats, who had come to the aid of Klobuchar's campaign by hosting high-profile rallies and fundraisers, saying, "We have a process here in Minnesota for choosing our candidates. We do not need the national party coming in here. This is not the party of Paul Wellstone if we let the national party come in here and tell us who the candidate's going to be" (Zdechlik 2006).[9]

This one example in 2006 of the intervention of Republican and Democratic Party elites trying to influence the nomination process in Minnesota is not the exception to the rule. Indeed, media coverage of primary races for federal offices is replete with anecdotes of party officials and party leaders, both Republican and Democrat and at both state and national levels, attempting to use their political clout and powers of persuasion to act as "kingmakers." These party elites regularly work to clear the field for a preferred candidate by discouraging others from running for public office. Paul Herrnson (1988) reported in the 1980s that officials from both national parties' campaign organizations indicated that dissuading individuals from running for public office was "one of their most important and difficult election activities," but these officials believed that it had to be done "to allow party members to unite behind and nominate their most electable candidates and then prepare for the ensuing general election," in order to avoid "the bitter aftermath that may follow a hotly contested primary" (54). From the 1980s to the present day, the mentality and objectives of party leaders have not changed. In the lead-up to the 2014 elections, Democratic Senatorial Campaign Committee executive director Guy Cecil, talking about candidate recruitment, said "It's the most important thing that we do. Without a good candidate, it makes your job a helluva lot harder" (Goldmacher 2013).

Yet in spite of these numerous anecdotes, modern scholarship on parties rarely affords them any attention in the nomination process. The

---

before the primary after expressing frustrations that the process was exclusionary and "not really democratic" (Doyle 2008).

[9] Paul Wellstone (D–MN) was renowned for his grassroots organization, especially because of his 1990 campaign against incumbent Senator Rudy Boschwitz (R–MN) when he "[built] on his success as a community organizer and [raced] through the state in a green school bus" and won, even when he was outspent by a ratio of seven to one (National Public Radio 2002). The organization Wellstone Action, founded by Wellstone's surviving children and his former campaign manager after Wellstone's death in a plane crash in 2002, continues to organize workshops focused on grassroots organizing.

decision to run for office, and a candidate's success in securing the nomination, have continued to be considered largely candidate-centered (Jacobson and Kernell 1981; Kazee and Thornberry 1990; Maestas et al. 2006; Maisel and Stone 1997). Instead, the scholarship on a candidate's decision to run for political office has focused on the characteristics and decision-making process of the potential candidate (Abramson et al. 1987; Butler and Dynes 2016; Lasswell 1948; Maestas et al. 2006; Matthews 1984; Rohde 1979; Schlesinger 1966, 1991) and the political environment (Abramson et al. 1987; Brace 1984; Jacobson and Kernell 1981; Rohde 1979).

This is not to say that scholars have not previously recognized that parties are active participants in the nomination process. Academic researchers have long recognized the efforts of parties to be active participants in recruiting candidates (Herrnson 2005; Kazee and Thornberry 1990; Maestas et al. 2005; Seligman 1961) and providing them with necessary resources (Dwyre et al. 2006; Herrnson 1986; Kolodny and Dulio 2003). Recent work has also found that recruitment plays a large role in getting potential candidates to run (Broockman 2014; Preece and Stoddard 2015).[10] In contrast, we know much less about the effectiveness of party efforts to discourage candidates from seeking the party's nomination (but see Niven 2006) or to influence the outcomes of primary elections (Dominguez 2011; Kousser et al. 2015; Masket 2009).

This book attempts to fill that gap and to bridge the differences between political scholars and political practitioners in the understanding of the role of parties in primary elections for US House and Senate by systematically answering the following questions: Are candidates, donors, and other political professionals connected to the party responsive to the cues of party leaders that are so well documented in the annals of campaigns across the country? Or are the decisions of party actors to support certain candidates made entirely on the basis of candidate viability? If party actors are responsive to party cues, are parties and party organizations effective and influential in shaping the options presented to primary electorates and in influencing the outcomes? These questions about the role of political parties in the primary election process are central to this book.

---

[10] Recent work has shown that personal characteristics and gender, however, do have an effect on how receptive individuals are to party recruitment appeals (Butler and Preece 2016).

## PRIMARIES AS A MEANS OF EXCLUDING PARTIES
## FROM THE NOMINATION PROCESS

While media coverage and the accounts of political insiders are rife with anecdotes detailing the parties' political maneuverings, scholars of congressional elections have been more skeptical of the ability of parties and party elites to intervene in the process. Primaries were an institution originally advocated by Progressives in the early 1900s as a way to minimize the influence of party bosses. Because party interests largely controlled nominations prior to the early twentieth century through nominating conventions manipulated through backroom politics, the idea behind the progressive reforms of the early 1900s that changed the nomination process from a caucus and convention system to a primary system was that this provided a way to take power away from these party bosses and turn it over into the hands of the people (Key 1949; Ranney 1975).

This view is clearly evident in the rhetoric of the progressive advocates of primary elections. Most notable of these early twentieth-century anti-party reformers, for his advocacy of the direct primary as a solution to the problem of too much influence exerted by party leaders, was Wisconsin's Robert La Follette. In 1896, La Follette had lost the Republican gubernatorial nomination on the floor of the Wisconsin Republican state convention. Coming into the party's state nominating convention, La Follette claimed to have enough pledged delegates to win the nomination on the opening ballot (Barton 1922; La Follette 1913). But party leaders were successfully able to wrest the nomination away from him through a variety of "persuasive" methods, because the "party's bosses preferred a more docile candidate" (Ranney 1975, 122). Having been thwarted by party bosses, he became a strong advocate of the direct primary as a means to stop party control. Speaking to the University of Michigan's Good Governance Club in 1898, he denounced the party machine and primary elections, explaining,

In this land of the free, dedicated to principles of democracy, climbing by the caucus and the convention, the machine has mounted to power ... It is not government by the people ... If bad men control the nominations we cannot have good government. Let us start right ... To accomplish this we must abolish the caucus and convention by law, place the nomination of all candidates in the hands of the people, adopt the Australian ballot and make all nominations by direct vote at a primary election. (La Follette 1898, quoted in Barton 1922, 106)

Passed over again in 1898 for nomination in the state convention, La Follette was able to rally his supporters and mollify the opposition within the party sufficiently to be nominated and elected Governor in 1900 (Phillip 1909). Once in office, however, La Follette returned with vigor to the cause of primary elections. Nor was La Follette satisfied with minimal progress. He vetoed a bill that would have implemented primary elections for only a small subset of offices, before finally being able to push through a comprehensive primary election reform bill in 1903, with the help of a sympathetic legislature, making Wisconsin the first state to mandate the use of the primary statewide.[11] By 1918, almost all other states had followed suit, mandating the use of primary elections as a means of nominating candidates for federal and statewide office.[12]

The clear rhetoric for the implementation of the direct primary was that it would take power out of the hands of the party organization. The predominant assumption was, and the initial analysis of these reforms indicated, that they were successful in their efforts to remove party influence from the nomination process (Burnham 1970; Lawrence et al. 2011; Merriam and Overacker 1928; Ranney 1975). In this view, the institution of primary elections and the removal of conventions and caucuses as a means of nominating candidates were a revolutionary takeover by Progressives. Antiparty reformers had triumphed over the more traditional party stalwarts and succeeded in wresting power from party bosses and delivering control of the nomination process to the people. Whereas party bosses had a strong influence on the selection of delegates to the party convention and also had the tools and resources to win over the small number of delegates needed to control the nomination process at

---

[11] There is some dispute about whether Wisconsin was actually the first state, as some may recognize Oregon or Minnesota as the initiators of the practice (Harvey and Mukherjee 2006). South Carolina was actually the first state to implement the direct primary as a means of nomination for federal office in 1896. As in other states in the South, however, this primary was not the mandatory way of nominating candidates. Instead, local party organizations could choose how to nominate candidates and use either a primary or a nominating convention, depending on the preferences of party leaders (The Green Papers 2016). South Carolina did not mandate the use of the primary statewide until much later, in 1915. These primary elections in a solid Democratic South ended up being tantamount to election, and provided a means to enact racial discrimination in order to prevent minorities from participating in the electoral process.

[12] A few states, including Connecticut, Delaware, and Utah, originally did not mandate primary elections, but rather had a system whereby individuals not nominated at the convention could choose to challenge convention winners through the primary system. These states have been joined by Colorado in recent years. Additionally in 1971, Virginia began permitting optional rather than mandated direct primaries, thus allowing party leaders to decide whether to hold a primary or a nominating convention, in a similar way to that followed in South Carolina's original system (The Green Papers 2016).

those conventions or caucuses, convincing the general public to support a candidate in a primary was perceived as a much more difficult task.

Opening up the nomination process to a vote by the general public theoretically reduced the ability of party leaders to control the process through backroom deals. The direct primary was put forward as a means of wrenching control of the nomination process out of the grip of party leaders and making elected officials and party nominees responsive to voters, rather than to party leaders. Writing shortly after the near universal adoption of the direct primary, political scientist Charles Merriam wrote

If the party organization fairly represents party sentiment, it will win whether the nominations are made directly or indirectly; but in case of serious conflict, the direct vote seems to give a better opportunity for popular success than the delegate method. (Merriam 1923, 6)

While party leaders may at times have been in agreement with the general sentiments of the rest of the party's partisans, at other times their preferences have not been aligned. The institution of primaries, theoretically successful because of a long history of antiparty sentiment in American political development (Burnham 1970; Hofstadter 1969), thus eliminated this mediator of public opinion and made officials directly responsible to the people. Writing in the middle of these reforms, Progressive leader William Allen White celebrated the success of the implementation of the direct primary, explaining that

Now [the people] are capturing the legislative branch through the primary, which to-day puts over half the United States senators under the direct vote of the people ... [who] will go directly to the people for nominations, and not to the railroads and the public service corporations of their respective states, in short, not to capital as they did ten years ago. (White 1910, 51)[13]

---

[13] Similarly, Senator George Norris (R–NE) argued in 1923 that "one of the objections that is always made to the direct primary is that it takes away party responsibility and breaks down party control. This objection is perhaps the most important of any that are made against the direct primary ... But this objection thus given against the direct primary I frankly offer as one of the best reasons for its retention. The direct primary will lower party responsibility. In its stead it establishes individual responsibility. It does lessen allegiance to party and increase individual independence, both as to the public official and as to the private citizen. It takes away the power of the party leader or boss and places the responsibility for control upon the individual" (Norris 1923, 23, cited in Hofstadter 1955, 263).

Although it is not clear that the institution of primary elections actually did result in the party's immediate loss of control over the nomination process or change party influence in Congress (Hirano et al. 2010; Ware 2002, but see Lawrence et al. 2011), until recently, the common perception has been that primary campaigns are not reliant on the support of party elites and that to win nomination candidates must appeal directly to primary voters (Jewell and Morehouse 2001; Morehouse 1990). In short, as V.O. Key (1964) explained, "throughout the history of American nominating practices runs a persistent attempt to make feasible popular participation in nominations and thereby limit or destroy the power of party organizations."[14] Direct primary elections were seen as the final step in turning that power over to the people rather than leaving it in the hands of party leaders to control the process.

This view of nominations as the decisions of voters has only been reinforced in recent years as debates over changes to primary election rules have largely been framed as debates over what group of people should have a say in the nomination of candidates for public office (e.g. Schumer 2014). Recent debates about the success or lack of success of outsider candidates Donald Trump and Bernie Sanders, for example, have focused in part on the nature of the rules surrounding primary elections (Noel 2016; O'Keefe 2016). While California's Proposition 14 of 2010, which eliminated party primaries in favor of a single primary ballot listing all candidates for office, is the most notable recent alteration to a state's primary system, political parties and state legislatures are continuously changing who is eligible to vote in primaries. Likewise, in 2011 alone, lawmakers in six states introduced legislation to open primaries to unaffiliated voters, while legislatures in 13 other states considered legislation to close primaries to all but party registrants, in order to change the dynamic of who is able to influence the outcome of nominations (Bowser et al. 2011).

---

[14] Key (1964) actually makes the point that the nominating convention grew out of the people demanding a voice in the selection of candidates, which previously was made by the party's legislative caucus. The nominating caucus consisted of party members from both state legislative houses, who met together to determine who the candidates should be in each district, and by 1800 this was the predominant means of party nomination and was used to nominate presidents between 1800 and 1828. This caused obvious objections, raised by those who resided in districts where the seat was held by the opposition party, as such a district had no say in the party's choice of nominee for its own representative.

In short, the move from party conventions to primary elections has caused nomination contests to be framed as candidate-centered affairs, where candidates focus on party voters rather than on winning the support of party elites. In this view of the nomination process, candidates struggle to win over the support of the primary electorate, and the victor is ultimately the candidate who is most successful at taking the campaign's message to that electorate.

## PARTIES AS OFFICE SEEKERS

Only recently have scholars questioned the candidate-centric view of primary election campaigns. Part of the motivation for this change comes from a reconceptualization of political parties. The traditional concept is that of a party of leaders within the organization who are principally interested in the material gains received through holding political office. While the specifics of what constitutes the party may vary, this general view holds parties to be "a coalition of men seeking to control the governing apparatus by legal means" (Downs 1957, 24).

In this view, parties (and identifying and associating with a party) are tools of those who seek office and those who hold office. Parties enable ambitious politicians to accomplish their primary goal of having a successful career in political office (Aldrich 1995). By this account, while politicians may have other secondary goals, specifically the enactment of good public policy or the accumulation of power within government, their primary goal, on which all of these secondary goals rest, is reelection (Fenno 1978; Mayhew 1974). The formal party organizations and their abilities, thus, are designed only with the purpose of serving elected officials and helping them achieve their goals. As such, the party is not driven by ideological goals beyond the need to establish a consistent ideological message that enables voters to trust that parties will keep their campaign promises (Downs 1957; Sulkin 2009).

In this weakest theoretical form, the party is an organizational body designed to service individual candidates and their goals and aspirations. While the party's brand may influence the electoral fortunes of the party as a whole, individual candidates are free to campaign as they wish, and their actions have a much larger effect on electoral outcomes than the party brand does (Fenno 1978; Fiorina 1977; Jacobson 1978). The party's main functionality is as a coordinating mechanism designed to solve collective action problems that arise within the legislature and during

campaign season. Parties help make campaigning more efficient by combining some efforts, such as get-out-the-vote activities and managing
voter files (Aldrich 1995; Jacobson 2010; Kolodny 1998; Menefee-Libey
2000). If parties are merely the formal organizations set up by politicians
to further their electoral careers, it is easy to see why parties would have
little desire to intervene in a primary.

## PARTIES AS POLICY DEMANDERS

Recent research conceptualizing parties as more than just the formal party
organization or those holding or seeking public office has changed the
expectations of what influence parties and party elites might have on the
nomination process. Unlike previous theories of parties, which posit their
formation as the result of the work of enterprising politicians, recent
research has conceptualized parties as a loose network of individuals
and groups who act as policy demanders (Bawn et al. 2012; Koger et al.
2009).[15] Instead of consisting of those inside the party structure, whether
acting as party leaders or bosses or politicians, parties inherently consist
of an extended network of individuals outside of the formal organization,
who are interested in a specific policy agenda (Bawn et al. 2012).[16]

The groups that make up the party coalition are not interested in electoral positions for the sake of holding power or prestige, but rather they
are policy demanders interested in the specific policy outcomes that holding public office enables them to enact. These individuals or groups may
not, however, necessarily be "united for promoting ... some particular prin-
ciple on which they are all agreed" (Burke 1770, 110). Rather, parties are
a "long coalition" of a diverse set of interests and demanders with a wide
range of policy interests. Unable to win control of government unilaterally,
organized groups band together to work to enact policies that will please

---

[15] While this theory of parties has been widely termed the UCLA school of political parties,
because of its origins among a small number of UCLA faculty and graduate students in
the early 2000s, who were the primary proponents of the concept, this text will refer to
it as "the policy demander theory" of parties, believing this term describes the nature of
the theory more clearly.

[16] A third and slightly more nuanced view perceives parties to be a mixture of ideologically
driven policy demanders and office-seeking pragmatists. This argument posits that while
the coalition is made up of ideological activists and organizations, the central formal
party organizations are more likely to be populated with pragmatists who prioritize the
winning of elections over any specific policy (La Raja and Schaffner 2015). This argument is analyzed and tested in more detail in Chapter 7.

all members of the coalition. The negotiating and forming of these coalitions generates the ideological space over which partisan battles are ultimately fought (Noel 2013). Working together under the party umbrella, these individuals and groups coordinate in order to achieve common electoral and policy goals (Bawn et al. 2012; Cohen et al. 2008; Desmarais et al. 2015; Herrnson 2009; Koger et al. 2009; Masket et al. 2012; Nyhan and Montgomery 2015; Skinner et al. 2013), in part by sharing information and electoral tactics (Grossmann and Dominguez 2009; Koger et al. 2009; Nyhan and Montgomery 2015; Skinner et al. 2013).

## Formal Party Organizations as Party Coordinators

While much of the research surrounding the policy demander school of parties has focused on the extended network, there is still evidence that the formal party organizations have an important role to play in this network. Because this is a diverse coalition of groups and interests, the party network needs a means to coordinate its efforts. Previous research has shown that party networks, while consisting of a multitude of interests and groups, are centered on the formal party organizations. The extended party network is organized in a network structure that has national party organizations at the center (Koger et al. 2009). Studies of formal party organizations also find evidence that formal party campaign institutions continue to operate as a central mechanism for coordination of donations to preferred candidates, even while their own fundraising and contribution levels have declined in recent years (Currinder 2009; Dwyre et al. 2006; Dwyre and Kolodny 2003; Jacobson 2010). While parties are diverse, the formal party organizations and the leaders in those organizations are often the focal points that facilitate coordination across these diverse coalitions. This book focuses on party organizations as the coordinators of this larger network of party elites who control and utilize key resources to be used to their political advantage.

## Achieving Policy Goals

This coalition of groups and interests is not interested only in pooling resources to influence government from the outside. While outside groups can lobby government officials to implement their preferred policies, they are unlikely to win on the strength of argument unless they can convince these elected officials that the coalition's preferred policy is also preferred by a substantial portion of the electorate, or, at the minimum, the implementation of the coalition's preferred policy does not incur any costs for the elected official. Even if this organized coalition is willing to attempt to win over the public official by some monetary means, there are a number of substantial principal-agent problems that may prevent the principal (in this case the organized coalition of interests) from monitoring the actions of the agent (the elected official) to ensure that the official is not swindling them of their campaign donations. While open government reforms have made the monitoring of public officials easier in recent times, there continue to be substantial impediments to the ability of policy demanders to ensure compliance with the arranged deals between themselves and the public officials.

Given the limitations of outside lobbying in influencing policy outcomes, these groups know that the most effective way to ensure the implementation of preferred policy is to elect a champion into office, who will vigorously advocate for and defend the coalition's interests (Bawn et al. 2015). Thus, parties conceptualized as a coalition of a diverse but united set of policy demanders have a strong interest in nominating candidates whose interests align with those of the party, more broadly defined. Therefore, the theory of a party as an extended network of individuals and groups centered on the formal national party organization, that work effectively together rests on the ability of these networks to control the nomination process (Bawn et al. 2012). Political parties have an interest in ensuring that the right election candidate emerges from the party's nomination process to give the party the best chance of winning a majority of seats in the Senate and the House and ultimately of obtaining the policies they want (Bawn et al. 2012; Menefee-Libey 2000). Recent research arguing for a broader understanding of political parties has provided preliminary evidence that party support influences electoral outcomes in a small subsample of primary elections (Bawn et al. 2014; Dominguez 2011; Masket 2016) and more broadly in general elections (Desmarais et al. 2015), the most prominent of these being Marty Cohen, David Karol, Hans Noel, and John Zaller's book, *The Party Decides*.

Previous forays into the study of party influence on primary elections have provided some evidence that parties may be more influential in the process than previously assumed. The strongest support for this theory, *The Party Decides*, focuses on the presidential nomination process, however, which is substantively different from the processes of nominations for legislative positions. Moreover, the perceived failure of this book to explain Donald Trump's nomination and subsequent electoral victory in 2016 could be seen as a rebuke to a theory of party influence in nominations, but it could also be seen as an exception to a general trend, because of a unique set of circumstances (Cohen et al. 2016). Although not attempting to explain the presidential nomination process, this book attempts to take a wider view of nominations, in order to better understand the role of parties in the nomination process, how and when they might be influential in that process, and what the effects of their involvement in the primary are on political outcomes. While *The Party Decides* focuses exclusively on presidential nominations, the presidential nomination process is different from most nomination processes in the United States. To understand the ability of party elites to influence policy we need to understand how parties influence nominations more generally.

Studies of nomination processes other than the presidential nomination, which might present a wider and more comprehensive view of party influence in the nomination process, have run into roadblocks, limiting our ability to generalize their findings more broadly. The study of the influence of parties in the nomination process is rife with methodological and informational problems that inhibit the ability of scholars to study the process and draw firm conclusions. One of the major impediments to the scholarly study of the effect of party involvement in primaries has been the lack of public information about party support. In the past, when parties have become publicly involved in the nomination process, they have been subject to public criticism, which caused has serious divisions within the parties. Just as Minnesota Democrats criticized the heavy-handedness of the GOP leadership for getting involved in the GOP Senatorial nomination in 2006, public involvement by party organizations has nearly always invited media criticism from individuals both inside and outside the party, which is viewed by party leaders as detrimental to the public face of the party (Herrnson 1986).[17] As a result, the efforts of parties to clear the field in support of a preferred candidate have been largely clandestine. Simply put, a party's support of a candidate during the primary is generally not public information. Thus, while in private the party may be channeling supporters and nonmonetary resources to its preferred candidate, in public the party remains neutral. Without a clear measure of party support, the bulk of scholarly work has focused only

---

[17] One only need look to the criticism of party insiders mounted by supporters of Donald Trump and Bernie Sanders during the 2016 nomination campaign. Although potential for this criticism was particularly prominent in the 2016 presidential nomination process, it extends back decades, and perhaps even centuries (La Follette 1913; Herrnson 1988).

on what parties do to recruit or discourage candidates, rather than the effects of these efforts to choose primary winners or to clear the field for the party's preferred candidate. Scholarship on the influence of parties on the outcomes is much more limited in its scope and conclusions.

Additionally, even if the party's support is accompanied by an increase in the likelihood that a nonendorsed candidate will drop out of the race, before concluding that such actions were due to party influence one must reject an observationally equivalent alternative explanation, of a bias regarding the person whom party elites choose to support in a primary. It could be that parties are merely jumping on the bandwagon of stronger candidates, who are inherently less likely to drop out of the primary. When a party (or any political organization) holds private information about the likely fate of a candidacy in the primary, it may be tempted to use that information in making the decision to support or not support a candidate, in efforts to "back no losers" and maintain influence within the party (Rakove 1975). If this were the case, party support would merely be an indicator, rather than a cause, of candidate success. As such, it is essential to understand how the party cabal decides which candidate to support and if their decisions are based entirely on primary viability, or on the basis of other characteristics.

## OUTLINE FOR THE BOOK

These problems, however, are not insurmountable, and this book aims to understand better the role that parties and party elites play in shaping the nomination process for the US House and Senate, and how parties and the extended party network of party elites might influence nominations more generally. To do so, this book proceeds in the following way.

Before hurrying into any analysis of the magnitude of the influence of parties and party elites in primary elections, it is important first to outline and to develop a good understanding of *how* parties might be able both to sway the decisions of candidates to continue to run in the primary and to shape the outcomes of that primary race. In order for parties to control the nomination process, they must have a means of controlling the outcomes of primary elections. Chapter 2 delineates the resources available in the party network that are not easily available elsewhere and should have a strong influence on the dynamics of the race. Although parties control access to a multitude of resources that can benefit a candidate in their quest for electoral success, unlike the normal practice in the days when state conventions determined the nomination process, they do not select the nominee directly. Instead, those in the party network, centered on the formal party organization, must muster other resources to create a playing field that benefits the party's preferred candidate.

To identify the causal mechanisms by which party elites might be able to exert a significant influence on the electoral process, Chapter 2 draws on extensive interviews with party leaders and staffers, candidates and campaign staffers, and major party donors. These discussions and interviews provide extensive detail about the resources available through party networks. Because of their political nature, party networks contain a number of key resources, crucial to the development of a political campaign, that are in scarce supply outside that network. The deployment of these resources creates an uneven playing field that benefits the party's preferred candidates. While the specific dynamics may vary slightly by region and by party, party organizations have several assets available to them that can be utilized to help a candidate win and also to encourage undesirable or nonpreferred candidates to go away and find something else to do.

Just because the party network has the means to change and affect the outcome of the primary election, it is not necessarily the case that party elites use these resources to do so. Chapter 3 specifically addresses the question of causality. Are candidates more viable because parties are supporting them, or are parties supporting certain candidates because those candidates are more likely to win their respective primaries? If a party is merely jumping on the bandwagon of an already successful candidate, they merely may be running up the score, rather than changing the already determined outcome. Support for a theory of parties as a networked group of policy demanders, however, requires that parties influence the outcome to obtain their preferred policies in government. This chapter shows that under most circumstances parties are not supporting candidates simply because they are likely to be successful in the primary. Instead, the evidence presented in this chapter shows that party elites take other factors into consideration when deciding which primary candidate to support. While the group decision to support one candidate over another is not random, party actors do not reach such a decision on the basis of the likelihood of the candidate winning the primary election. Evidence from the interviews with party elites, donors, and national and state party officials and staffers from both parties shows that the search to coordinate on a particular candidate is focused on a mixture of a variety of factors including, but not limited to, a candidate's salience among party insiders, the perceived viability of the candidate in the general election, and the repercussions a particular candidate running for a particular office has on other elected positions.

This chapter also examines the question of causality quantitatively. It is here that a measure of party support is introduced and validated. Part of the reason why scholars have not been able to recognize the influential role of parties in primary elections is that national party organizations and networks act discreetly during primary elections, in order to avoid accusations of tampering with local party affairs. To work around this problem, the assembly of evidence in this book relies on a measure built around publicly reported campaign finance data linking parties to candidates. While this is a narrower conceptualization of parties than previously arrived at through looking at the policy demander party network, because party networks are centered on the party electoral committees as a means to encourage electoral victories, the formal party campaign committees act as coordinators of the larger party network in the electoral sphere (Herrnson 1988; Kolodny 1998). While a political party usually does not publicly endorse candidates, both the Republican and the Democratic campaign organizations act as facilitators between potential financial contributors and preferred candidates (Herrnson 1986, 1988; Kolodny 1998; Masket 2011; Menefee-Libey 2000). On this theoretical basis, the strength of the relationship between a candidate and the party can be measured using the candidate's and the party's fundraising networks. This measurement quantifies the levels of support within the party network and identifies the party's preferred candidate.[18]

After having established a means of quantifying the party's support of a primary candidate, the book uses this measure to show that party support does not follow candidate viability. The evidence shows that party support has a strong influence on the subsequent success of the campaign by performing important campaign functions. In contrast, however, campaign success, in most cases, does not predict future party support. This analysis helps confirm the findings from the discussions with party leaders and elites.

---

[18] To show the relationship between this measure and actual connections between a political group and a candidate in a practical manner, the Appendix to Chapter 3 also provides evidence that the strength of a candidate's connection to an interest group increases immediately after the interest group's endorsement, even when controlling for factors such as ideology, partisanship, and fundraising.

While Chapters 2 and 3 show that parties do have the political resources necessary to influence the primary election process and outcomes and that party elites are not merely jumping on the bandwagon of already successful candidates, Chapters 4, 5, and 6 examine the effect of being a party-preferred candidate on the likelihood that a candidate will stay in the primary and ultimately win the nomination. The book proceeds by first exploring the ability of the parties to influence the candidacy decisions of primary candidates running for the US Senate and House. Chapter 4 measures the party support each candidate received in every senatorial primary race between 2004 and 2014 and explores how the strength of that relationship between the candidate and the party influences a candidate's decision to stay in the race. Chapter 5 does the same for candidates in primaries for the US House. Analysis in these chapters provides strong evidence that a candidate's party support significantly increases the likelihood that a Senate or a House candidate will remain in the primary race.

Yet not all candidates are responsive to their party's pressure. Chapter 6 examines what happens when candidates buck the party's preference that they exit the race and instead continue to fight for the nomination. Consistent with earlier accounts, in Chapter 2, party-supported candidates are significantly more likely to win primary elections. Contrary to the hopes of the progressive reformers, all of this evidence shows that primary elections are not a foolproof blockade against the influence of parties in primary elections. Party-supported candidates consistently gain access to the resources and tools that they need to run successful campaigns, while candidates without party support struggle to do so. Because of these resources, party-supported candidates enjoy significantly more success at winning a party's nomination than do candidates without party support.

Finally, after the effect that party insiders have on the ability of candidates to win party nominations has been established, the book's concluding chapter discusses some of the normative implications of these findings on the primary elections process. While a full detailing of the normative implications of these findings would comprise a book in itself, this book looks at the impact of party control of the nomination process on the polarization of American politics.

One recent argument pertains to the perceived need to increase the strength of parties in order to combat increasing polarization. This argument is based on the premise that while a party may be a network of policy demanders, there are many actors within the formal party organization that are more likely to be pragmatists than pure ideologues or strict policy demanders. According to this theory, these pragmatists are more likely to be found within the party organization and there they work to support more moderate ideological candidates. Because the formal party organizations act as coordinators of the larger party network, Chapter 7 uses the measure of party support to test how candidate ideology differs between candidates with and without party support. While party-supported candidates are generally more moderate, the balance of evidence suggests that the party's preference for moderate candidates is most likely the result of sincere ideological preferences rather than for pragmatic or strategic reasons. In primary elections that lead to competitive general elections, the ideology of party-preferred candidates is not significantly or substantively different from those of the alternative primary candidates that parties could choose to support. As a result, party influence in primary elections has reduced polarization. This moderation, however, may be subject to change as different actors take control of the party apparatus.

All of these chapters, combined, provide a clearer picture of the nature of the party's influential role in primary elections and the impact it has on our political system. In short, this book argues that parties play a larger role in the nomination process than previously recognized and that the influence that parties have has a significant effect on the outcomes of the American democratic process. Primary elections are not the impenetrable wall, preventing the influence of party elites and power brokers, that the Progressives intended them to be. While it is not in the proverbial "smoke-filled back room" where parties nominate candidates through brokered conventions and backroom deals, parties do play a role in the choices presented to primary voters. Rather than being disinterested and uncoordinated individuals who merely respond to a candidate's ambition and political abilities, party elites are actively engaged in determining the choices available to voters in primary elections and in influencing the outcomes of the primary elections. This evidence fundamentally alters our understanding of primaries, candidate emergence, and the roles of parties in these processes. Parties are not merely neutral players. Their involvement in the process has a significant and substantial influence on nomination outcomes and also on the choices presented to voters. Such evidence supports a wider view of a party as an extended network, centered on the formal party organization which is interested in ensuring the nomination of a preferred candidate. This network, when effectively coordinated and acting in a unified way, enjoys substantive success in its efforts to usher its preferred candidate through the nomination process in hopes of winning public office.

# 2

# The Sources of Party Strength

*[To get the right candidates] we use all the tools in our toolbox. Some of them are sharp; some of them are blunt; some of them are softer. But we use every tool.*
— Representative Steve Israel, Chair of the Democratic Congressional
Campaign Committee in 2013[1]

Party kingmaking requires the political resources necessary to crown a nominee. It was these resources that were on display in the 2008 Republican Primary for the US Senate in Nebraska as party elites worked to clear the field for then US Secretary of Agriculture, Mike Johanns. Going into the 2008 election cycle, incumbent Republican Senator Chuck Hagel recognized that he was facing a tough reelection campaign as national Democrats were pushing hard to recruit former Nebraskan Governor and US Senator Bob Kerrey to run for the seat. Hagel's struggle for reelection, however, would start within his own party. By 2008 and even by early 2007 many of his public positions, specifically those on immigration and the Iraq War, had left him at odds with many of the groups in the Republican Party coalition. Hagel had been quick to criticize the Bush administration's handling of the Iraq War, calling the administration full of "arrogant self-delusion reminiscent of Vietnam" (Scott 2007), calling the 2007 troop surge "the most dangerous foreign policy blunder in this country since Vietnam, if it's carried out," and saying about Vice President Dick Cheney's assertion in 2005 that the insurgency was in its "last throes" that "if that's winning, then he's got a different definition of

---

[1] Quoted in Goldmacher (2013).

winning than I do" (Reeve 2012; Whitlock 2012). Likewise, Hagel had staked out a more liberal position than that of his Nebraskan colleague Ben Nelson on the subject of immigration reform, supporting a policy position dubbed by conservative activists as amnesty for illegal immigrants (Pore 2007). Not coincidentally polls in late 2006 showed that Hagel actually had a higher approval rating among Democrats than he did among his fellow Republicans (SurveyUSA 2006).

In light of the obvious dissatisfaction that several of the factions within the Republican Party coalition felt with Hagel, several credible primary challengers, encouraged by these dissatisfied groups within the party, began to express interest in running for Senate regardless of whether or not Hagel kept his promise to serve only two terms. In the early spring of 2007, two prominent Republican public officials, former congressman and Omaha mayor, Hal Daub, and sitting State Attorney General, Jon Bruning, began to make plans and to lay the groundwork for their campaigns to seek the nomination even if it meant challenging an incumbent for the nomination (Tysver 2007c; Walton 2007b).[2] Later that spring internal polls released by Bruning's campaign showed Hagel losing head-to-head matchups in the Republican primary, an ominous sign for the incumbent Senator (Walton 2007a). The presence of the looming (and likely successful) primary challenge encouraged Hagel to keep his promise and abide by his self-imposed term limits in September of that year. Almost immediately thereafter both Bruning and Daub would convert their exploratory committees into official campaign committees seeking to secure the party's nomination (Walton 2007d).

Yet, almost as soon as they got into the race, both Bruning and Daub got right back out. Just ten days after officially declaring his candidacy, Daub abruptly reversed course and announced that he would not contest the primary, saying that it would not help the national Republican Party's efforts. "It's too important for me to put political consideration ahead of the country and of the state's best interests," he explained upon announcing he would withdraw from the race (Tysver 2007b).

At a more personal level, however, Daubs realized he was not going to get the support of the extended party network. State and national party leaders both, this time with the explicit support of the Bush White House, had moved quickly to support Mike Johanns even before Johanns

---

[2] In obvious reference to the objections that several groups within the party had to Hagel's policy stances, in his announcement speech in early 2007 Bruning indicated that his chief issues would be the war in Iraq and illegal immigration (Tysver and Reed 2007).

had announced his candidacy (Thompson 2007). The support of the party and the network surrounding it provided Johanns with substantial resource advantages, against which Daub recognized that he would not be able to compete. "The system has decided that Mike Johanns will be the frontrunner, and (he) will have a substantial [campaign and fundraising] advantage," Daub explained (Tysver 2007b).[3] The resources which the party was able to provide for its preferred candidate were the motivation for Daub to exit the race.

In dropping out of the race, Daub indicated that concerns about a competitive general election had encouraged Republican elites to consolidate quickly around a single candidate and that as a result other candidates would struggle to get the resources they needed to mount a competitive primary campaign. At that point in time former Democratic Senator Bob Kerrey was considering running for the seat. Daub explained that there was a "Kerrey fear factor [among Republicans] that seems to have swept into the national thinking about why they're so intent on focusing on this primary race in Nebraska" (Tysver 2007b).[4] Motivated to eliminate the anticipated negative effects of an extended and possibly bitter and expensive primary election, party elites consolidated quickly behind Johanns. Reading clearly the writing on the wall, Daub dropped out of the race almost a month before Johanns would even officially enter the race. Bruning would follow Daub's exit just a month after Johanns' official announcement, bowing to strong pressure from state and national party leaders, including the White House, leaving Johanns as the only credible candidate in the Republican primary (Tysver 2007a).[5]

---

[3] Daub had previously expressed frustration when NRSC chief John Ensign had called each member of the Nebraska congressional delegation individually as well as the current governor (all of them Republicans) to gauge their opinions on the Senate race and encourage them to support Johanns, if he were to enter the race. At the time, Daub pushed back forcefully, saying that "The outsiders should keep their noses out of Nebraska Republicans' business" (Thompson 2007).

[4] Ultimately Kerrey would not run. Johanns would waltz into the Senate, beating his opponent, businessman Scott Kleeb, by almost 20 percentage points.

[5] Bruning claimed that the decision to exit the primary around Thanksgiving of 2007 was his decision and not that of the national Republican Party. "This decision was not made in haste or under pressure. This decision was mine and mine alone," he explained, on leaving the race. However, many others thought otherwise, pointing to a President Bush fundraiser for Johanns that would occur shortly after Bruning dropped out and other signals of a clear national party preference for Johanns (Tysver 2007a). Talking about the events that led to Bruning's exit, Daub remarked, "I see it as indirect [party] pressure. And I think it's just as pernicious as the obscene costs of running for office" (Tysver and Reed 2007).

This chapter takes a closer look at what campaign resources party organizations might be able to offer candidates, that are difficult to obtain elsewhere. While the 2008 Republican primary for the US Senate in Nebraska provides a good example of a clear national party preference for a particular candidate, more importantly this example also provides insight into a number of crucial resources that the party was able to provide for their preferred candidate, which gave Johanns a substantial electoral advantage. Although parties have a vested interest in ensuring that the right sort of candidate makes it through the primary, in order to get the candidate through the process they must also have the resources or power to do so. Political insiders can claim that party leaders act as kingmakers, but without any tools that bestow political leverage, the party's preferred "king" would gain no particular advantage in the fight for the nomination.

As part of the process of examining any claims of influence the alleged kingmakers might have, it is essential to first scrutinize the resources that parties might have at their disposal to help candidates. Are the claims that parties are influential in the process even politically feasible? What tools and resources do parties have that would be of benefit to a party-supported candidate? Is there a documentable process that would allow political party elites to wield influence over potential candidates and to direct those candidates down different political paths or otherwise thwart their efforts to secure the nomination?

While the example of the Nebraska Senate Primary indicates that access to the party network provides at least one additional resource that can significantly aid candidates seeking the nomination, most notably the support of the President and the access to important campaign funds, this chapter looks more carefully at the variety of resources that the party can provide through the perspective of those engaged in the party nomination process. A better understanding of the power of political parties and the tools at their disposal enables us to understand not only how much parties influence the nomination process, but how and why party support is influential in nomination politics. Before proceeding to examine the magnitude of any effects that parties have, it is important first to understand the process by which they might have an effect on candidate success. This understanding alleviates concerns that party elites are merely flocking to already viable candidates as opposed to driving the process. Looking deeper, understanding the origins of party power provides a clearer assurance that the effects we find are the product of party influence. Furthermore, a clear knowledge of the tools parties have also allows us to understand the nature of that power, and how it might change in the future as the political environment changes and as different types of candidates with different backgrounds emerge on the political scene.

Tracing the pathways through which the power of political parties flows is difficult. Most of what parties do and the means by which they do it is highly sensitive. As a result, the efforts of parties to clear the field in support of a preferred candidate are largely clandestine. Although we see glimpses of party maneuvers and how they influence the actions of candidates in the vignette that opens this chapter, we rarely get the complete picture. Parties and party elites have a large incentive to keep their internal discussions and processes secluded and private. Political parties must act discreetly in support of candidates to avoid being perceived as improperly intervening in the local democratic process. Although political parties have taken public stances on primary candidates on rare occasions in the past, those stances have prompted undesirable media scrutiny as well as criticism both from within the party and from opponents (Herrnson 1988; Lopez 2006b). When multiple candidates of the same party compete for the nomination, the party must be careful to avoid the appearance of meddling, so as not to provide fodder for opponents and not to offend potential general election supporters.

Yet, a knowledge of the tools available to parties and the process of party coordination and support is essential to gaining a complete understanding of whether or not parties influence and affect the nomination process, and if so, how. Without a good comprehension of the origins of political party power, we lack insight into how that power works and when it might increase or decline.

## THE INSIGHTS OF POLITICAL INSIDERS

To appreciate better the resources at play which may not be clearly visible to an outside observer, this chapter chronicles the source of party influence as seen by those within the inner circles of the party. The evidence documenting party resources comes from interviews and conversations between 2013 and 2015 with twenty-six party elites, donors, and national and state party officials and staffers from both parties active in party politics in California, Colorado, Connecticut, Florida, Georgia, Iowa, Maine, Minnesota, Montana, Ohio, Pennsylvania, and Washington, DC.

These interviews draw upon the work of prominent scholars such as Richard Fenno (1978), whose interviews and open-ended surveys provide insights into the behaviors of political elites. The chapter also relies upon analysis of news coverage from many of the competitive federal election primaries for House and Senate in the last decade and a half, both in races where candidates fought until the end and in instances where candidates dropped out before the primary date. Examining these resources and talking to individuals intricately involved with the party allow for a better understanding of how party support advantages primary candidates favored by the party. By better understanding the tools and resources available to party elites that are not available outside the party network, we can gain insight into the process by which party support helps candidates win and encourages other candidates to drop out. Knowing first the origins of party power can help us to understand better why and when parties are influential.

While not a fully representative sample of political operatives and party elites active across the United States, these individuals come from both large and small states, are from both parties, and have many years of political experience. The choice of states where interviews were conducted was made to provide a diverse group of states and to maximize the utility of personal connections and the connections of acquaintances from both parties. A more detailed explanation of the sampling and interview methodology can be found in the Appendix to this chapter.

The snowball-sampling process resulted in a sample of eighteen Republicans and eight Democrats. These interviews did reveal some differences in unity and in network structure between Democrats and Republicans, but the political aspects described in this chapter were well detailed in both parties.[6] While there are differences between (and even within) states in regard to the structure and organization of party elites (Bawn et al. 2014; Masket 2009), no information from these interviews is included that was not confirmed from multiple sources. In addition, many of the individuals interviewed had worked in more than just one state and mentioned specific experiences in other states when answering the questions posed.

Consistent with previous work that details the structure and flow of party networks surrounding campaigns, many of these individuals had held a number of different roles in the party and on different campaigns

---

[6] One of the ways in which respondents repeatedly indicated that Republicans and Democrats differed in their coordination on candidates was that Republicans were more likely to fall in line, while group conflicts within the Democratic Party at times made coordination more difficult. In many ways, these responses echo many of the findings of Grossmann and Hopkins (2016) about the differing ideological and issue-oriented approaches of the Republican and Democratic Parties, respectively.

(Masket et al. 2012; Nyhan and Montgomery 2015; Skinner et al. 2013). All individuals interviewed had been involved in a significant way in the campaign process, and many had held multiple positions in formal party organizations or in campaigns or both.

Sixteen of the interviews were in-person interviews, with the rest being conducted by phone. Because talking openly could involve some risk, respondents were notified in the initial request for an interview, and reminded again in the informed consent form, that the identity of the interviewees would be concealed except in the cases where the respondent mentioned a specific individual who was a public personality and the interviewee's involvement with the individual named was publicly known. Therefore, many direct quotes are edited to withhold information that might provide insight into the identity of the respondent.

In all the interviews, respondents were asked about their role and involvement in campaigns and party politics and about their initial entry into party politics. Depending on their background, these political insiders were also asked questions about how they and other party members decide to support particular candidates. In their responses, many of these individuals elaborated on their own experiences and about the role that the party had played in specific primary campaigns in which they had been participants or close observers. All individuals were also asked about the effect of party support and how and why parties (and party elites) might be influential in affecting primary outcomes.

Individuals on both sides of the transactions between parties and candidates identified three resources that, while found in abundance within the party network, are scarce outside of that network. There was a general consensus among political elites that parties had privileged access to political campaign resources, monetary resources, and media connections in a way that those outside of the system did not. These essential resources are key components of a successful political campaign, without which candidates struggle to communicate with party members and donors and ultimately to win votes in the primary. Many of these resources are interconnected as well, leading to a cycle that reinforces early candidate success. Lastly, candidates and party elites also indicated that they viewed parties as the pathway to political influence even outside of the formal government structure. This perception of the pathway to power allows parties not only to influence immediate outcomes, but also to shift the long-term expectations of politically ambitious individuals. Parties thus controlled access to the political status and influence which ambitious politicians sought.

## CAMPAIGN STAFFING RESOURCES

In response to questions about why candidates without party support who seek the nomination might face an uphill battle, party elites identified three essential campaign resources which, while found in abundance inside the party network, are difficult to obtain outside of that network. The first of these essential political resources is competent and experienced campaign staff. To run an effective campaign, candidates are increasingly reliant on professional campaign staff who have experience in the many aspects of campaigning that are critical to electoral success. Campaigns must create television advertisements, produce and distribute direct mail, manage voter lists, put together capable fundraising infrastructure, and organize and coordinate volunteer operations. The knowledge and expertise required to perform all of these tasks has increased to the point where specialized expertise is essential to getting a candidate's message out effectively (Hassell and Marn 2015; Johnson 2007; Medvic 2001). Getting individuals with the experience and the expertise necessary to manage all of these different technical aspects of the campaign is much easier when a candidate has the help and support of the party network. Asked to elaborate on why party-supported candidates have inherent electoral advantages in primary elections over candidates without party support, one party official explained,

There are two reasons the party's preference is upheld. One, people don't run. And two, if they do run, they run inept campaigns. The smart campaign people get behind the party's candidate and there's no one left for the candidate that wants to challenge the party's candidate.

Convincing high-quality campaign staff to join the campaign team is best accomplished through the party network. Finding individuals with the necessary experience and ability to carry out the many demanding tasks of a campaign is difficult to do outside the network of the party.

Party leaders and elites also have a strong influence on the ability of candidates to adequately staff their campaigns. One party staffer related an instance in a Senate primary where a campaign had asked party leadership for a recommendation to fill a high-profile position in the campaign leadership. Party leaders and elites were concerned about the strength of that candidate in the general election and as a result, party leadership intentionally recommended the candidate hire a political staffer whom party leaders perceived to be under-qualified to fill that position. Campaign consultants and staff are an intricate part of the party network, and party-supported campaigns are connected to competent staffers through these networks (Nyhan and Montgomery 2015).

Furthermore, the right staff also allows the candidate to connect further with other influential players within the network. As one major campaign fundraiser explained,

Candidate success has to do with who they're putting on their team. If you're running for statewide office and you want to be successful you've got the best political strategist, and the best fundraiser, and the best whatever. And then you've got a finance committee of people that are actually willing to pick up the phone and say, "Hey, I'm supporting candidate X, I want you as my golfing partner to support candidate X, and I want you to come to my house and hear him, and then I want you to write him a check." You can spend a lot of time recruiting volunteers and people on your team, and if they're the wrong people. Guess what? You lose.

In addition, having the right campaigns staff also allows candidates to tap into party networks outside of their direct connections within the party. One party staffer elaborated on this idea clearly,

Candidate success has to do with who they're putting on their team. Staff choices are very important because they've gone through the political battles. They know that if I want to do well in a particular county and win a particular section of the state I need to get Ron and Mary on my team because Ron and Mary control this local political organization (the donors and the volunteers) and this area and if I don't have them, I can write this one off. What you end up with is a small group of people who know who the players are, and you have to get that small group of people on your team to succeed.

Outside of the party network there is a dearth of competent and experienced campaign staff who know how to run a successful campaign and who can facilitate the political connections necessary to leverage support across the state. Without a competent staff, a candidate's campaign struggles to gain traction with donors willing to give to political candidates and has trouble connecting with and persuading primary voters.

## MEDIA ATTENTION

In addition to the connections to political resources that the party provides, the political elite also have close working relationships with members of the news media, which enables them to promote party-preferred candidates. As one former party chairman explained,

One of the biggest resources the party can bestow is perceived credibility. They'll drop the person's name to Politico or Daily Caller or organizations like that and suddenly that candidate has hit the radar. They can create the buzz that this person looks like they're an up and comer who has a lot of people rallying behind them whether that's true or not, but they can create the media hype and the perception that they're a leading player.

The party's access to the media and its professional working relationship with individuals in that profession allows its senior members with media connections to plant information that boosts the candidacy of a preferred candidate. Candidates with professional campaign staff are much more likely to express a belief that the message communicated through the media is representative of the campaign's overall message than are candidates without a professional staff (Hassell and Marn 2015). Without party connections candidates struggle to gain the attention of the media or to gain any traction around their candidacy. Because individuals within the party have extensive connections with the media and use those connections with frequency, it is easy for them to get the media to create the perception among party elites and even among primary voters that the party's preferred candidate is the best choice and also the most viable general election candidate.[7]

This media attention, and the creation of a perception of electoral inevitability, especially in political outlets, are also important for the influence they have on political donors. This media coverage provides the candidate with material it can use to leverage the support of major donors. As one party leader explained,

The party will put the word out on the street through the various political journals. So if the party drops the line to some political journal that I'm the best candidate and the best shot to win and they publish that I'm going to take that and print it out and blast the donors with it.

This is effective because of the desire of major donors to be able to have access to public officials. As this particular leader further explained,

Donors are business people, they've made their money because of good business decisions, and most of them look at it as an investment. They want to go with a winner and they want to make sure they have access. So they want to put their money on somebody who can win the general election, or they're led to believe is going to be the winner. And so the perception that the party creates can become the reality because the candidate that doesn't have the perception because the

---

[7] There is an extensive literature on the effect of horse-race political coverage which provides benefits to the front-runner and pushes voters to have a more favorable disposition toward and to support the perceived front-runner both with votes and financially (Ansolabehere and Iyengar 1994; Hinckley and Green 1996; Mutz 1995).

powers that be haven't put that behind them, they're going to find it hard when they knock on that donor's door to get them to give that $2500 or $5000 or whatever the max is.

Party connections with the media create the proper perceptions about a candidate that are necessary to sway donors who, in order to facilitate their access to public officials, are looking to contribute to candidates who will win.

### MONETARY RESOURCES

Media attention is not the only means whereby party support can swell the campaign coffers of aspiring candidates. Many party leaders and elites are donors themselves. Just like campaign talent, candidates recognize that without party support it will be difficult to acquire the monetary resources necessary to compete in a competitive primary. As Hal Daub explained when he dropped out of the primary to replace outgoing Senator Chuck Hagel in late 2007, "I was in Washington (last) Monday and Tuesday and came away convinced (Mike) Johanns was (the party's) chosen spearcarrier. He will have all the money he needs" (Walton 2007c). Daub recognized that the resources which the party would provide for Johanns would make it difficult for him to compete in the primary.

Some of these messages to key party donors are even communicated directly from party leaders. As one former party leader explained,

If all of a sudden someone in the party sends you a message saying this is the guy we think is best positioned, well you're more likely to get a big check as opposed to somebody who's coming in when the party is pointing to somebody else.

While not often vocalizing it clearly in the public sphere, because of concerns about possible charges of antidemocratic actions, party leaders are not shy about funneling staff or supporters or donors to particular candidates.

Alternatively, party actions can effectively dry up the sources of funding for other candidates. At times, party leaders actively discourage donors from giving to particular candidates whom they do not want to run. As one former campaign staffer for Representative David Minge (D-MN), who was running for Senate in 2002, indicated, the party's efforts to discourage Rep. Minge from running were targeted at the donor class.

(The Minority Leader Dick) Gephardt, or his people, went to all the major donors or people who could help out with fundraising and told them basically to not give money. I don't think it was a hard sell for them, basically telling them to hold off, or let the field develop, or see what happens if a better candidate emerges, and so David couldn't raise the funds because they had all been told to wait.[8]

Party elites, leaders, and candidates all indicated that direct party messages are highly influential in encouraging donors to give or to refrain from giving to party-preferred candidates.

Even without obvious party cues or connections with major party fundraisers, party donors pick up on the party's subtle cues because of the close party network. As one fundraiser explained,

The donors are all connected to each other. They all know each other. And if they don't know each other, they all know somebody who knows somebody who knows them. It's a small group and they talk, they know where each other stand and there's a lot of information out there about who they're supporting and why.

Party donors are also likely to share information and take cues from each other. Because these donors are highly connected within the party, many of their decisions to donate to a candidate revolve around their connections. As one donor explained, "How can I not support this person, I've known them since my first race? Or I've known them since 1984. That's generally how I make all my decisions now." Even if donors are not actively involved in the party's decision-making process, they still benefit from their connections within the network. As one major party donor explained about a less attentive fellow donor,

When I go to talk to [Vincent Hartford], who doesn't or is no longer actively attending local party meetings or involved in the process, he's always trying to pick my brain about what's going on and where things stand so that he can get a better idea of who he should support.

The effect of party support on the fundraising success of potential candidates is not entirely the result of the message that the party leaders send either directly or indirectly. Part of the inability of candidates without party support to gain traction with party donors also stems from a lack of well-connected campaign staff. Both Republican and Democratic

---

[8] This will be addressed in more detail in Chapter 3; for now, note that Gephardt was not concerned about the ideology or viability of a Minge candidacy. Rather he was concerned about getting someone who could win Minge's district if Minge left to run for Senate.

Party elites indicated that having well-connected fundraisers on the campaign team is essential to gaining access to acquire the necessary monetary resources. As a fundraiser in one state explained,

It's a small pool of major donors, people who will give more than $500 in a single check. It's a small group of people. And the people who work the 500 or 600 major donors is a very small group of people ... It's not rocket science to figure out that to run a good campaign you need those individuals [the key fundraisers]. You need access to the major donors.

Candidates without party support struggle to access the donor network necessary to mount a successful campaign. One candidate explained,

I had donors I would call who would go 'ppphh, who are you? Please, be serious' ... and hang up on me basically. A lot of them would meet with me to see if there was more behind that, but I would say that more from the realists in politics, the—not the zealots—but the people who are there all the time, it was more from them, just giving it a practical analysis saying 'I don't think there's any way, I don't know why you're wasting your time.'

Without party support, many candidates feel they are "wasting their time" in their attempt to drum up the financial resources necessary to fund a successful campaign.

These facts are often clearly communicated to potential candidates in an attempt to persuade those candidates not to challenge the party's preferred candidate or to discourage them from entering the race in a particular year. As one local party official explained,

The local party doesn't do a whole lot of trying to talk people out of races, but the national party has a different stance on that. There are a lot of people that, in their eyes, aren't viable right off the bat. I've been in conversations along the lines of asking candidates to maybe reconsider or just being very blunt with them that they're not going to get the support of national Democrats because they don't have what it takes to be a viable candidate.

The support of party elites and major players in the political network is essential to facilitate the candidate's acquisition of monetary resources within the party network. Having access to and support from party elites opens up streams of financial resources within the party network which are essential in running a fully operational and successful primary campaign.

## POLITICAL ASPIRATIONS

The last of the reasons that candidates and party officials mentioned repeatedly as a motivation for candidates to get out of the way of the party's choice was the perception of the political influence which parties have on the political careers of the politically ambitious candidate in the longer term. Not only does running against the party's choice present an uphill campaign, but also such a quixotic campaign risks offending key players within the party network whose support may be essential in enabling politically ambitious individuals to realize their future political aspirations. Ruining relationships within the party network reduces opportunities for future influence in other political spheres. Most candidates are unwilling to damage the relationships within the party that are critical to their political future because the chances of immediate success in the primary when running against a party-supported candidate are perceived as small. One former candidate in a Republican congressional primary explained that challenging the party-backed candidate would not help him achieve his goal of winning office. When asked about why he ultimately decided not to challenge an opponent in the primary, he responded,

Ever heard of Reagan's 11th commandment? Ok, I think the truth behind that, and there is truth to it, and there's good cause, but the truth is that newspapers are generally more left of center and they will jump at the chance to print something about somebody on the right...So, if you want to [challenge the party's candidate], you can get press, but it's like Benedict Arnold. The Brits didn't want him because he was a traitor and he certainly wasn't going to go back to America, and it's the same kind of thing. If you do that, as a Republican, you're done. So you get ostracized from the party and the Democrats aren't going to pick you up. The media will take you and use the heck out of you and spit you out and you're going to be partyless after that.

One of the party's chief sources of power is the party's potential support, neutrality, or even antagonism shown for the ambitious candidate, in future attempts for office. Both former candidates and party officials explained that part of the reason why candidates exit the primary is because they have aspirations to political office in the future. As one former party leader explained,

Why piss off a bunch of people you're going to need someday? That's the other thing, when you run against the "anointed one" all you end up doing is pissing off people you might need someday, and you look like the hero when you announce that you're not going to run against the "anointed one."

Candidates who aspire to elected office recognize that by bucking the party they are doing so at the cost of future opportunities. Thus, only when candidates can see a clear pathway to victory in the nomination that same year will candidates continue forward even without the support of the party elites and perhaps even in opposition to party elites. As we will see in Chapter 5, the pathway to a primary victory in the face of party opposition is rarely an easy one, and therefore candidates are loath to traverse it and risk forgoing future political opportunities.

In brief, while a frustrated candidate may be inclined to buck the party, the bottom line is that most have political ambitions which are best realized through political parties and the networks that surround them. By acting on an urge to ignore the wishes and preferences of the party, these ambitious politicians would be forgoing that future opportunity in exchange for an outside chance at the nomination in the present.

## CONCLUSION

Most candidates who run for federal office have strong political ambitions. Even if they are most interested in pursuing a specific set of policy outcomes, they must first hold office in order to realize those goals. These individuals have aspirations to hold political office and to be influential in the political process. Achieving those goals requires resources, both political and monetary.

The commentary from party leaders, party elites, candidates, and staffers indicates that the political class perceives the best source for these resources to be the party network. Support from the party helps encourage skilled campaign staff to join the candidate to run the multifaceted high powered operation that is a successful campaign. Support from the party provides easy access to the media and its ability to boost the perception of candidates and propel them to the front of the pack. In low information environments, the ability of the media to make salient one candidate or another provides crucial benefits. Support from the party provides access to needed financial support. The party's access both to media and staff creates additional pathways for candidates to collect the monetary resources necessary to run a successful campaign. Support from the party opens doors to major donors who are willing to finance political campaigns in the hope of receiving political access once the party is in office.

All of this makes it more difficult for candidates without party support in their pursuit of the party's nomination. Successful political campaigns are not easy to put together and to run. Without access to the party's network, candidates find that job much more difficult. Combine that with concerns that a candidate who runs in opposition to the party will jeopardize a relationship with party leaders and elites that could be useful in future runs for office, and it begins to make sense why unsupported candidates may decide to drop out and pursue other opportunities or to spend more time with their family. The resources at the disposal of the party network appear to be formidable. The power to influence the making of kings appears to be present in the party network. The next step is to understand whether parties are effectively using that power to create kings.

## APPENDIX TO CHAPTER 2

### INTERVIEW METHODOLOGY

Interviews were conducted between 2013 and 2015 with party leaders, staffers, donors, and former candidates who had been active in party politics in California, Colorado, Connecticut, Florida, Georgia, Iowa, Maine, Minnesota, Ohio, Pennsylvania, and Washington DC. States in which interviews would be conducted were initially chosen to represent a diverse selection of states and also to utilize personal connections and the connections of acquaintances in both parties. Potential interviewees, present and former party leaders and staff, past candidates, well-connected donors and fundraisers, and national party operatives in each location were identified, and an initial request for an anonymous conversation was made via email. At the end of each interview respondents were asked if they knew any additional individuals who might be willing to talk about the relationship between parties and candidates, following standard snowball-sampling techniques (Lynch 2013).

This process resulted in a sample of eighteen Republicans and eight Democrats from these states. The sample of respondents comes disproportionately from the upper Midwest (Minnesota and Iowa), but many of these individuals had political experience in many other regions of the country. While there are differences between (and even within) states regarding the structure and organization of party elites (Bawn et al. 2014; Masket 2009), no information from these interviews is included that was not confirmed from multiple sources. In addition, many of the individuals interviewed had worked in more than just one state and mentioned specific experiences in other states when answering the questions posed.

TABLE 2A.1  *Positions held by Interviewees*

| | |
|---|---|
| Candidates or Campaign Managers | 6 |
| Campaign Staff (not including Campaign Managers) | 6 |
| Party Staff | 14 |
| Party Leadership | 5 |
| Major Donors/Fundraisers | 6 |
| **Total Individuals Interviewed** | **26** |

*Note*: The numbers do not add up because many individuals held more than one role.

As with previous work on the party networks of campaigns (Masket et al. 2012; Nyhan and Montgomery 2015; Skinner et al. 2013), many of these individuals had held a number of different roles in the party and in different campaigns. Fourteen respondents had worked for a party organization as a paid party staff member (not including elected party leadership) during an election cycle. All individuals interviewed played significant roles in the campaign process, as indicated by Table 2A.1. Many held multiple positions; nine individuals each held two roles and one had been involved in three different capacities. In each of the categories listed below there were at least two individuals from each party. All but four individuals were still fully active in politics through the 2014 election cycle. Three of those individuals were active in politics up until the mid to late 2000s (one individual continues to participate, but in a more limited capacity). The last individual was active in party politics up until the late 1990s (and continues to participate on a limited basis but in a significantly reduced role).

Sixteen of the interviews were in-person interviews, with the rest done by phone. As explained in Chapter 3, anonymity was a key component in gaining access to some of these individuals. Immediately prior to the interview, each respondent was given an informed consent form which detailed the process for recording and storing interview material. Because talking openly could involve some risk, respondents were notified in the initial request for an interview and reminded again in the informed consent form that the identities of interviewees would be concealed except where the individual involved was a public personality and the interviewee's involvement with the individual named was publicly known. In keeping with Cornell College Institutional Review Board procedures, respondents were also told that they could stop the interview at any time or refuse to answer any of the questions. They were also informed that if they requested it they would be sent a copy of the transcribed interview so that they could provide any clarification needed. Only one individual took up that offer, and made no changes to the interview transcript provided.

Before the interview began, respondents were asked if they would agree to having the interview recorded. All but three individuals agreed. Those interviews not recorded were transcribed from memory immediately following the interview. In two interview recording sessions, the respondents provided additional information after the recording device had been turned off. On both occasions, permission was granted to include those remarks that had not been recorded, which were transcribed immediately after the interview.

Each respondent was asked about their role and involvement in campaigns and party politics and how they had begun to be involved. Depending on their background, respondents were asked appropriate questions about how they and other party members decide to support a particular candidate. They were prompted to comment on their own experiences and their personal knowledge about the role that the party had played in specific primary campaigns. All individuals were asked about the influence of party support on the campaign and how and why parties (and party elites) might be influential in affecting party outcomes.

# 3

# The Choosing of the Candidate

*The path to getting a general election candidate who can win is the only thing we care about ... I'm going to do whatever I need to do to win ... This is politics, and we ultimately are in the wins business*
—Rob Collins, Executive Director of the National
Republican Senatorial Committee in 2013[1]

*I think the Republican Party has been very lazy in its recruitments: Who has high name ID, who is independently wealthy, who is well established. Often the party overlooks a strong candidate who doesn't have some of those characteristics.*
—Matt Hoskins, Head of the Senate Conservatives Fund[2]

The defection of Jim Jeffords of Vermont from the Republican Party in 2001, shortly after winning his reelection campaign as a Republican, was a blow that stung the party. Fresh from the Republican Party having just won narrow control of the House, the Senate, and the White House all together for the first time since 1953, Jeffords' decision to switch parties gave control of the Senate back to Democrats and had a drastic effect on the ability of the Republican Party to enact its preferred policies (Karon 2001). Jeffords' decision to retire prior to the 2006 election cycle, then, was seen by many Vermont Republicans as a redemptive chance to win back the seat for the party. Nor was Vermont seen as a place where a Republican

---

[1] Quoted in Hunt, Kasie. 2013. "In Shift, GOP Vows to Fight for More Electable Candidates in Senate Primaries." *NBC News*. (November 5), and in Bump, Philip. 2013. "Why Would the GOP Think It Can Affect Its Primary Results?" *Atlantic Wire*. (November 3).
[2] Quoted in Goldmacher (2013).

victory was unimaginable. In addition to electing Jeffords as a Republican in 2000, the state had elected Republican Governor Jim Douglas in 2002 and reelected him in 2004 with almost 60 percent of the vote.[3]

Although the race would not be an easy Republican win, in part because the Republican nominee would have to beat popular independent Congressman Bernie Sanders in the general election to win the seat, there was no shortage of quality candidates who expressed interest in running for the seat, including Lieutenant Governor Brian Dubie, State Senator Mark Shephard, and wealthy business executive Richard Tarrant.[4] Dubie was viewed by many political observers as the obvious frontrunner, having been elected in 2002 and reelected by a comfortable margin in 2004. In Vermont, the Lieutenant Governor is elected independently from the Governor, and Dubie's political profile and success in that position provided him an excellent jumping-off point for a competitive run for the Senate. In early June of 2005, Dubie began the process of gearing up for a run for the nomination, and in August he had formed an official exploratory committee to advance his candidacy (Gram 2005; Porter 2005a).

Yet, in spite of Dubie's experience, some party leaders were hesitant to support Dubie over the less experienced Tarrant, for a number of strategic reasons. Party leaders were concerned with more than just winning a single Senate seat and were aiming to maximize the success of the party in controlling a number of public offices. Specifically, because of the lack of a deep Republican bench of potential candidates, Republicans were concerned about their ability to retain the Lieutenant Governor's office if Dubie decided to vacate it in a run for the Senate (Associated Press 2005). In addition, while Dubie's strong antiabortion positions were popular among the Republican base and would help him in the primary, many in the Republican Party leadership feared that his strong conservative ideology would not resonate with voters in the general election in a liberal state where issues rather

---

[3] Vermont is one of two states that elect governors for terms of two years as opposed to four years. The other is Vermont's New England neighbor, New Hampshire.

[4] Activist Greg Parke was also running for the Republican nomination. Although Parke had never before held public office, he had been the GOP's nominee for Vermont's only congressional seat in both 2002 and 2004. In 2004, Parke had raised significant controversy by portraying his opponent, Bernie Sanders (VT-I), in a television ad as enjoying "long walks on the beach with child pornographers and pedophiles, candlelight dinners with illegal aliens, and cozy evenings by the fire with al-Qaida terrorists." The ad was quickly pulled, but not before being denounced by state Republican Party leaders (Marx 2004). Parke had lost to Sanders by over 40 percentage points in a race that also included a Democratic Party nominee (Sanders running then as an independent). Needless to say, few in the Republican Party leadership were enthusiastic about a Parke candidacy.

than competence would be a major focus (Parker 2005; *Times Argus* 2005). Wanting to win the seat, party elites indicated they were willing to make sacrifices in ideological purity if that meant an increased chance of success. Thus, party leaders put significant pressure on Dubie to forgo a run for the Senate and instead to run for reelection as Lieutenant Governor.

As a result, Dubie, once perceived as the frontrunner for the Republican nomination, did not last long in the race for the Senate nomination. Less than a month after officially forming the exploratory committee, Dubie dropped out of the electoral contest, clearing the way for Tarrant to cruise to the nomination.[5] State Republican leaders were secretly pleased, expressing confidence in their ability to maintain their control of the Vermont executive branch. State Republican Chairman James Barnett expressed delight at Dubie's decision, saying Dubie's name on the ballot for Lieutenant Governor would help form "what will eventually be the strongest statewide Republican ticket since Vermont was solidly a Republican state" (Porter 2005b).

This chapter examines how parties make the decision about which candidates to coordinate behind and support. Knowing how parties decide to support particular candidates is important for understanding party influence in primary elections. If parties consistently choose to support candidates who are already strong favorites to win the nomination, correlations between party support and primary election success are likely to be spurious. However, in this example, the party's preference for Tarrant over Dubie was not the result of the party's jumping on the bandwagon of the most viable primary candidate.[6] But is the example of party support for Tarrant instead of Dubie representative of party action broadly, or is this case an exception to the rule?

The mere fact that parties have the resources to shape the processes and outcomes of primary elections does not mean that they do shape

---

[5] The year 2006 was a rough year for Republicans in general and Tarrant did not fare well, losing to Bernie Sanders by 33 percentage points. Dubie, on the other hand, won reelection as Lieutenant Governor handily and would serve another two terms before running for Governor when Republican Jim Douglas announced he would not seek reelection in 2010. Dubie would lose the gubernatorial contest in 2010 by fewer than 5,000 votes.

[6] If the leadership of the Republican Party were to jump on the bandwagon of the most viable primary election candidate, they would have supported Dubie. Many observers recognized that Dubie would have been the clear favorite to win the primary election. In September 2005, just before Dubie initially announced his formal candidacy, Middlebury College political scientist Eric Davis, a scholar of Vermont politics, expressed that "Dubie likely would win a primary if he gets into the race and was likely to be the toughest challenger the Republicans could offer Rep. Bernie Sanders" (Parker 2005).

those outcomes. One of the key sources of political power is a professional reputation inside the political world (Neustadt 1960). While it would not necessarily get them a candidate who will champion their causes, party elites may be strongly tempted to choose to use the electoral weapons available to them only in support of a winning cause in order to protect, or even bolster, their reputation within the party.[7]

At the same time, supporting candidates who breeze through the primary election process, only to fail spectacularly in a general election, can also seriously damage the reputation and power of party elites. Party elites work together because they are interested in policy outcomes and policy outcomes cannot be achieved unless the right people hold office.

Likewise, supporting a candidate who wins both the primary and the general election but fails to contribute to the achievement of preferred policy outcomes once in office can also damage the power and standing within the party of those who supported that candidate (Bawn et al. 2014).[8] Thus, while the resources at the disposal of the political elites discussed in Chapter 2 are formidable, the bigger question is whether parties are using them decisively to pick winners and to dissuade other candidates from running, or if these tools only are utilized in support of candidates who were already likely winners.

Because political elites may have a number of potential reasons to support primary candidates and because each of those reasons has different implications for theories of partisan primary influence, it is important to examine why party elites support the candidates they do. Are party elites using the vast array of resources available to them to attempt to influence primary outcomes? Or are they utilizing these resources in support of candidates already likely to win? Because party elites are interested in political power, one may suspect them of trying to burnish their political reputation as kingmakers by supporting a candidate whose victory in the

---

[7] This has been a noted difficulty in identifying the influence of interest group endorsements and support on election outcomes as well. Interest groups, because of their interest in having access to public officials who are in office, are often hesitant to support candidate who are not likely to win (Ansolabehere et al. 2003; Brunell 2005).

[8] Donald Trump may turn out to be a classic example of this latter phenomenon. Although he won the party's nomination, many party elites and party operatives refused to work for his campaign or associate with him because they feared that associating themselves with that campaign would cast a certain stigma on their professional career and reduce the power and influence they had within the party organization (Bade and Bresnahan 2016; Peoples 2016). Although not to the same extent, following the downturn in popularity of President George W. Bush's presidency in 2007, many Republicans attempted to downplay their connections to him and his associates (Kaplan 2014; Tankersley 2005a).

primary is already inevitable. If party elites are merely joining the bandwagon of an already successful candidate, claims of party influence are simply not credible. In short, without preliminary evidence delineating the process by which these party elites come to support specific candidates, inferring the influence of party elites in the nomination process is elusive.

While it might increase a successful candidate's margin of victory, party bandwagoning would only reinforce the vision of a candidate-centered model of elections, where party preferences take a back seat to candidate ability and motivation. Without understanding the process by which party elites come to coordinate behind a candidate, identifying whether primary election processes and outcomes are candidate-driven or party-driven is impossible. Therefore, if we want to understand the nature of party influence, we must first understand the party coordination process. This chapter attempts to do just that.

Before rushing to analyze the correlation between party support and primary outcomes, which we will focus on in Chapters 4 and 5, we must first understand how party elites identify which candidates to support and which candidates to discourage from running. Understanding how parties come to support certain candidates and shun others provides a means to distinguish whether the correlation between party support and party outcomes that we find is evidence of party influence in the nomination process or merely the result of an attentive group of party elites latching on to the primary election frontrunner. Understanding the process of party coordination, rather than just looking for statistical correlations between party support and primary outcomes, provides a clearer understanding of how to interpret the relationships between party support and primary outcomes and to understand whether parties are influencing the process or merely going along for the ride.

As with the evidence presented in Chapter 2, to understand the process of party coordination we turn first to the explanations given by party elites. This allows us a glimpse into the possible range of explanations for party support of a candidate. As part of the interviews described in Chapter 2, respondents also elaborated on the process of how party elites identify which candidates to support and how parties come to coordinate behind those candidates. These questions about party coordination posed in the interviews were aimed at getting a better understanding about what party elites say their motivations are in supporting particular candidates.

These interviews with political practitioners can help clarify why and how party elites coordinate and collectively choose to support preferred candidates. This line of questioning provides insight into and answers to the following questions: Are party elites merely following the primary candidate with the best ability to appeal to an ideological primary base (rendering party support endogenous to primary outcomes that were already foreordained)? Or do they use other factors in identifying a preferred party candidate, thus suggesting they have a larger role in influencing primary elections?

The interviews presented in this chapter illuminate the perception of party elites about their own and their colleagues' motivations for supporting particular candidates. These insights provide a picture of the process by which party elites coordinate in support of a particular candidate. The perception that elites have of party coordination is that it is not motivated by primary viability but rather is a product of a mix of issues related to general election electability, the facilitation of party coordination, and, as the example of the 2006 Vermont Republican primary shows, other strategic considerations related to maximizing the number of political offices the party holds. These findings counter assumptions that party support is driven by a candidate's primary election viability. Instead, this qualitative evidence suggests that party elites are not driven to support a candidate on the basis of that candidate's primary election viability. Rather, they are concerned about finding candidates within the party network who can win the general election while at the same time attempting to maximize the spread of good candidates across races to maximize the number of party office holders. More importantly, however, the interviews with party elites provide valuable insight into the informal and ongoing conversation between party elites about which candidate to support, and they help to understand the process of party coordination.

Quantitative analysis presented later in this chapter also supports the idea that parties are not merely jumping on the bandwagon of the most viable primary election candidate. Together, both sources of evidence point to a clear conclusion that party support does not generally follow perceived candidate primary election viability. Party elites act strategically to increase coordination and to increase the probability of securing favorable policy outcomes after the election.

## THE PROCESS OF COORDINATION

As should be expected in view of the large number of actors that make up the party network, coordination of party elites in support of a single candidate is not a simple process. Unlike the glamorized accounts of party politics in the age of the party machine, all individuals interviewed indicated that there is no one individual, or even one formal organization, whose unilateral decision to support a candidate causes party elites to line up behind that candidate. As one former Democratic state party chair explained,

> It's more shifting coalitions, rather than a center, command and control type of model. As chair, I remember walking around often saying "Where's the back room? Where's the room where I get to go smoke cigars and make all the decisions, because I haven't found the door."

Republicans also indicated the same thing, though some considered the process a little less fragmented. One former Republican Party official explained the process of coordination, saying,

> I wish I could give you a scientific formula, or even a rule of thumb, but I can't. Really, it's all situational. It's all the perception of who can win [the general election], and that perception is not driven by one individual in the system. I can't think of it in the abstract. I think of it in terms of personalities. Where's this big donor going to go, where's that big donor going to go? What does this former party leader think, what does that guy think? People are attentive to what's going on in their social circles. They're all important people in their own right, so they're not intentionally following one of their peers, but there tends to be a consensus or a bandwagon effect. There usually tends to be one person towards whom people tend to gravitate.

Neither the Republican network of elites nor the Democratic network of elites are political operations where commands of action come down from superiors and are obeyed with strict discipline. Instead, coordinated action requires forging consensus across the network of party elites. And consensus in a large group requires an informal and ongoing (but disjointed) conversation. Unlike the smoke-filled back rooms of olden times, these discussions do not happen when all major players are together. Rather this coordination and decision-making happens through signaling across the various social and professional networks that tie party elites together.

Coming to an agreement across such a network is not easy. To facilitate coordination, party elites identified numerous different factors within this informal conversation that drove consensus. The specific factors that enabled coordination often varied significantly by party and region. However, across party and region there did emerge three key general principles that appeared to guide the process: perceived general election viability, strategic party goals, and salience within the party network.

## PERCEIVED GENERAL ELECTION VIABILITY

Although the specific processes and channels of communication among elites vary by region and party, in the interviews, party elites in both parties repeatedly mentioned several considerations which transcended specific party structures and which motivated their decisions and the decisions of their colleagues to support particular candidates. In the informal conversation that takes place among party elites there are a number of factors which they appear to consider. The first of these was perceived general election viability.[9] While party leaders have not removed ideology from their coordination efforts, they explain much of their actions as being pragmatic. As the executive director of the National Republican Senatorial Committee, Rob Collins, explained in the run-up to the recruitment season before the 2014 midterm elections, "We're not anti-conservative. We're just anti-people-who-can't-win" (Cassata 2014). Party elites say they care about winning, and winning requires both good candidates and unity within the party.

In interviews, party elites indicated that they were always looking at candidates with an eye to the general election. While ideology is a strong bond that ties parties together, these individuals suggested that a party-preferred candidate need not necessarily fit the ideological mold that might normally be necessary to satisfy the party's primary election voters. As one individual explained,

Higher up the [political] food chain, there's less idealism. It's more about winning. Not to say that there's not idealism, but it becomes pragmatic idealism. Higher level activists, donors, party officials want to back someone ... who also can win.

---

[9] There is a big difference between perceived general election viability and actual general election viability. Individuals within parties are often more likely to perceive candidates who share their own ideological preferences as more electable because a message that contains that set of ideological appeals resonates with them. In addition, electoral success may be achieved in a many different ways as majority electoral coalitions can be formed from appeals to a number of different segments of the electorate. As a result, the ideology required for a candidate to be perceived as viable by one set of individuals may be different that required by another. This is addressed further in Chapter 7. Thanks to Boris Heersink for our conversations on this point and for his work documenting the use of electability as an argument for party branding (Heersink 2016).

Party elites often described an increase in tension that developed between the party and the party's base as the party worked to nominate a candidate that local party members did not want. Party leaders indicated numerous times that they were willing to overlook a lack of ideological purity if it increased the likelihood of holding public office. Primary viability was not important to them; general election viability was. As a Democratic party official stated,

The reality is that we need to elect Democrats ... and at the end of the day if I or others tried to find a candidate who fit the party [and just focused on satisfying primary voters] as opposed to the district, we'd lose. So first and foremost when you're recruiting candidates you've got to find a candidate who ... can win the general election.

Parties and partisan elites indicated they were concerned with holding office. All of them recognized that holding office necessitated winning the general election. Many of them expressed a belief that primary outcomes were more likely to be pliable as a result of variable turnout and lower information environments, while the general election's outcome was perceived as less so.[10]

General election viability was mentioned as influential in the decision to recruit and derecruit candidates for public office. One party staffer explained that while national party regional staffers had met with a number of viable candidates in a competitive primary, national party leaders directed the regional staffers not to reach out to one competitive candidate, because the candidate "didn't have a chance in the general election." That undesirable candidate would ultimately win the hotly contested congressional primary and then go on to lose by a large margin in the general election (without any party support) in what had previously been perceived as a potentially competitive seat. Likewise, another former state party staffer indicated that he and other staffers gave preferential treatment to some congressional and senatorial candidates and responded more slowly to requests from other competitive candidates in the primary because "if they won the nomination we'd be embarrassed

---

[10] Because of the highly variable turnout in primary elections, the ideological placement of the median voter in the primary is much less certain (Ensley 2012; McCarty et al. 2014). These primary voter abstentions may actually encourage elites to believe they have more flexibility in identifying a preferred candidate. This (in addition to the pragmatic arguments that they often highlight to win over ideological voters) allows them to support candidates who may not necessarily be the most acceptable to the primary electorate.

in the general election, and there's no way we'd have wanted that." The previous chapter mentioned an instance of national party leaders recommending that a candidate hire a staffer whom party officials regarded as the least competent of those available to fill a major role in the campaign in a competitive Senate primary, because they viewed that candidate as a significantly weaker general election candidate. All of these accounts show how party elites generally frame their actions around their perceptions of candidate general election viability.

This is not to say that party elites are ignoring their own ideological preferences. Previous researchers have theorized that voters have a limited ideological perception, which creates a blind spot in their ability to identify precisely the ideological preferences of certain candidates (Bawn et al. 2012). As long as candidates are not obviously outside that blind spot, they do not suffer any electoral penalty for ideological positions that are farther away from the media voter than those of their opponents. While this ideological blind spot is undoubtedly smaller for a more attentive primary electorate, it is reasonable to expect that it is still present for many voters, especially in the absence of clear partisan cues that enable voters to have more ideological constraint across issues (Campbell et al. 1960; Converse 1964; Sniderman and Tomz 2005). Thus party elites may perceive some flexibility in the choice of whom to support as a viable general election candidate.[11]

In addition, party elites' indications that they were most interested in supporting candidates who could win the general election does not preclude their coordination behind the candidate that also most closely aligns with their own ideological preferences (which may or may not align with the preferences of primary voters). In the 1960s, both moderates and conservatives in the Republican Party advocated for candidates who were most closely aligned with their own ideological preferences, claiming it would improve electoral viability and increase the size of the party's caucuses in the House and the Senate (Heersink 2016). Moderates argued that by supporting a more moderate brand, they would be better able to appeal to moderate factions in

---

[11] One individual indicated that the negative aspects of Christine O'Donnell's candidacy for party leaders in Delaware, where she defeated party-preferred candidate Mike Castle in the primary, was not her ideological conservatism. What troubled them was her penchant for outlandish and offensive statements and her inexperience and inability to campaign well. In no other example was this more clear than her "I'm not a Witch" television ad, which gained her additional national notoriety and focused the campaign even more on her past history of engaging in witchcraft (Farber 2010).

the northeast and would compete better with liberals, while conservatives advocated for the support of more conservative candidates to broaden the party's appeal in the south. Both moderates and conservatives, in addition to arguing that their ideological preferences made for better policy, argued that their preferences could lead to better electoral outcomes. Similar arguments continue to exist within both parties (see for example Greenfield 2015).

While the actual meaning of the term "general election viability" is not entirely clear, at every juncture, party elites made it clear that they were unconcerned about a candidate's perceived ability to win the primary and more concerned about finding a candidate who they thought would be competitive in the general election, and that they perceived their colleagues to be focused in the same way.

### STRATEGIC COORDINATION

Many individuals explained that party elites, rather than supporting the best candidate or the candidate most likely to win the primary, strategically supported certain candidates, with the goal of maximizing the number of victories they could win in a general election. In efforts to extend their influence over government and public policy, parties attempt to control as many public offices as possible. This, of course, requires winning as many elections in an election cycle as possible. This is one of the factors that confronted the Vermont Republican Party as they considered the candidacies of businessman Richard Tarrant and Lieutenant Governor Brian Dubie. When Dubie ultimately dropped out of the race, clearing the field for Tarrant, the Associated Press reported that Dubie "acknowledged that he faced pressure from leading Republicans to defend a seat that they feared they would lose if he sought a move to Washington" (Associated Press 2005).

Although many viable candidates may express interest in running for a seat, the party has an incentive to try to encourage good candidates not to congregate in a single race. As one party official involved in the candidate recruitment process explained,

It's partially the party making sure that they have good candidates in every race. They're going to try and convince people to get into races where they have a chance. You don't want two good candidates running in one race and a crappy candidate running in another especially when you've got a good political environment on your side.

Rather than waste good candidates in a primary election, parties want to maximize their potential for general election victories. At times, this means discouraging well-qualified candidates from running because they are needed in other electoral races.

In all cases, the goal is to maximize the number of seats held in both the House and the Senate. At times, this may require heavy-handed tactics to dissuade candidates from pursuing higher office, even though they are viable general election candidates. One former staffer for Representative David Minge (D-MN1) indicated that these strong-arm tactics were used to dissuade Minge from running for Senate in 2000 and running for reelection in the House, for this very reason.[12] This campaign staffer explained:

> Minge had announced he was running for Senate in mid-1999. Well, [House Minority Leader] Dick Gephardt got this news and went absolutely apoplectic because he was going to lose that congressional seat because he was in a rural Republican district and David was the only one who could win that and if he didn't run they were going to lose that seat. So Gephardt, or his people, went to all the major donors or people who could help out with fundraising and told them basically to not give money ... So by October of '99 David came to us and said, "I've got a decision to make, I can either say 'Screw you Gephardt,' or I can admit that he was right, and the bottom line is that I want to be a member of Congress." So he dropped out, and ran for his old seat.

In a similar manner the initial efforts to push the mayor of Cranston, Rhode Island, Steve Laffey, out of the Republican primary in that state against the incumbent Republican Senator, Lincoln Chafee, centered on encouraging Laffey to run for a different office. In his book documenting the party's efforts to foil his campaign, Laffey records the following phone conversation between himself and Republican National Committee Chair Ken Mehlman, in the lead-up to the Senate primary:

---

[12] A similar dynamic, with fewer strong-arm tactics and with less success, appears to have played out in 2012 in Indiana. Joe Donnelly (D-IN2) was recruited by the DSCC to challenge incumbent Senator Richard Lugar. Donnelly described the recruitment process as a tug-of-war between the DSCC and the DCCC, as leaders in the latter organization were afraid they would lose Donnelly's seat if he ran for Senate. As Donnelly explained, "It's probably fair to say, [DCCC chairman] Steve [Israel] said, 'Hey, buddy, don't ditch me'" (Goldmacher 2013). In this case, however, Donnelly did choose to run for Senate. Although Donnelly would win the Senate race (after incumbent Republican Richard Lugar lost the Republican primary), the Democrat nominated for Donnelly's old seat (Brendan Mullen) would be defeated by Republican Jackie Walorski.

| KEN [MEHLMAN]: | I've heard you've done such wonderful things in Cranston (as Mayor) ... I heard you might be running for Senate. |
|---|---|
| ME: | I haven't made any decisions yet, Ken, but I appreciate the call. |
| KEN: | Well, we think it might be a good idea for you to run for lieutenant governor. |
| ME: | Really? Why? |
| KEN: | To help grow the Republican Party (Laffey 2007, 25). |

While these efforts were undoubtedly partially an attempt to protect a vulnerable incumbent and to ensure the nomination of a candidate considered more electable in the liberal state, the conversation also indicates that party officials were concerned with preventing candidates from clumping together in a single primary race in which good candidates who lost the primary election would be wasted. Getting Laffey to run for Lieutenant Governor would also give Laffey the additional exposure and experience needed for campaigns for higher office in the future. One party official in charge of recruitment explained,

We're focused on building a pipeline of future candidates ... [getting candidates to run for lower office] and start establishing themselves and positioning themselves for a run for higher office down the road. We always have an eye on candidate development, first and foremost, which is developing off a bench.

Accomplishing the enactment of preferred public policy means having candidates in general election contests that they can win and thus hold the public offices where they can control policy outcomes. Inefficient distribution of good-quality candidates across races limits the ability of parties to control public office and enact their preferred policies. Developing a pipeline of good candidates also helps develop party strength over time.

Strategic recruitment and derecruitment by the party or certain party elites within the party may even extend to considerations of political leadership. In March 2015, the *New York Times* reported that Minority Leader Nancy Pelosi was working to convince Congressman Chris Van Hollen (D-MD8) not to run for Senate because of her desire that he succeed her as House Minority Leader (Steinhauer 2015). Likewise, in 1996, Speaker of the House Newt Gingrich was active in dissuading certain candidates from running, in part because of considerations about who would chair certain important committees (BuzzFeed 2012).

Thus, while parties prioritize getting what they perceive as the best general election candidate to run for a particular office, they are at the same time concerned about maintaining control of the current offices they hold and maximizing the opportunities to seize control of additional political offices both now and in the future. Doing so necessitates an efficient distribution of quality candidates across the range of offices. Having too many good candidates in one race may hamper efforts to expand party influence to other areas, and for this reason parties may encourage even strong candidates to run for other offices.

### FOCAL POINTS OF COORDINATION

Finally, in their efforts to coordinate behind a single preferred candidate, parties may restrict the scope of their search for acceptable candidates to the inner network of the party in an attempt to facilitate party coordination. As the size of the group increases, coordination becomes more difficult, in the absence of a single individual with the power to direct action. In the party politics of today, the bosses of old who might have fulfilled that dominant role are generally nowhere to be found. Coordination problems stem from insufficient shared information about individuals' preferences and may prevent collective action even when there is agreement that coordination is important. As anyone who has ever tried to arrange a meeting time for a large number of people or to achieve a consensus about a group activity in a large extended family gathering knows, the larger the group becomes, the harder such tasks become. In many cases, as the group gets larger, coordination may be generally unachievable without the use of focal points or salient cues that help individuals identify a limited set of available options. A focal point is merely a point of coordination that is most obvious to the individuals involved (Schelling 1960). Coordination of large numbers of individuals is not an easy task and, in the absence of a single coordinator (such as a party boss), is best done when the point of coordination is a focal point (Lewis 1969; Schelling 1960).

Coordination of party elites behind a single candidate poses the same problem as any other attempt at coordination of large numbers of actors. Party elites want to coordinate behind the best candidate, but identifying and unifying behind that candidate as a group poses challenging coordination problems. To mitigate and help find a solution to these coordination problems, parties generally search for well-known candidates within the party network in order to help facilitate coordination in their search for viable general election candidates.[13] These salient potential candidates act as focal points for coordination. Many individuals interviewed acknowledged that the perspective of party elites was limited to their extended network and those in public prominence. Echoing the complaint from Matt Hoskins that heads this chapter, some party insiders even complained that the party failed to support the best candidates simply because they were outside the party's network. As one former party official involved in the candidate recruitment process explained,

The party has become such an inside game. I mean you say "give me a candidate for any office" and the first thing they do is name ten state legislators. People in the party tend to gravitate towards the legislators. They go with people that they know.

Another party leader highlighted connections within the party network that were essential for being recruited to run.

In leadership … you had a good feel for politics. You looked at numbers and said, "ok, these are marginal districts. Let's go and try to recruit somebody." And then you just reach out to those people who had some connection to party donors or other elected officials.

Even when looking beyond the current slate of office holders within the party, the identification of viable candidates occurs within the circles of the political elite. As one former state Republican Party Chair explained,

If the NRSC or the NRCC is looking for candidates, they're most likely going to call people they know and respect, people like the [former Congressman] of the world. So they'll call [this former congressman], and they'll say "Who's out there in your state?" And it's people like them that really provide the information. If he doesn't know, he'll call people in his network and ask who's a possible up and comer. And then he'll will go back and say "here's who you should talk to." So, even if he doesn't know the person, he's been told by his people that this is the guy that they should back. So, it's all about who knows who and connections … [When] the national party members are looking for candidates they gravitate towards people who are known commodities.

---

[13] One might use the well-worn analogy of a drunk searching for his keys under the streetlamp, as parties generally search for good candidates where they know the light is good and can see and gather information on potential candidates. (However, many of those interviewed would object to the comparison of political parties to an inebriate.)

The reasons for a party's selective search, however, do not appear to be the result of an intentional effort to exclude outsider candidates or certain ideological preferences, but rather a function of facilitating coordination. As one major donor explained after listing a number of nominees with a wide range of ideological profiles within the party,

It's a boon to have some sort of a profile in politics. If you're in elected office, and if you're not [you should] have some sort of connection or relationships in the business community or in the community at large.

Coordination on a candidate is easiest when potential candidates are restricted to individuals well known among those individuals who are trying to coordinate.[14]

The successful coordination of donors and party elites behind a single candidate relies on recognition within the network. Candidates who are salient focal points facilitate party coordination. This is true not only in the recruitment process but also once candidates have emerged. One well-networked major party donor explained his choice to support one candidate or another as a matter of social connections: "How can I not support this person? I've known them since my first race! Or I've known them since 1984! That's generally how I make all my decisions now." While party elites are interested in getting the most viable general election candidate through the nomination process, in order to facilitate coordination the list of potential candidates is often limited to individuals who are salient in the party network. Even when viable alternatives present themselves, partisan elites have a harder time coordinating on individuals outside the network.

PARTY SUPPORT AND CANDIDATE VIABILITY

The substance of these interviews helps to clarify the relationship between party support and candidate primary electoral success (Lynch 2013; Mosley 2013). Evidence from these interviews strongly suggests that party coordination efforts are not the result of bandwagoning on a

---

[14] This might also partially explain the higher success of experienced politicians (Jacobson and Kernell 1981). Because they are more likely to be well known within the party network where key political resources are readily available, experienced politicians are likely more able to attract key party resources such as those mentioned in Chapter 2 than other equally qualified and competent campaigners.

candidate already destined to win the primary. Rather, party elites consider other factors, separate from primary electoral viability, in deciding who to support. Instead of focusing on primary election viability, they mobilize in support of candidates with the intent of maximizing their chances in the general election in that race, distributing good candidates across races efficiently, and facilitating the solution to coordination problems that they face in getting behind a single candidate.

The question remains, however, whether or not systematic empirical data corroborate these party insiders' perceptions and beliefs about the nomination process. Even though party insiders indicate that they do not choose whom to support on the basis of primary election viability, concerns about the validity of these statements still remain (Bleich and Pekkanen 2013). If party elites are trying to preserve power by "backing no losers," they may be hesitant to acknowledge such a fact because of the implications it might have on their professional reputations (Rakove 1975).[15]

Therefore, it is important to validate the statements of party insiders about the process of coordination through other means. We need some independent validation of whether party support is or is not predicated on candidate success. To achieve this, we need to consider quantitatively whether or not measures of candidate viability effectively predict future party support. We should be able to look at other signs of campaign health and vitality to gauge whether party elites are merely following the strongest campaign or coordinating on the basis of other factors, as they claim to be. If other factors predicting candidate success do not predict subsequent changes in party support, we can be more confident that party elites are not merely jumping on the bandwagons of successful candidates.

Moreover, showing that party support during a specific period has a strong influence on future campaign viability can generate more confidence that the outcomes we look at in the next few chapters are a result of party support, rather than a result of parties supporting candidates who are already likely to win. If party support predicts increases in future measures of candidate viability, we can be even more confident that any

---

[15] Parties are hesitant to take any action that might limit their power. As one Chicago committeeman famously explained to Milton Rakove (1975), "I got two rules. The first one is 'Don't make no waves.' The second one is, 'Don't back no losers'" (11). While Rakove focuses most of his efforts on the first rule, the second rule is the focus of this chapter. Indeed, it is easy to see how picking primary losers could be detrimental to the perceived power of party elites.

relationship between party support and primary outcomes is driven by party resources and not by candidate inevitability. As shown below, measures of primary viability do not influence future levels of party support. Instead, party support influences primary viability.

TESTING PARTY BANDWAGONING

To more fully understand whether party elites are leading or following candidate primary viability, we need to examine the effect of party support on candidate viability. Examining this effect quantitatively requires that we have some dynamic measure of both party support and candidate primary viability for candidates running in primaries for House and Senate. In order to do so, we start with a list of individuals who declared their candidacy for the US Senate or the House of Representatives and who filed with the Federal Election Commission (FEC) between 2004 and 2014. This includes candidates who only formed exploratory committees and candidates who withdrew or switched to a different race shortly after announcing their intentions to run for either the House or the Senate.[16]

### Measuring Party Support

First, we must come up with a way of identifying the candidates that party elites are coordinating behind. Because parties generally do not make public endorsements in primary elections, we need some alternative way of measuring the coordination that is occurring behind the scenes.[17] As a measure of the strength of the relationship between party elites and

---

[16] The FEC requires that any candidate who raises more than $5,000 must register a campaign committee within 15 days with the FEC and report any donations greater than $200. While the list of candidate committees recorded by the FEC is not a complete list of all candidates who were on primary ballots in various states or even a list of all those who actively campaigned for office, most candidates who do not appear on this list were not viable candidates and did not run competitive campaigns. It is a reasonable assumption that these candidates were not running with a realistic hope of winning office, but rather were more interested in the experience of running for office (Canon 1990).

[17] Previous researchers have also attempted to measure party support in other ways, most notably through tracking party elite endorsements of candidates (Cohen et al. 2008; Dominguez 2011). Despite their usefulness, previous researchers have also argued that we need to find "other proxies of this partisan support" because previous measures "are cumbersome to gather for large numbers of candidates" (Dominguez 2011, 542). More details about these alternative measures are available in the Appendix to this chapter.

a candidate, the analysis in this book relies on the number of donors who donated money to the candidate and also either the party's Senatorial Campaign Committee (the Democratic Senatorial Campaign Committee for Democrats and the National Republican Senatorial Committee for Republicans), for Senate candidates, or the party's Congressional Campaign Committee (the Democratic Congressional Campaign Committee for Democrats and the National Republican Congressional Committee for Republicans), for House candidates.[18] The analysis focuses on the years between 2004 and 2014, as that time was marked by consistent campaign finance regulations governing the amount of money individuals were allowed to give to candidates and to parties. These regulations came into effect with the passage of the Bipartisan Campaign Reform Act in 2002 and continued until the FY2015 Omnibus Appropriations bill changed regulations on donations to parties starting in 2016.[19] The consistency in these regulations (in spite of changing regulations regarding donations to SuperPACs and other outside groups) allows for a cleaner comparison of effects across time.[20] The FEC's requirement that

---

[18] Although there is some evidence that parties prefer candidates who can finance their own election campaigns, both in the interviews and reiterated in one of the quotes at the head of this chapter, the measure used to quantify party support in this book does not account for party support of self-funded candidates. However, if parties do support wealthy self-funders, the effects of party support on a candidate's ability to win and stay in the primary are likely to be underestimated, because these candidates, when they are supported by the party, will be identified as candidates without party support. This misclassification merely acts to decrease estimates of dropout rates and increase estimates of win rates among candidates who do not have the support of the party.

[19] Although the fundamental authorization legislation did not change, the FY2015 Omnibus Appropriations legislation allowed a donor to give almost $300,000 to a party for the purposes of supporting party conventions, providing for the acquisition and renting of buildings, and funding recount or other legal efforts, in addition to the $32,400 of donations donors were already able to give to parties for political activities. These increases harken back to a previous era, when parties could accept unlimited donations for "party-building activities" (Garrett 2014).

[20] The analysis for this book also tested models that excluded from the count of party donors those individuals who gave to both major political parties' Hill Committees (Senatorial Campaign and Congressional Campaign committees). There is no difference in the results. Bipartisan party donors made up less than 1 percent of the sample of party primary donors. While there may be some concern that bipartisan party donors are not part of the party and are merely interested in access, this is less of a concern in a primary than in a general election. Eliminating these individuals, however, does not give an accurate representation of the role that parties play in connecting donors (both bipartisan and partisan) to preferred candidates. As noted below, party organizations regularly bundle money on behalf of candidates, including money from donors who give to both parties (Herrnson 1988, 2009; Kolodny 1998). Not including these individuals

candidates and party organizations report donor information quarterly allows us to calculate party support on a quarterly basis. Having, therefore, a measure of party support on a quarterly basis provides a way to test the dynamic effects of party support on perceived candidate viability.[21]

While at first glance this measure may appear to make sense, we must also validate it theoretically and quantitatively to show that it is a good gauge of party support. Fortunately, there is a good theoretical motivation behind the use of this measure to quantify the relationship between parties and primary candidates. Using the number of donors a candidate shares with his or her party's senatorial committee as a measure of party support matches accounts of the party organizations as the center of a coordinated effort to direct campaign funds to favored candidates (Herrnson 1988; Kolodny 1998). Party elites routinely take cues from the Hill committees.[22] Donors who give to the party committees are well connected within the party network (Herrnson 1988, 2009; Koger et al. 2009; Kolodny 1998). Even when parties do not transfer funds directly to candidates, they often mobilize party-connected donors on behalf of these candidates.

In addition, using a similar measure to connect candidates with various interest groups on both the left and the right of the political spectrum shows that an interest group endorsement strongly correlates with a subsequent increase in the number of donors a candidate shares with an endorsing interest group. A more detailed explanation of the measure of party support is available in the Appendix to Chapter 3. In short, however, the use of shared donors as a measure of a candidate's support from the party matches accounts of party actions as coordinators of party donors. In addition, we also find that the number of shared donors does increase when a political organization makes an endorsement if we look at other political organizations that do offer explicit endorsements. These two factors suggest that measuring party support by calculating

---

eliminates an important part of the parties' efforts to coordinate in support of preferred candidates.

[21] Also considered was the use of other measures of party support that take into account the relative standing of candidates (see for example Norrander 2006). These models can also be considered a measure of factionalism within the campaign. Models with this alternative specification of relative party support show much the same results and are available in the Appendix of each chapter, where the party support variable is used.

[22] Calling the parties' senatorial and congressional campaign committees "Hill committees" refers to their original location in the Capitol Building on Capitol Hill (Herrnson 1988, 154)

the number of shared donors between the party and the candidate reflects accurately the support that a candidate has from the party.

## Measuring Candidate Viability

In addition to measuring party support we must also identify a dynamic measure of candidate viability. The largest predictor of success among nonincumbent candidates in primary elections is candidate fundraising (Jacobson 1980; Jewell and Morehouse 2001). Although candidates may spend a lot of their own money, it is candidate fundraising, not candidate spending, that is an indicator of candidate success (Brown 2013; Steen 2006). Even though quarterly polling numbers and media coverage are unavailable for many House and Senate primaries as a means to measure the primary election viability of each candidate, quarterly fundraising totals provide the same indicator of success.[23] Using fundraising as a measure of candidate viability, we can assess whether connections to the party committees are determined largely by a candidate's primary election viability or whether party donors support candidates through different coordination mechanisms, as the interviews suggest.

### EXPECTATIONS FOR PARTY BANDWAGONING IN HOUSE AND SENATE PRIMARIES

Before testing the relationship between party support and candidate viability in primary elections for the House and Senate, it is important to delineate how party coordination efforts might differ between House and Senate nomination contests. There are some significant structural differences between elections for the House and those for the Senate, and these differences should shape the actions of party actors in their efforts to coordinate behind a preferred candidate.

For the purposes of understanding party coordination efforts, primaries for House and Senate differ in two key ways. The first and obvious difference is the number of primary elections held in each election cycle and the number of candidates who run. When dealing with House elections, party elites and party leaders must monitor races in 435 congressional

---

[23] Previous studies of presidential nominations have found no statistically significant effect of media coverage or polling numbers on levels of party support, just as fundraising does not predict party support, as is shown here (Cohen et al. 2008).

districts, compared to roughly 33 in the Senate.[24] On average, 170 candidates file with the FEC to run for Senate each election cycle, compared to an average of 1,278 candidates for the House.[25]

The large number of races and candidates on the House side makes coordination more difficult. Efficient resource allocation is more critical on the House side than it is on the Senate side. Allocating resources to a primary in an uncompetitive Senate race can have a significant impact, where funding an uncompetitive House race will not. Senate races are on the top of the ticket and the quality of the Senate candidate on the general election ballot can have significant effects on the fortunes of the down ballot candidates. The same is not as true for House candidates, who draw much less media attention. Moreover, parties must be more selective about where they allocate their attention and resources for House races because of the large number of contests and the impossibility of funding them all.

In addition, considerably more House seats are unwinnable for one party or another. Previous work on open seat House races has shown that parties are much more likely to attempt to coordinate in primaries in congressional districts where it is anticipated that the general election will be competitive and where choosing the right candidate can make a difference in the likelihood of victory (Dominguez 2005). While the small number of Senate races each year allows party leaders to be cognizant of the status of every race, the sheer volume of House seats and the number of candidates running makes uncompetitive seats less of a focus than they are in the Senate. Talking about one safe Democratic congressional district primary, one major Democratic donor said, "I don't think [the party] got very involved. I mean this is a safe seat so the DCCC didn't get very involved with [the campaign] and certainly not in the primary." Because of the large number of elections for seats in the House every year, parties have little reason to pay attention to safe seats and unwinnable seats, choosing instead to focus on races where their influence might make a

---

[24] This number may increase slightly, depending on whether there are special elections to fill the remaining terms of an incumbent senator who has left office for one reason or another. These elections are often held concurrently with the fall general elections.

[25] The number of House candidates who filed with the FEC ranged from 1,113 in 2004 to 1,718 in 2010. On the Senate side that number ranges from 151 in 2006 to 260 in 2010. The difference in these ranges explains why party coordination is achieved much more easily in the Senate than in the House. With fewer options it is easier to get more information about each candidate for the Senate, while getting information about candidates for the House is much more difficult.

difference to the outcome. Thus, while there may be an interest in ensuring that there is a candidate running in an unwinnable district where there might otherwise not be, the quality of that candidate is of less interest (Seligman et al. 1974). So, while the party might be actively involved in all or most Senate primary races because of their greater impact down ballot and greater visibility, parties are more likely to focus only on competitive elections in House races.

Second, compared to Senate primaries, House primaries are low information environments, even those that are competitive. Although parties have a similar goal, of coordinating efforts behind an acceptable and formidable general election candidate, in both Senate and House primaries, the information and resources they have to accomplish this task are distinctly different. Congressional campaign committees must deal with much lower-level information environments than senatorial campaign committees. While statewide races often generate substantial media coverage, races for local congressional districts are often overshadowed by other news and by races on the top of the ticket. Thus, the ability of the party to gather information about preferred candidates, or that of nonpreferred candidates to pick up on party cues, may be limited. As a former congressional primary candidate, political scientist L. Sandy Maisel, wrote,

When I reviewed my campaign shortly after its conclusion, I was amazed by how little I knew when I decided to run. I did not know who my opponents would be; I did not know how I was perceived through the district, by the political leaders or by those at the grassroots; I did not know how much money I could raise, nor what others could spend against me; I did not know in a precise way what [the incumbent's] weaknesses were. The list could be expanded. (Maisel 1982, 19)

Even with the advent of technological improvements, media information about general election races, let alone primary elections for the US House of Representatives, is still extremely limited (Clarke and Evans 1983; Hassell and Oeltjenbruns 2016). While the flow of information has improved drastically with the advent of political blogs and internet media since the 1980s, information about candidates running in House primaries continues to be scarce and hard to find. There is much less information available about House candidates than about those running in presidential or senatorial primaries (Hassell and Oeltjenbruns 2016; Maisel 1982). Candidates may be able to gauge their own support, but they are often unable to determine the strength or the origins of the support for their opponent.

Because current, relevant, and even accurate information is difficult to come by, we expect party elites to be more likely to rely on other shortcuts, such as previous elected office, to determine which candidate to support. Thus, we should expect parties to use salient and readily available information about a candidate's past political experience, when such information is available, in House primaries. These are the same cues that make candidates more attractive in the eyes of voters and lead to candidate success (Jacobson and Kernell 1981). Only when competing candidates have similar levels of past experience should we expect party coordination to influence candidate viability, rather than the other way around. The large number of races in each election cycle and the limited information available about many candidates suggest that party support will cause rather than follow candidate viability only in competitive districts, where there are not clear differences in the experience of the primary candidates.

As a result of the low information environment, where there are clear differences in candidate quality, the party is more likely to use candidate quality as a shortcut in decisions about whom to support. Likewise, in races where the party has either no chance of winning or a sure chance of winning, party elites should coordinate behind candidates who also have other structural advantages. Parties will also be more likely to let the situation play out and to back candidates who garner outside support when whoever wins the primary is unlikely to have an effect on the outcome of the general election.

However, parties are more likely to lead, and less likely to jump on the bandwagons of already viable candidates, in House primaries in competitive districts where there are no differences in candidate quality as measured by elected experience. When obvious differences in candidate quality do not exist, party elites are forced to coordinate in making a decision about which candidate to support. Given this situation, party support should cause an increase in candidate viability only in important primaries where other information is not available.

Senate primaries do not have the same institutional constraints. Because they are on the top of the electoral ticket and have an effect on down-ballot races, parties have a strong incentive to become involved. Moreover, because there are fewer races to consider, party elites do not have to choose which races to pay attention to. In addition, because they are statewide races, which the media covers more extensively, and most Senate candidates are well-known and information on all races is readily available.[26] Even in uncompetitive states, there is an abundance of

---

[26] If there is not an abundance of information about a Senate candidate, it is unlikely that that candidate have the qualities that either voters or party elites are looking for.

information about potential candidates. We should expect, therefore, that party support should cause measures of candidate viability to increase in all Senate primary races, regardless of competitiveness or differences in candidate quality.

These key differences between primary elections for the House and those for the Senate lead to two entirely different expectations about the role of political parties in primaries for these offices. For the Senate, we can reasonably expect the party to be involved in most, if not all, races. Because of the limited number of races each year, parties do not have to overextend themselves in order to try to influence outcomes in all primaries. Party support in Senate primary races should cause increases in candidate viability in all cases, while measures of candidate viability would not generally be expected to influence future party support. For the House, we can expect party support to have a causal influence on candidate viability only when there are not clear differences in candidate quality and only when these candidates are in races in districts where it is anticipated that general election campaigns will be competitive.

## CAUSALITY IN THE SENATE

We begin by looking at the Senate, where we should expect parties in all instances to coordinate on the basis of factors other than candidate primary election viability. To examine quantitatively the relationship between candidate viability and party support in House and Senate primaries, this analysis relies on a Granger test of causality between the number of party donors who give donations to a candidate and candidate fundraising. A Granger causality test is a simple statistical test that provides the ability to distinguish here whether past party support predicts future fundraising, or whether past fundraising predicts future party support, or whether there is not a clear causal relationship between the two. Party support can be said to Granger cause candidate fundraising if the values of party support predict future fundraising, but the values of fundraising do not predict future party support when both lagged values are included in both models.[27] This test helps identify which comes first in the causal process, party support or candidate viability.

[27] These models include long-shot candidates and challengers to incumbents. When long-shot and incumbent candidates are excluded, the results are the same. These models also include observations where there was only one candidate, or where all but one candidate had dropped out of the race. Again, if these races are excluded, the results are the same.

TABLE 3.1 *Granger causality tests of fundraising and party support for US Senate primary candidates*

| | All candidates | | Primaries with candidates with the same level of experience | |
|---|---|---|---|---|
| | Logged fundraising | Party support | Logged fundraising | Party support |
| Party support (t-1) | 0.005** | 0.907** | 0.004** | 0.807** |
| | (0.001) | (0.072) | (0.001) | (0.040) |
| Logged fundraising (t-1) | 0.736** | 0.258 | 0.724** | 0.377 |
| | (0.033) | (0.417) | (0.064) | (0.358) |
| Constant | 2.711** | 2.271 | 3.015** | 5.008 |
| | (0.348) | (2.945) | (0.711) | (3.924) |
| Observations | 2,969 | 2,969 | 948 | 948 |
| R-squared | 0.497 | 0.706 | 0.510 | 0.623 |
| RMSE | 2.47 | 32.47 | 2.31 | 39.91 |

OLS coefficients with standard errors clustered by candidate in parentheses. Asterisks indicate the coefficients are statistically significant.
**$p < 0.01$, *$p < 0.05$.

Table 3.1 shows the relationship between party support and fundraising in Senate primaries. The first pair of models examines all primary candidates. The results indicate a clear causal relationship between party support and candidate fundraising, with party support having a statistically significant effect on future fundraising. While there is a statistically significant effect of party support on future fundraising, there is no effect of fundraising on future party support. From these numbers we find that an increase of 100 additional party donors causes roughly a four percent increase in fundraising the following quarter. However, while increases in the party's support of a candidate cause that candidate's rate of fundraising to increase in the subsequent quarter (as shown in the first column in Table 3.1), increases in candidate fundraising rates do not have any statistically significant influence on future party support (as seen in the second column of Table 3.1).

It is still possible, however, that party support and fundraising are both motivated by candidate viability. It could be that both the general public and party elites are paying attention to indicators of candidate quality such as past political experience. If this is true, party support would not cause an increase in candidate viability, but rather both fundraising and party support would be caused by differences in candidate characteristics. To tell whether this is the case we can restrict our analysis to only those situations where candidates had the same level of experience. In these instances, because the candidates in the race have similar levels of experience in elected office, it cannot be differences in candidate quality that cause both party support and fundraising to increase. As is evident in the second set of Granger causality tests (under the heading "Primaries with candidates with the same level of experience") in Table 3.1, the results are the same if we look only at races where all candidates had the same level of experience. Even after eliminating any possible confounding influence of candidate viability, party support continues to have a statistically significant positive effect on a candidate's future fundraising abilities. This analysis corroborates the accounts of party insiders that party elites are not reacting to candidate viability in Senate primaries; instead, party support predicts future candidate viability.

## CAUSALITY IN THE HOUSE

We can do the same thing to examine the relationship between party support and candidate viability as measured by candidate fundraising in House primaries as well, using a Granger test of causality between the number of party donors who give donations to a candidate and the candidate's fundraising rate.

The expectations for party causality for House candidates, however, are different than they are for Senate candidates. As outlined earlier, the number of House primaries and candidates running in them, combined with the low levels of information available about many of these contests, creates an environment where parties seek to change candidate viability only in competitive races where there is no clear distinction in candidate quality among the candidates running. In other races, we expect party coordination to follow or to move together with candidate success, as they use the same information about candidate experience as the general public does to evaluate candidates. Given these assumptions, the analysis here presents two tests. The first test examines the causal relationship between party support and candidate fundraising for all candidates. By including candidates running in noncompetitive races and races where there were clear differences in candidate quality, we should expect that party support does not independently improve candidate viability as measured by fundraising. Instead, given cues provided about candidate quality and the level of interest in the race, we expect that party insiders will follow candidate viability rather than risk offending the party base over a race where the specific choice of the candidate is unimportant, because the seat is either safe or unwinnable.

Likewise, even in primary races in competitive districts, when there is a clear difference in candidate quality we should expect that candidate quality would advantage one candidate over another in fundraising and in party support. As others have previously pointed out, both a candidate-centered model and a party-centered model would predict that party elites would coordinate behind higher-quality candidates who have more elected experience (Dominguez 2011). Given what we know about party preferences for winning public office to achieve policy goals, it is unlikely that party elites would back a less experienced and lower-quality candidate. In instances where one candidate had a recognizable advantage in experience and ability, both the general public and the political elite should be expected to move in support of the more experienced candidates. In House primaries, candidates with more political experience are likely to be those who both raise more money and garner more party support, because they are more likely to have the qualities that party elites seek. Thus, with both the general public and the party moving together, it is difficult to identify a causal process.

The second set of tests examines primary races in congressional districts where the general election race is expected to be competitive, and where there was also no difference in quality between at least two candidates running in the primary. It is these races where we have hypothesized that party coordination would Granger cause candidate viability, as party coordination provides resources that strengthen a candidate's ability to succeed when there are not clear differences in the levels of electoral experience among the candidates. In this select set of primary contests, we expect to see party support cause changes in future candidate viability.

To measure the competitiveness of the race, the analysis here relies on the first available report from the Cook Political Report of competitive House races in the election cycle (Campbell 2010). For all election cycles, these were the reports issued in January of the election year. More importantly, Cook Political Reports issued these reports before any of the primary elections had been held. For purposes of simplicity, the models use a measure of competitiveness that combines the five-part ranking by the Cook Political Report into a single measure indicating whether or not the general election race was expected to be competitive.

TABLE 3.2 *Granger causality tests of fundraising and party support for US House primary candidates*

| | All candidates | | Primaries in competitive districts where candidates have the same level of experience | |
| --- | --- | --- | --- | --- |
| | Logged fundraising | Party support | Logged fundraising | Party support |
| Party support (t-1) | 0.018** | 0.723** | 0.027** | 0.942** |
| | (0.001) | (0.027) | (0.005) | (0.062) |
| Logged fundraising (t-1) | 0.717** | 0.269** | 0.717** | 0.098 |
| | (0.010) | (0.035) | (0.046) | (0.078) |
| Constant | 2.752** | −0.975** | 2.713** | 0.427 |
| | (0.101) | (0.240) | (0.489) | (0.653) |
| Observations | 21,307 | 21,307 | 1,542 | 1,542 |
| R-squared | 0.452 | 0.473 | 0.403 | 0.517 |
| RMSE | 1.884 | 7.110 | 2.075 | 7.865 |

OLS coefficients with standard errors clustered by candidate in parentheses. Asterisks indicate the coefficients are statistically significant.
**p < 0.01, *p < 0.05.

The results from this first test of causality in all House primaries, in both competitive and noncompetitive districts, are presented in the first two columns of Table 3.2. For all primary candidates, regardless of the competitiveness of the district and the relative quality of their opponents, we find that party support and candidate viability influence each other in a way that makes causality difficult to distinguish. In essence, party support and fundraising both influence each other. Thus, while suggesting that party support does have an effect on candidate fundraising, the origins of that party support are not independent of a candidate's previous fundraising success. In the full set of House primaries, party support both causes and is caused by candidate fundraising.

In contrast, in competitive districts where there is no difference in candidate quality, we find similar results to our findings for Senate candidates. In these races, candidate fundraising does not have a significant effect on future party support. The second set of models in Table 3.2 shows that party support has a statistically significant positive effect on future candidate fundraising. Because there are no differences between these candidates in candidate quality, we also can be more confident that these effects are not being driven by some aspect of candidate experience or quality. In these races, party elites are not simply following the candidate with the highest fundraising totals. Instead, party support acts as a guide for other potential donors and influences future fundraising. In these instances, namely primaries leading to competitive general election contests where there is no difference in the past political experience of the candidates competing for the party's nomination, party support is driving the viability of the candidates in the primary election.

In these situations, party donors are not reacting to candidate fundraising; rather, party support predicts future changes in candidate fundraising. Ultimately, these two tests of causality show that in Senate primary races, and in a select subset of House primary races, party support causes an increase in future candidate fundraising, rather than the other way around. Simply put, these results give credence to the argument that party coordination is not the result of party elites jumping on the bandwagon of candidates already likely to win.

### CONCLUSION

This chapter began with the question of whether party elites were leaders or followers. Party elites participate in a game where reputation is a powerful and useful coin of exchange. For those reasons, before beginning to attempt to understand whether the tools described in Chapter 2 are effective, we needed to understand the process by which parties coordinate behind a preferred candidate and to mitigate concerns about the notion that party elites might have to only "back no losers."

The evidence presented here suggests that, for the most part, party elites are not merely jumping on the bandwagon of the most viable candidate. Party elites do not perceive themselves as bandwagoning, nor does the statistical analysis suggest that they are in most cases. The only instances where the causal process is not entirely clear are in House races, where party elites either already have a strong incentive to support a strong candidate with a weak primary opponent, or in House primaries, where the identity of the nominee has little effect on the likelihood of victory in the general election, or both. In Senate primaries, and in primaries in competitive House districts where candidates are equally qualified, party coordination is not the result of candidate fundraising success. In these instances, party coordination behind a candidate causes and is not caused by candidate fundraising success.

In short, parties coordinate and act to increase candidate viability where there are not clear distinctions in candidate quality and when they have a vested interest in picking between two candidates because of the potential impact of candidate choice on a highly competitive general election and. In these cases, party actions have a significant impact on future candidate fundraising and the viability of the candidate in the primary. Parties coordinate together not with the goal of building up their reputation by supporting the candidate who will win the primary election, but rather with the goal of supporting and helping through the primary the candidate that they perceive as having the best chance of winning the general election. Party elites do care about winning, but only the type of winning that leads to office holding.

As such, if party elite coordination correlates with primary outcomes it is not because partisans are strategically choosing to support only candidates who are already likely to win. Partisan elites, especially those in positions of power, do not support candidates merely on the basis of viability in the primary election or of their ability to appeal to the party base and those most likely to turn out to vote in the primary. Rather, parties act with the hope of maximizing their influence in government and do so in a way that helps to facilitate coordination among the many individuals involved in the process. With this knowledge, we can turn now to the effect of party support on primary outcomes with confidence that, in most primary races, party support is independent of other measures of candidate viability that might drive the outcomes of primary elections.

## APPENDIX TO CHAPTER 3

Part of the reason why scholars of primary elections have struggled to find evidence of party influence during the primary is the lack of quantifiable measures of party support. As is evident from the frustration expressed by Senator Grams, as detailed in Chapter 1, and that of many other frustrated candidates who found the party explicitly supporting their opponent in the primary (La Follette 1913; Laffey 2007; Zdechlik 2006), political parties must act discreetly in support of candidates in order to avoid public criticism for intruding in the local democratic process. Opposition candidates and parties often take this public criticism and use it as fodder for criticism leveled against the nominee and the nominee's party in the general election. Although political parties have occasionally taken public stances on primary candidates in the past, those stances have prompted criticism from the media, criticism from within the party, and criticism from general election opponents (Herrnson 1988; Lopez 2006b). Therefore, when multiple candidates compete for the party's nomination, the party must take care to avoid the appearance of meddling, so as to not to offend potential general election supporters.

Even if parties are active behind the scenes, party organizations, party leaders, and even many party elites rarely choose to announce publicly their full efforts on behalf of nonincumbent candidates in a primary. While the party and party elites may remain publicly neutral, behind the scenes they are privately encouraging capable staff and rich donors to support the party's favored candidate.[28] Because of the clandestine nature of party activity in primary elections, scholarly accounts of party efforts in primary elections have relied on interviews or other historical and anecdotal records to demonstrate that parties are involved in the primary election stage of the process (Herrnson 1988; Menefee-Libey 2000). As a result, we know a lot about what parties do, but little about the magnitude of their influence.

To overcome this problem, in recent years researchers have turned to other ways of measuring party support, such as calculating the share of endorsements or using community detection methods to discover in-network and out-of-network candidates. In their work on the role of parties in presidential primaries, Cohen and his colleagues argue in *The Party Decides* that party elites play a coordination game with their endorsements to winnow the presidential field down to a single candidate, that being the eventual winner (Cohen et al. 2008). Dominguez uses a similar measure of candidate endorsements in her studies of congressional candidates, but because of the amount of time and effort required to collect this information for all 435 congressional races in multiple years, her study is limited to open seat primaries in 2002 (Dominguez 2011).[29] More recently, Desmarais and his colleagues (2015) used network community detection algorithms to locate central candidates within the network of PAC donations during general election campaigns. All of these

---

[28] One recent salient example of party efforts in support of a candidate behind the scenes is the 2016 Democratic presidential nomination. While publicly neutral, DNC chairwoman Debbie Wasserman-Schultz and other high ranking DNC officials strongly favored Hilary Clinton over Bernie Sanders and made concerted efforts to promote Clinton's presidential candidacy (Shear and Rosenberg 2016).

[29] In her Ph.D. dissertation Dominguez (2005) used a composite measure of party support that includes a wide range of components, including endorsements and donations from party-loyal donors (donors who gave only to party candidates).

alternative methods, however, are either time-intensive or computationally and theoretically complex. Previous researchers examining the role of parties in select congressional primaries have argued that we need to develop "other proxies of this partisan support" because previous measures "are cumbersome to gather for large numbers of candidates" (Dominguez 2011, 542).

To create a measure of party support, this analysis builds upon previous research that has described the central role of the official party Hill committees in coordinating party elites on a national scale.[30] While individual party elites may have little knowledge about the vast number of races and candidates, national party organizations are perfectly positioned to connect party elites with deserving and viable candidates who need support to run successful campaigns. To measure the strength of the relationship between party elites and a candidate the analysis in this book uses a count of the number of donors who donated money to both the candidate and the party's Hill committee (the DSCC and NRSC for the Senate and the DCCC and NRCC for the House). This Appendix provides more detail about the theoretical basis for the use of such a measure of party support. It then provides additional tests of this measure's usefulness as a measure of group endorsement by constructing an identical measure of interest group support (the number of donors shared between a candidate and the interest group) and documenting that measure's relationship to interest group endorsements.

PARTY HILL COMMITTEES AS COORDINATORS

Using the number of donors a candidate shares with his or her party's senatorial committee quantifies accounts of the national party organizations as the center of a coordinated effort to direct campaign funds to favored candidates (Herrnson 1988, 2009; Koger et al. 2009; Kolodny 1998). While congressional campaign committees can and do give direct donations, their primary role is to connect candidates and donors in what scholars have termed "conduit activities" (Herrnson 1986, 1988; Kolodny 1998).

---

[30] The work of others has shown that coordination on the local scale is often more difficult, especially in districts where the party is likely to win regardless of the nominee (Bawn et al. 2015; Dominguez 2005). Here, however, we are looking at the ability of the national party to coordinate party elites on a national scale.

The national party connects donors to its preferred candidates by encouraging its own donors also to donate to its preferred candidates and by acting as a party coordinator. Talking about the National Republican Senatorial Committee (NRSC) in the 1990s, Robin Kolodny (1998) explained, "the NRSC does not spend more than the legal amount but provides a critical link for funneling additional funds to candidates by encouraging these NRSC donors to give money to targeted senatorial candidates" (151). The established relationship between the party and its donors enables the party to push its own donors to preferred candidates. The national parties put together many fundraising programs designed to assist candidates in their tasks of raising money by acting as the bridge between high-profile donors and candidates whom they view as viable general election candidates (Cantor et al. 2010; Goldmacher 2013).

While official party organizations do not have the same financial clout that they once did, they continue to act as a coordinating mechanism for influential donors (Herrnson 2009). Party elites, as part of the *extended party network*, continue to be organized in a network structure that has national party organizations at the center (Koger et al. 2009). Studies of formal party organizations corroborate this account.

In the late 1980s, the National Republican Senatorial Committee (NRSC) faced a new dilemma, having raised more money than it could legally transfer to candidates. Although accounts differ about when it began to happen, the NRSC began bundling money to candidates as part of the solution (Herrnson 1988, 71–3; Kolodny 1998, 151). Bundling is a procedure by which an organization gathers a large number of donations on behalf of a candidate. The organization then "bundles" these checks and gives them to the targeted candidate. What began in the late 1980s and early 1990s with the NRSC now is common practice for both the NRSC and its Democratic counterpart (Currinder 2009; Dwyre et al. 2006; Dwyre and Kolodny 2003; Jacobson 2010; Kolodny 1998). Even if they are not asked explicitly, attentive donors pick up on cues from party elites about which candidates they should support (Masket 2011; Sinclair 2012).

The party also connects donors to candidates by acting as a campaign bundler. By relying on bundlers, a candidate raises money on the established credibility of the bundler. Because of their longstanding reputation, party organizations are adept at directing hundreds of thousands of dollars to targeted candidates (Hasen 2008; La Raja 2008). Paul Herrnson explains that, "in its conduit role the [party] committee encourages individuals and PACs to make campaign contributions to particular ... candidates" (Herrnson 1988, 72). Indeed, party organizations have found that directing donors to a particular candidate is just as effective as a direct contribution from the party, but does not invite public criticism (Dominguez 2005, 158).

Large donors who are interested in access to elected officials are also attentive to cues from the party. As Herrnson explains, "large individual contributors who are attuned to the politics of campaign finance recognize high levels of national party support to be *de facto* endorsements from these committees" (Herrnson 1988, 69). Even without an explicit endorsement, those in the party network are able to recognize signs that the party supports one candidate or does not support another. With their experience, habitual donors involved in party activities are trained to pick up the subtle cues that indicate a party's endorsement or lack thereof.

Even if they are not actively involved with the party, attentive donors, as previously noted, easily pick up on cues from other party elites about which candidates they should support (Masket 2011). As one major party donor interviewed for this book explained about a less attentive fellow donor: "When I go to talk to [Vincent Hartford] who doesn't or is no longer actively attending local party meetings or involved in the process, he's always trying to pick my brain about what's going on and where things stand so that he can get a better idea of who he should support." Even when donors do not pay attention to the national party committees, this kind of evidence indicates that elite donors are highly connected and take cues from one another and from the party network (Sinclair 2012).

Parties not only point donors to candidates, they also point candidates to donors. Party organizational leaders encourage their own donors to give to targeted candidates, but they also point candidates to other potential sources of campaign revenue, thus connecting candidates and donors (Kolodny 1998). Parties, and well-connected individuals within the party, may share fundraising lists, and in some cases party organizations may allow candidates to host fundraisers on party property, which gives credibility to the campaign. Candidates who receive many donations from individuals well connected to the national party organization are more likely to have a stronger link to the national congressional or senatorial campaign committee.

## VERIFICATION OF THE MEASURE AS AN INDICATION OF ORGANIZATIONAL SUPPORT

Although party support as a measure of the number of shared donors makes theoretical sense, it is also important to corroborate this logic with some more tangible evidence. This section of the Appendix lays out some of the evidence that supports the use of the number of donors a candidate shares with the party organization as a measure of party endorsement or support.

Unfortunately, we cannot easily verify that this measure of party support is tantamount to a party endorsement, because party support of candidates is normally not explicitly broadcast. Simply, if we had a clearer measure of party endorsement, we would use it. We can, however, look at some high-profile instances in primaries where there was an establishment candidate perceived as party-supported and also a credible and well-funded outside candidate. In these cases, does this measure match what journalists and political insiders indicate? In these instances, the anecdotal accounts match the data extremely well.

The 2010 election cycle saw a number of these Senate primaries which had candidates explicitly recognized as outsider candidates running against candidates who were believed to be well connected to the party network. These races included the Alaska Republican primary (Lisa Murkowski versus Joe Miller), the Arizona Republican primary (John McCain versus J.D. Hayworth), the Arkansas Democratic primary (Blanche Lincoln versus Bill Halter), the Colorado Republican primary (Jane Norton versus Ken Buck) and Democratic primary (Michael Bennett versus Andrew Romanoff), the California Republican primary (Carly Fiorina versus Tom Campbell and Chuck Devore), the Delaware Republican primary (Mike Castle versus Christine O'Donnell), the Kentucky Republican primary (Trey Grayson versus Rand Paul), the Nevada Republican primary (Sue Lowden versus Sharon Angle), and the Pennsylvania Democratic primary (Arlen Specter versus Joe Sestak). In all of these cases except one – the Nevada Republican primary, where the party establishment objected strongly to Angle but was not able to recruit its preferred candidate, Congressman Dean Heller, into the race (Riley 2009) and was left with a variety of other candidates about which it was not enthusiastic – the party-supported candidate, as so described by the media, was also the candidate who received more support from donors who had given to the party organization.[31] Simply, the measure of party support of candidates in a primary matches well

---

[31] Even in the Nevada Republican primary, in three of the five quarters during which Sharon Angle was in the race, more party donors gave to her opponents than gave to her candidacy. In the last quarter of 2009, the candidate with the greatest level of party support was Danny Tarkanian, who would go on to become the Republican Party's nominee for the 4th congressional district in 2012 and for the 3rd congressional district in 2016.

the party's actual preferences in cases where we know who the party's preferred candidate in the primary was from the media coverage of that primary race.

### Interest Group Endorsements and Shared Donors

As another means of validating this measure as a measure of institutional support, we can also look at the relationship between candidates and interest groups which do make candidate endorsements and see how those endorsements affect those groups' support of the candidate through donor networks. Parties are not the only organizations that attempt to act as coordinators of support. Many nonparty organizations both give endorsements and also act as campaign bundlers and fundraising organizers in much the same way that parties do. While we cannot verify this measure of party support by the use of explicit party endorsements, we can construct a parallel measure of the strength of the connection between a candidate and an interest group and can look at how this measure of group support is affected by the explicit endorsement of an interest group.

EMILY's List is one example of a group that uses its resources and political clout to direct donors to particular candidates. While collecting information on past endorsements by interest groups is not easy to do in retrospect, this analysis uses complete information on EMILY's List's endorsements for nonincumbent candidates running for Senate in 2006 and for all candidates for both House and Senate in 2010.[32] For each of these years we can also create a measure of the strength of the support of EMILY's List for each declared candidate, using the same measure that is used to connect candidates to the party organization in this chapter. This time, however, because we are interested in the strength of the relationship between the candidate and the interest group, the measure is the number of shared donors between the candidate and EMILY's List rather than between the candidate and the party organization.

In 2006, EMILY's List endorsed two nonincumbent candidates, Amy Klobuchar of Minnesota and Claire McCaskill of Missouri. More importantly, these endorsements did not coincide either with the candidate's declaration of candidacy or with the candidate's victory in the primary election. Thus, we can get a good sense of what effect an endorsement

---

[32] Interest groups tend to scrub their institutional memories of any candidates which they supported that lose the election.

by EMILY's List has on the shared connection between candidates and the organization by way of the donor network. Figure 3A.1 shows the strength of the connection between these two endorsed candidates in each full quarter of the election. The solid line between quarters three and four of the election year is the timing of the endorsement. EMILY's List endorsed both Klobuchar and McCaskill on September 29, 2005, at the end of the third quarter of that election cycle.

The effect of EMILY's List's endorsement is clear. In both instances, the effect of the endorsement was to double or triple the number of shared donors between EMILY's List and the candidate. Prior to EMILY's List's endorsement, Klobuchar and McCaskill had 35 and 44 shared donors with EMILY's List, respectively. That connectivity increased dramatically, to 94 and 116 shared donors, in the subsequent quarter and continued to rise throughout the election cycle, even as it became apparent that Klobuchar's race would not be competitive.[33]

This early surge in the strength of the connection between EMILY's List and these nonincumbent candidates is even more starkly apparent when compared to the position of other similar nonincumbent candidates in competitive races. Figure 3A.2 shows the number of donors each quarter that five other Democratic candidates in competitive races shared with EMILY's List in that same election cycle.

While some of these candidates later did share a strong connection through shared donors with EMILY's List, especially as their races became more competitive at the end of the election cycle, none of them had as strong a connection early in the election cycle before the primary. All of the large increases in the connections between EMILY's List and these nonendorsed candidates came at the end of the election cycle, when it was clear that these candidates were in a competitive race. Although at the end of the election cycle it was clear that Amy Klobuchar was going to win her election easily, her relationship with EMILY's List is stronger than the relationships that all the other candidates in competitive races had with EMILY's List. Many candidates in competitive races never received any noticeable support from EMILY's List.

---

[33] While the campaign between Amy Klobuchar and Mark Kennedy for the Minnesota Senate seat was initially expected to be competitive, and Cook Political Report, in their first report issued in 2006, rated it as a seat that leaned toward the Republicans, it became evident in late summer that the race was not close. Klobuchar won the race by 20 percentage points, with 58 percent of the vote to Mark Kennedy's 38 percent, with third-party candidates winning the remaining 4 percent of the vote.

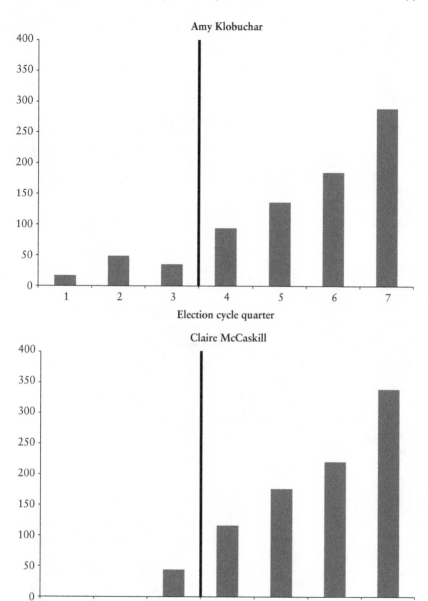

FIGURE 3A.1 *Effect of EMILY's List endorsement on number of shared donors*
*Senate candidates share with EMILY's List candidates in 2006*
Note: Line in graph indicates the point in the election cycle
when EMILY's List endorsed the candidate.

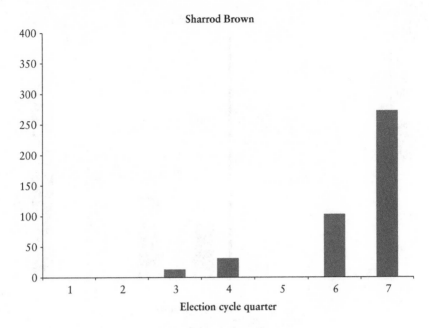

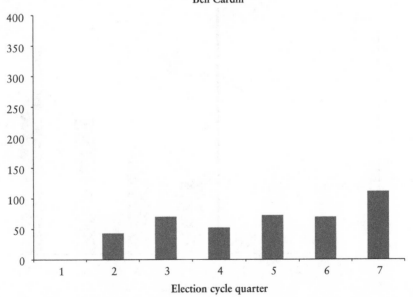

FIGURE 3A.2 *Number of donors that non-endorsed non-incumbent Senate candidates in competitive races share with EMILY's List in 2006*

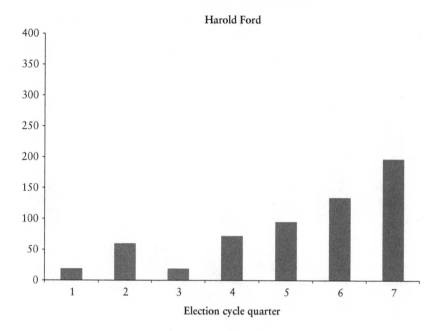

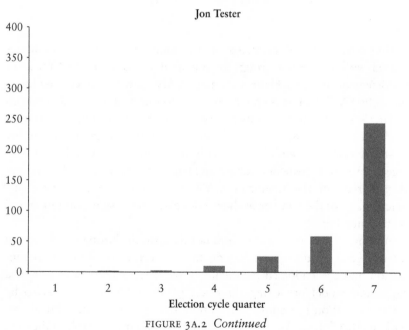

FIGURE 3A.2 *Continued*

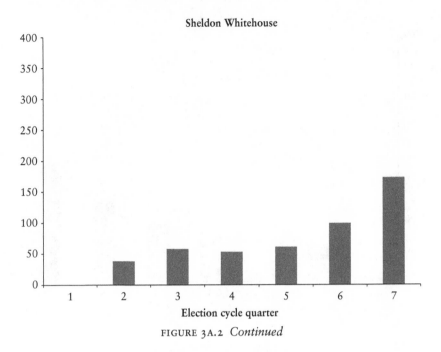

FIGURE 3A.2 *Continued*

The effects of endorsements on the number of donors candidates shared with an interest group are similar if we look at EMILY's List's endorsements in 2010. Figures 3A.3 and 3A.4 show the effect of endorsements by EMILY's List on the number of donors a candidate shares with EMILY's List for nonincumbent Senate and House candidates, respectively. Just as in 2006, an endorsement dramatically increased the number of shared donors a candidate has with the organization. Candidates who received the endorsement doubled and tripled the number of donors that they shared with the organization. While an endorsement is not the sole determinant of the number of shared donors, it has a significant influence on that number.

Adding a series of controls does not dampen the strong effect that an interest group endorsement has on the connection between the organization and the endorsed candidate. Table 3A.1 shows the result of a regression model predicting the effect of an endorsement in 2010 by EMILY's List on the number of donors that a House candidate shares with EMILY's List. As well as including a dummy variable indicating whether the candidate had been endorsed, the model includes controls for party identification, incumbency, candidate quality, as measured by

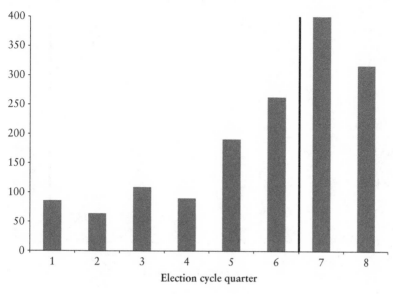

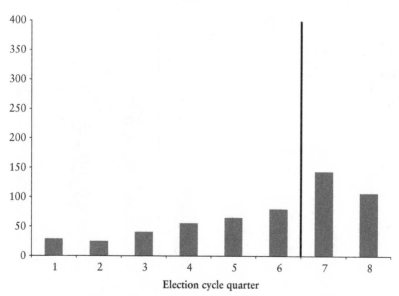

FIGURE 3A.3 *Effect of EMILY's List endorsement on number of donors non-incumbent Senate candidates share with EMILY's List in 2010*
Note: Line in graph indicates the point in the election cycle when EMILY's List endorsed the candidate.

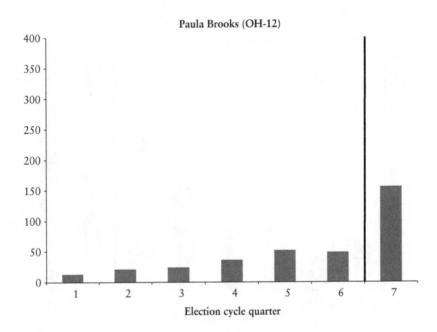

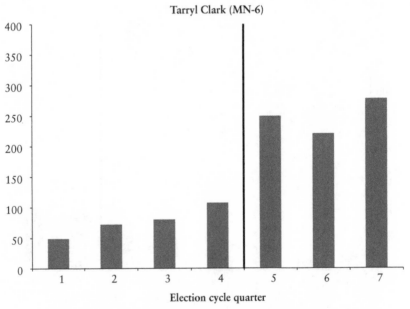

FIGURE 3A.4 *Effect of EMILY's List endorsement on number of donors non-incumbent House candidates share with EMILY's List in 2010*
Note: Line in graph indicates the point in the election cycle when EMILY's List endorsed the candidate.

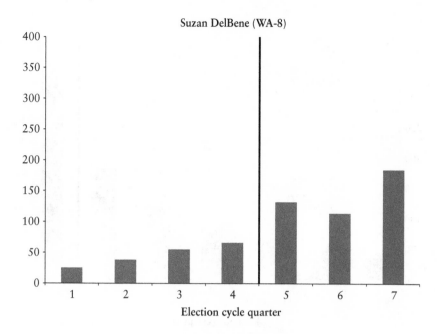

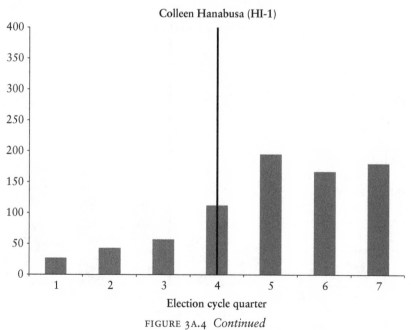

FIGURE 3A.4 *Continued*

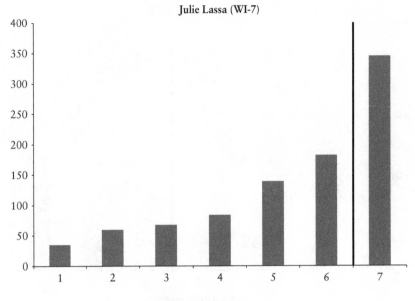

Election cycle quarter

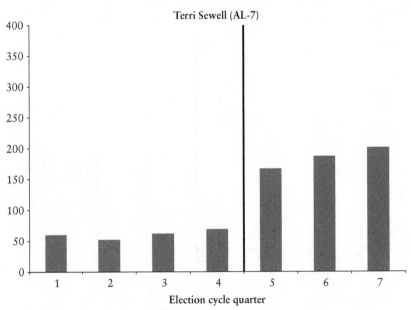

Election cycle quarter

FIGURE 3A.4 *Continued*

TABLE 3A.1 *Effect of EMILY's List endorsement on House primary candidates' shared donors with EMILY's List*

|  | Shared donors with EMILY's List | Shared donors with EMILY's List (Democrats only) |
|---|---|---|
| EMILY's List endorsed | 17.440** | 17.501** |
|  | (1.077) | (1.757) |
| Incumbent | 0.287 | 0.331 |
|  | (0.292) | (0.745) |
| Candidate quality | −0.001 | 0.074 |
|  | (0.263) | (0.805) |
| Competitive district | 0.865** | 2.358** |
|  | (0.213) | (0.586) |
| Democrat | 1.415** |  |
|  | (0.223) |  |
| Shared donors (t-1) | 0.984** | 0.979** |
|  | (0.006) | (0.010) |
| Constant | −0.373* | 0.543 |
|  | (0.173) | (0.495) |
| Observations | 8,363 | 3,129 |
| R-squared | 0.863 | 0.852 |
| RMSE | 9.037 | 14.72 |

OLS coefficients with standard errors clustered by candidate in parentheses. Asterisks indicate the coefficients are statistically significant.
**$p < 0.01$, *$p < 0.05$.

whether the candidate had held any previous office to which they'd been publicly elected, a dummy variable for the competitiveness of the race as measured by Cook Political Reports in January of the election year, and a lagged measure of interest-group support.

As can be seen in Table 3A.1, the regression analysis confirms the findings from the figures above. An endorsement from EMILY's List has a strong effect on the number of shared donors between EMILY's List and the endorsed candidate. Endorsed candidates on average share 17 more donors each quarter with EMILY's List than do nonendorsed candidates,

TABLE 3A.2 *Effect of EMILY's List endorsement on Senate primary candidates' shared donors with EMILY's List*

| | Shared donors with EMILY's List | Shared donors with EMILY's List (Democrats only) |
|---|---|---|
| EMILY's List endorsed | 76.634** | 76.821** |
| | (11.085) | (18.215) |
| Incumbent | 4.980 | 9.697 |
| | (4.744) | (10.946) |
| Candidate quality | 2.557 | 7.532 |
| | (3.187) | (8.685) |
| Competitive state | 4.695 | 11.218 |
| | (2.998) | (7.762) |
| Democrat | 6.654* | |
| | (3.123) | |
| Shared donors (t-1) | 1.003** | 0.997** |
| | (0.013) | (0.021) |
| Constant | -3.725 | -3.926 |
| | (2.687) | (7.284) |
| | | |
| Observations | 1,221 | 476 |
| R-squared | 0.912 | 0.906 |
| RMSE | 50.677 | 81.162 |

OLS coefficients with standard errors clustered by candidate in parentheses. Asterisks indicate the coefficients are statistically significant.
**$p < 0.01$, *$p < 0.05$.

even after controlling for other key determinants of candidate success. Over the course of the entire election cycle this can amount to almost 400 more shared donors.

Table 3A.2 shows the same result, but for Senate candidates. As shown, the results are similar, although an endorsement of a Senate candidate has an even greater influence on the number of shared donors. An endorsement increases the number of shared donors by 76 donors per quarter, or over 600 across the entire election cycle.

Nor does this seem to be just an artifact of EMILY's List. This finding is consistent with other similar findings documenting how endorsements shape the relationships of interest groups with candidates through their donor networks on both sides of the political spectrum. Similar effects of endorsements can be found for organizations supporting conservative candidates, such as the Club for Growth and Campaign for Working Families, and for organizations that support liberal candidates, such as NARAL and the Sierra Club (Hassell 2012; Sclar et al. 2016; Skocpol 2016).

All of this evidence suggests that party support, as measured by the number of donors that a candidate shares with an organization, accurately reflects the support of that organization. As the number of shared donors between a political organization and a candidate increases we can be reasonably confident that there is a strong relationship between these two entities. While party organizations may not officially and publicly endorse a candidate, the actions of those connected to the party provide a clear insight into the preferences of the party network. Knowing the number of donors that a candidate shares with the party organization thus allows us to gain a clear insight into which candidate the party is supporting in the primary election.

# 4

# Clearing the Senate Field

*What kind of third world politics does [the party chair] want to impose on the Republican Party? The delegates won't be elected for another year. The convention is 18 or 17 months away and he wants to have a single name on a slate. That's kingmaking. I thought the role of the party ... was to encourage all good candidates to run.*

—Former Senator Rod Grams (R-MN)[1]

On March 17, 2005, President George W. Bush announced that he was nominating Congressman Rob Portman (R-OH2) to fill the vacant position of US Trade Representative. Shortly thereafter, Portman announced that he would resign his House seat upon his confirmation by the Senate. Portman's resignation would prompt a special election in August of that same year for his congressional seat in a district that had long been considered to be safely Republican. In the previous two decades, no Democrat had managed to win more than 35 percent of the vote (Reuters 2006), and Portman had won 70 percent or more in every election, beginning with his victory in a special election in 1993. To run for Portman's House seat, Democrats would nominate Paul Hackett, a Marine whom the *New York Times* described as "a lean 6-foot-4 ... garrulous, profane and quick with a barbed retort or a mischievous joke" (Dao 2005). Hackett was a political outsider with limited political elected experience, only having previously served briefly on the city council in a suburb of Cincinnati. One reporter, however, explained that "Hackett's freshness is not confined ... to his resume. It is also abundantly evident in

---

[1] Quoted in Stassen-Berger et al. (2005a) and Homans (2005).

88

his language, which may not be especially raunchy for a Marine, but is definitely salty" (Auster 2005a).

Hackett's political journey was not strategically calculated, either. He jumped into the race on the day he got back from his tour of duty in Iraq, just five months before the special election. Knowing that Hackett had political ambitions, the idea of running for Congress was planted by one of Hackett's friends, who greeted him at the Cincinnati/Northern Kentucky airport with the news of Portman's resignation. The decision to run was not hard, and as Hackett explained, "I don't think we made it to the (Ohio River) before we decided I was going to do it" (Budd 2005).

Hackett's military service in the Iraq War and his conservative views on guns and gun control made him a strong candidate in a heavily Republican district, and his candidacy drew national attention (Horstman 2005). Although he did not win the special election in August of 2005, Hackett came incredibly close to knocking off highly favored Republican Jean Schmidt, losing by less than 4,000 votes out of over 115,000 votes cast. It was Hackett's prodigious performance in a race where few would have given a Democrat any chance, and the high volume of media attention that surrounded the special election, that vaulted Hackett's career into the national spotlight (Sewell 2005b).

While party leaders strongly supported Hackett's campaign in the special election, it was their actions after the special elections that influenced the political decisions of Paul Hackett. Basking in his status as a liberal darling after his close defeat in what had seemed a quixotic campaign, Hackett revealed he was uninterested in an attempt at a rematch against Republican Jean Schmidt. He knew from personal experience that winning a seat in Ohio's 2nd Congressional District would be difficult, so that his chances of succeeding were slim and even if he did win, the seat would be hard to defend and retain. Instead, Hackett expressed a desire to run in a more winnable race and indicated that he was interested in a statewide campaign for some other position (Hershey 2005).[2]

At the same time as Hackett's decision not to run for Congress a second time, Senate Democrats were struggling to find a candidate to challenge incumbent Senator Mike DeWine (R-OH). Despite strong efforts on the part of national Democrats, their first choice to run against the incumbent

---

[2] Nor was Hackett focused on any one particular race. In addition to floating the idea of running for Senate, Hackett also indicated that he might be interested in running for State Attorney General, as the Republican incumbent had announced that he was likely to leave the seat to run for Governor (Hershey 2005; Sewell 2005c).

Republican, Democratic congressman Sherrod Brown, indicated that he was passing on the opportunity to return to his House seat (The Blade 2005).[3] While admitting that the polling numbers that the DSCC had shown him for his candidacy "were pretty good," he was unwilling to give up a safe seat in the House to challenge a Senator who had won over 60 percent of the vote just a few years before (Provance 2005).

Unable to convince Brown or any other Democratic member of the Ohio congressional delegation to run, party leaders turned quickly to recruit Hackett to challenge DeWine (Tankersley 2005d). Hackett received strong encouragement from prominent individuals in the party, both nationally and at the state level. Representative Tim Ryan (D-OH17) indicated that party leaders were aggressive in their attempts to recruit Hackett, saying that "After Sherrod had announced that he wasn't running, (Senate Minority Leader) Harry Reid asked me to encourage Paul Hackett to run because he's a good candidate ... I was asked by the highest-ranking Democrat in the country to help get somebody in this race" (Collins 2005b). Just a little over a month after his narrow loss in the congressional special election, Hackett met with party leaders, including DNC chairman Howard Dean, Senate Minority Leader Harry Reid, and DSCC chair Senator Chuck Schumer, to ponder his political future as the party attempted to persuade him to enter the race (Collins 2005a; Hammer 2005; Tankersley 2005c).

The party's efforts to recruit Hackett were successful. Just a few weeks after initially being courted by party leaders and encouraged to run for the Senate, Paul Hackett announced that he would bypass other opportunities and would seek the US Senate seat held by Senator DeWine (Auster and Koff 2005). As part of that decision, Hackett and those close to him pointed specifically to the strong influence that party elites had on his decision. One of the key reasons Hackett's spokesman gave for Hackett's decision to run was the "overwhelming support from the leaders of the Democratic Party, campaign organizations, and staff," and he indicated that "Mr. Reid gave Mr. Hackett the confidence to run" (Tankersley 2005c). Hackett even indicated later that he had talked with other potential Democratic candidates, including Congressman Sherrod Brown, and

---

[3] Hackett was not even the second choice of Senate Democrats to run. Party leadership also encouraged Representative Tim Ryan (D-OH17) to run against Senator Mike Dewine. However, Ryan's relatively short term as a member of Congress and his relative anonymity to statewide voters ultimately played a large role in his decision not to run for Senate (Krawzak 2006).

they had indicated that they were not going to run and had encouraged him to jump into the race (Hammer 2005). It was Democratic Party elites who had given him the confidence to throw his hat into the ring. Party efforts to recruit a challenger they believed could defeat incumbent Republican Mike DeWine had landed them Paul Hackett.

However, it was party efforts which began a few weeks later that would also push Hackett out of the race he had just entered. Almost at the same time as Hackett announced that he was running for Senate, Sherrod Brown indicated to party leaders that he was reconsidering his decision not to challenge DeWine (Tankersley 2005b). Although Brown cited the resolution of several issues of House business that he was deeply concerned about as the reason for his change of heart, many saw Brown's reversal as a move driven by strategic political ambition, as the political events in late 2005 changed the political environment into one that seemed strongly to favor Democrats in the upcoming midterm elections (Tankersley 2005a).[4]

Brown's decision to run quickly caused party elites to change their position toward Hackett. Although they had clamored for Hackett to announce his candidacy just a few weeks before, party leaders now rallied behind Brown and clamored for Hackett to get out of the race. Party leaders were not shy about encouraging Hackett to get out, either. Rather than sticking to the ordinary clandestine political pressure, party leaders were public about their desire for Hackett to get out of the race. Citing a need for a competitive candidate in the 2nd congressional district, DCCC chair, Rahm Emanuel, said explicitly, "This isn't talking behind the scenes; I'm saying it publicly ... I'm petitioning Paul Hackett to run for Congress" (Hammer 2006).

Consistent with the evidence presented in Chapter 3, this decision to support Brown and encourage Hackett to drop out was not merely party elites jumping on the bandwagon of a candidate who was more popular among primary voters.[5] In their explanation of their preferences, party leaders pointed to the differences in general election viability between Hackett and Brown. "It boils down to who we think can pull the most votes in November against DeWine," said Chris Redfern, chairman of the

---

[4] In reference to the electoral effect that an unpopular President George W. Bush would have on the election in Ohio, Cook Political Report Analyst Jennifer Duffy said that "There's definitely a Bush drag out there. And really, Ohio, it's radioactive. It's so toxic for Republicans, they're starting to glow" (Tankersley 2005a).

[5] Hackett's rise had given him considerable support among grassroots activists and the online community of liberal activists (Daily Kos 2005; Sewell 2005c).

Ohio Democratic Party. "And in Ohio, Brown's name is golden. It's just that simple" (Urbina 2006).

In addition, because Republican Senator Mike DeWine was perceived as vulnerable, party elites indicated quite clearly that they did not want an expensive and divisive primary to ruin that electoral opportunity (Tankersley 2005a). As a spokesman for Senator Schumer explained "We've told both Sherrod Brown and Paul Hackett that avoiding a primary will make it easier to win the Ohio Senate seat" (Urbina 2006). Thus, Brown's reversal of his decision not to run for Senate, which gave party elites their preferred candidate, also changed how party elites treated Hackett. While Hackett still maintained his media star status and attracted strong support among party bloggers and liberal activists, party elites now saw a potentially loose cannon who might do significant damage to the party's eventual nominee in a competitive primary election (Auster 2005b; Sewell 2005b).

Brown's decision to jump back into the race infuriated Hackett and made it even more crucial to party leaders that Hackett be convinced to drop out of the race. Hackett was known for his coarse nature and language, and party elites in the Democratic Party were concerned about the political damage that Hackett might do to Brown (or to himself) in a contested primary (Auster 2005a). As political analyst Stuart Rothenburg explained, "There are signs that Hackett seems a little embittered. If he runs an aggressive race that attacks Sherrod Brown, it could divide the party, and that's an issue that the Democrats have to be concerned about" (Sewell 2005a).

But what was more infuriating to Hackett was how party leaders rallied to Brown after he changed his mind about a Senate run, and Hackett was quick to vocalize his opinion about party leaders. "They have some relationship with (Brown). They're all professional politicians, and I think they'd be happy if I went away," he said, while also reiterating his commitment to the Senate race when it first became clear that party elites were now pressuring him to get out of the race (Hammer 2005).

Yet, despite his adamancy that he was not going to withdraw his candidacy, just four months after declaring his intentions to run for Senate, Paul Hackett announced he was leaving the race. In doing so, he made quite clear the pressure party leaders had put on him. "For me, this is a second betrayal," Hackett said, upon announcing he was dropping out of the race. "First, my government misused and mismanaged the military in Iraq, and now my own party is afraid to support candidates like me" (Urbina 2006). Hackett also made it clear that the party had been intimately involved in "behind-the-scenes machinations that were intended to hurt my campaign" (Chancellor 2006). The same party leaders who persuaded him to throw his hat into the Senate race were those who pressured him and ultimately were successful at getting him to step aside (Urbina 2006).

## A BULWARK AGAINST PARTY INFLUENCE?

In this case, and in the examples from previous chapters, the party's influence on the primary election process seemed to have fundamentally changed the considerations of candidates as they contemplated their potential candidacies. Hackett got into the Senate race because of party elite encouragement and left the race because of explicit party pressure to do so. Yet, this is not how many conceive of the role of parties and party elites in primary elections. For the most part, the American public has largely considered primary elections a bulwark against the corrupting influence of party leaders. The origins of the direct primary go back to local party nominations in the 1840s in Crawford County, Pennsylvania. Yet primaries were not implemented as a means of nominating candidates for statewide and federal office until the early 1900s, when the progressive antiparty movement began to advocate for them as a means of eliminating the influence of corrupt party bosses on the electoral process.

As is discussed in Chapter 1, the progressive movement's main objective was to eliminate corruption in government. Parties, corporations, and other large groups of individuals seeking influence were seen in the eyes of progressive reformers as anathema to democratic ideals. Progressives advocated for the opening up of government and the direct influence of the general public as a way of reducing party influence in electoral politics. Key to these efforts was the implementation of the direct primary to wrest control of the nomination process out of the hands of party bosses and to give it to the public citizen.

However, while Wisconsin Governor Robert La Follette and his fellow Progressives strongly advanced the direct primary as a means of reducing party control over the nomination process (and as a means of advancing their own political careers), it was partisan actors in government who largely encouraged the adoption of such measures (Ware 2002). Conventions caused their own sets of problems for party elites, and some accounts suggest that the implementation of primary elections solved many of these problems, while still allowing party bosses to play a significant role in the process. Indeed, primaries are perhaps not as strong a barrier as the public supposed, as subsequent analysis has shown that the changes in the nomination system ultimately had minimal influence on legislators' voting behavior or the levels of party unity in state legislatures or Congress (Hirano et al. 2010; Masket 2016).

Whether or not the actual implementation of the direct primary was a revolt against party bosses or not, the progressive movement was effective in using antiparty rhetoric to mobilize support for a cause that grew to attract wide support from the general public. Even those more critical of the influence of the progressive movement in the adoption of the primary have recognized that areas of high partisan competition tended to adopt the direct primary more quickly because of its popularity, and that the antiparty movement effectively "channel[ed] debate so that the direct primary was always likely to emerge as the subject of legislation" – and to be the solution to the problem (Ware 2002, 213–14).

Thus, regardless of whether or not the direct primary was actually embraced and enacted because it limited party power, the perception among the public and in the general discourse has been that it is the "most radical of all the party reforms adopted in the whole course of American history," meant to work by "breaking the bosses' power over party nominations" and giving power directly to the people (Ranney 1975, 121). It was the antiparty tradition in America that made direct primaries appealing to the public as a reform.

Yet, if progressives intended the direct primary to change the type of politician that was nominated and to eliminate party control over the process, it is not entirely clear that primaries have done their job (Hirano et al. 2010; Ware 2002). Whether or not the almost universal adoption of the direct primary in the United States had the desired effect of reducing partisanship and polarization by leveling the playing field for politicians who were not as loyal to their party, however, is still debatable. As evidence of the minimal effect these reforms had, changes to the party system did not bring on a significant change in the political behavior of elected officials (Masket 2016). The adoption of the direct primary had only moderate effects on the ideological voting patterns of Senators and Representatives, now nominated through the direct primary rather than by caucus or convention (Hirano et al. 2010).

However, while the voting patterns and behaviors of politicians have been shown not to have changed, there has been little analysis of whether party elites still control the primary election process by which House and Senate candidates are nominated. It could be that changes to the nomination process reduced party control, but did not change voting behavior in the legislature. Indeed, not everything that party insiders want from politicians in office may be documented through roll call votes. This chapter and the next two chapters focus on analyzing whether party elites continue to wield significant influence in the nomination process in the House and the Senate. Specifically, it is this chapter and Chapter 5 that seek to determine whether parties are influential in clearing the field for preferred candidates. Chapter 6 then examines the ability of parties and party elites to secure the nomination for those candidates.

## WHY PARTIES WANT TO CONTROL NOMINATIONS

Regardless of the rules in place governing the process, nominations are the opportunity for the party to put forward a candidate that best represents its interests, is best able to win the general election, and is the most likely to enact preferred public policies (Bawn et al. 2012).[6] The party has an interest in ensuring that a general election candidate emerges from the party's nomination process with aligned policy preferences and who will give the party the best chance to win a majority of seats in the Senate and the House, and thus be able to enact preferred legislation (Herrnson 1988). As such, party leaders have a strong incentive to become involved in the process of preventing unelectable candidates, or candidates who will not pursue acceptable party policy goals, from being nominated.

Not only do party organizations have an interest in who wins the primary election, they also are concerned about the process. As evident in the comments from party leaders about the potentially contentious primary between Sherrod Brown and Paul Hackett, parties and candidates worry about the potential negative effects that a divisive primary may have on the eventual nominee. While scholarly studies are inconclusive about the effect of competitive primaries on general election vote totals (Bernstein 1977; Born 1981; Hacker 1965; Jewitt and Treul 2014; Lazarus 2005; Miller et al. 1988; Piereson and Smith 1975), the media and political practitioners view competitive and divisive primary elections as

---

[6] The party's preference for Sherrod Brown over Paul Hackett in the Ohio Democratic Party primary for the US Senate district in 2006 could also be seen as a clear indication of party elites and policy demanders preferring a candidate that they knew they could trust and who would enact their preferred policies. As Richland County (OH) Democratic Party chairman Joe Mudra explained, "I can tell you the things that Sherrod Brown stands for. I can't tell you what Hackett stands for" (Auster 2005b).

detrimental to the eventual nominee.[7] Party elites fear the damage that a fierce primary battle could do to their eventual nominee. These concerns are not isolated to primaries with ex-Marine candidates known for being loose cannons on the campaign trail, either. In their study of primary election competition, Alvarez et al. (1995) found over 500 news articles referring to competitive primary elections, almost all of which mentioned the detrimental effect the competitive primary would have on the party's general election chances. In the last two decades not much has changed, as news stories routinely cite the parties' concerns about divisive and negative primaries and the effect those primaries would have on the party's ability to win public office (Cataluna 2010; Martin 2010).

In addition, regardless of the actual tone of a competitive primary election, parties are also concerned about the financial cost that a competitive primary might have. Party officials and candidates want to avoid expensive intraparty primary fights that leave the winning candidate in a financial hole. Most party elites would prefer that their preferred candidate be able to save scarce resources for electoral conflict where winning means holding a legislative seat. In his book on party campaign activity in the 1980s, Paul Herrnson (1988) reported that officials from both national parties' campaign organizations indicated that dissuading individuals from running for public office was "one of their most important and difficult election activities" (54). Unfortunately, previous research work on this important party function of candidacy dissuasion has been primarily anecdotal in nature, not delving into the effects of national party activities on actual candidacy decisions (but see Niven 2006).

As Paul Herrnson paraphrases campaign committee officials, "certain candidates must be discouraged from running" in order to allow the party to join forces behind a single candidate rather than spending

---

[7] Scholars have argued both that divisive primaries are harmful to a party's general election candidate (Bernstein 1977; Hacker 1965; Johnson and Gibson 1974; Kenney and Rice 1984, 1987), that they are helpful to a party's general election candidate (Dowdle et al. 2013; Galderisi et al. 1982; Jewitt and Treul 2014), and that their effect depends in part on the nature of the primary challenge (Ezra 1996; Johnson et al. 2010; Lazarus 2005). Competitive primaries are beneficial to the eventual nominee if a competitive primary increases interest and activity among less interested partisans (Galderisi et al. 1982). However, competitive primaries also increase the amount that a candidate must spend to win the primary, which he or she cannot subsequently spend in the general election (Ezra 1996; Goodliffe and Magleby 2001). Similarly, primaries that feature two candidates focusing their attacks upon one another instead of the opposition are also more likely to lose the support of members of their own party in the general election (Djupe and Peterson 2002; Johnson and Gibson 1974; Kenney and Rice 1987).

campaign resources fighting within the party in an election that does not result in the winning candidate's holding public office (Herrnson 1988, 54). Rather than face a tough primary election, parties would prefer the best candidate to sail through an uncompetitive nomination process, thus remaining politically unscathed.

The question that this chapter addresses (as does the next) is whether parties have the power to clear the field for a preferred primary candidate. In Chapter 6, we will turn our attention to whether parties can influence the outcomes of contested primary elections where the party was not fully able to clear the field. In regard to party influence in primary elections, current political theory would leave parties and party elites rather discouraged and the old progressive reformers celebratory. As detailed in Chapter 1, until recently, studies of the candidate emergence process have focused on the characteristics of candidates and their ambition and the political environment (Dynes et al. 2016; Jacobson and Kernell 1981; Key 1949; Maestas et al. 2006; Prewitt 1970). Political campaigns, especially their aspects regarding candidate emergence, have almost uniformly been declared "candidate-centered." In the election process, parties have been thought to play only a small role in candidate emergence at best, let alone a role in clearing the field for preferred candidates.

The previous chapters in this book have sketched out the possibility of a significant role for parties in primary election races where the party's actions might shape the decisions of candidates to run for office and influence their success in this political endeavor. Political scientists have begun to document the coordinated action of party elites in support of candidates in primary elections at different levels of government (Bawn et al. 2014; Cohen et al. 2008; Dominguez 2011; Hassell 2016; Masket 2009, 2011). These studies have begun to show that parties are neither passive observers nor merely service organizations for the candidate but instead coordinate their actions strategically in support of a candidate. This chapter explicitly tests the effects of those coordinated actions on the ability of parties to clear the field for a preferred candidate across a wide range of nomination contests.

Previous chapters have laid the groundwork for understanding the tools that parties have at their disposal and documenting the fact that they use these tools not just in support of inevitable winners. This chapter and the two that follow examine whether those tools actually have any influence in shaping the options presented to primary voters for the Senate and the House. These chapters show the ability of a political party to clear out the field for a preferred candidate. Party action in support of primary candidates does have a strong influence on the decision of these candidates to remain in the race for the nomination.

### CLEARING THE PRIMARY FIELD

Prior to the implementation of primary elections, the party's nominee was often nominated in a "smoke-filled back room." While the individuals in these positions of power within the party no longer have exclusive control over the nomination (nor do they often meet in a smoke-filled back room), they still have a number of tools that enable them to exert a strong influence on the decisions of candidates to run for office.

As outlined in Chapter 2, the party has access to resources that are critical to a successful campaign. By promising to mobilize these resources in support of a candidate, parties can encourage potential candidates to run for office. The incentives which parties and other party-connected organizations have to offer candidates provide a strong impetus to run for office. Parties, and groups connected to the parties, strategically influence the pool of candidates by encouraging certain candidates to run (Broockman 2014; Fox and Lawless 2010; Preece and Stoddard 2015).

Likewise, party officials can discourage candidates by offering strong support to a candidate's ambitions in the pursuit of another office, or by simply making it clear that the party is going to support another candidate (Herrnson 1988, 54–6). As explained in Chapter 2, ambitious candidates take these factors into account with the knowledge that if they buck the party and lose, they will have trouble receiving support in their future political aspirations. While previous chapters have laid the groundwork for understanding why parties might be influential, this is the first foray into measuring the role parties play in changing the decisions of candidates to compete for the nomination. If we are to ask if parties are influential it is not sufficient merely to point to their resources and their decision-making process, but it is also necessary to demonstrate the magnitude of the influence of the party's support on candidate actions.

### DATA SOURCES AND PROCEDURES

Given that the party's decision to coordinate in support of a preferred candidate is not merely a bandwagon effect, as demonstrated in Chapter 3, we can directly examine how the support of parties influences the decisions of candidates to compete in the primary. Can a party effectively convince a candidate to drop out of a primary to clear the way for another candidate? One of the biggest concerns that progressive reformers had was that party elites were limiting the choices available to voters and forcing voters to accept their handpicked candidates. This chapter specifically looks at the ability of parties to clear the field in Senate primaries for their preferred candidates so that, in the words of one major party executive, "the other guy can have an easy primary race and concentrate on the general election" (Herrnson 1998, 54).

To examine the party's ability to clear the primary field, as before, in Chapter 3, this chapter relies on the data of all individuals who declared their candidacy for US Senate and filed with the Federal Election Commission (FEC) between 2004 and 2014.[8] This includes candidates who only formed exploratory committees and candidates who withdrew shortly after announcing their intentions to run for Senate. Because we are interested in the ability of parties to clear the field, the data also identify whether the candidate dropped out of the primary race prior to the primary election. If a candidate withdrew before the primary, the data include the date when the candidate dropped out of the race, gathered from local media sources. When no information about a candidate's date of withdrawal was available, the dropout date was set as a week after the last recorded donation to the campaign, or the date of the state's candidate filing deadline, whichever was earlier.

For each declared candidate, the data also include information on fundraising totals from individual donors during each quarter in the primary. Candidates have an incentive to ensure that quarterly reports of fundraising totals and donor lists are accurate, because they must file a report with the FEC on a quarterly basis, and campaigns use these reports to signal the strength of their candidacy. Most importantly, the data on party support and candidate fundraising used here are specifically limited to the primary and do not include donations occurring after the primary election. The data also contain information about whether the candidate had held previous elective office at any level (Jacobson and Kernell 1981; Lublin 1994).

It is important to note that by looking only at candidates who declared their candidacy for office, we are likely greatly underestimating the effect

---

[8] The end of Chapter 6 contains a discussion of the 2016 election cycle. Although Republicans may have been unable to push out Donald Trump from the presidential primary, both Republicans and Democrats were successful at pushing out a number of Senate contenders that were not their party's preferred candidates.

that parties have on the process. Many of the actions that parties take
in an effort to clear the field are taken well in advance of the primary
election, when potential candidates are actively gauging their chances of
successfully obtaining the nomination (Smith 2001a). Candidates routinely consult with party leaders and elites to try to determine where the
party is going before jumping into the race. Party pressure on individuals
who have expressed interest in running for office to stand down for the
party's preferred nominee does not necessarily begin when the candidate
declares his or her candidacy for public office. Many candidates send
out feelers to gauge how their candidacy would be received, and many
of those feelers reach important individuals within the party network.
Even while potential candidates are deciding whether to declare their
candidacy they are taking cues from party elites. Thus, while this chapter
shows that parties are successful at getting candidates who have declared
their candidacy out of the race, these estimates of the magnitude of the
effect that parties have on the choice of candidates available to primary
voters are most likely underestimates of the true overall effect.

## Measuring Party Coordination

Because we are interested in the effect of party support on candidate
behavior we must have a good measure of party support. As explained
in Chapter 3, to measure the strength of the relationship between party
elites and a candidate in each quarter, the analysis uses a count of the
number of donors who donated money to both the candidate and the
party's Senatorial Campaign Committee as a measure of party support.[9]
Using the number of donors a candidate shares with his or her party's
Senate or House campaign committee quantifies accounts of the party
organizations as the center of a coordinated effort to direct campaign
funds to favored candidates (Herrnson 1988, 2009; Koger et al. 2009;

[9] Also tested were models that excluded from the count of party donors those individuals who gave to both major political parties' Hill committees. There is no difference in
the results. Bipartisan party donors made up less than 1 percent of the sample of party
donors. While there may be some concern that bipartisan party donors are not part of
the party and are merely interested in access, this is less of a concern in a primary than
in a general election. Eliminating these individuals, however, does not give an accurate
representation of the role that parties play in connecting donors (both bipartisan and partisan) to preferred candidates. As noted in the text, party organizations regularly bundle
money on behalf of candidates, including money from donors who give to both parties
(Herrnson 1998, 2009; Kolodny 1998). Not including these individuals eliminates an
important part of the parties' efforts to coordinate in support of preferred candidates.

Kolodny 1998).[10] While official party organizations do not have the same financial clout that they once did, they continue to act as a coordinating mechanism for influential donors (Herrnson 2009).[11]

These donors are party elites and are major players in the process. Around one third of these donors gave more than $1,000 to the party, and many gave much more. More importantly, these individuals are attentive to signals from the national party. Even if they are not asked explicitly, attentive donors pick up on cues from other party elites about which candidates they should support (Masket 2011). Even when donors do not pay attention to the national party committees, this and other evidence indicates that elite donors are highly connected to each other and take cues from each other and the party network (Sinclair 2012). In addition, party elites, as part of the extended party network, continue to be organized in a network structure that has national party organizations at the center (Herrnson 2009; Koger et al. 2009). Studies of formal party organizations have also found evidence that parties continue to operate as the central mechanism for coordination of donations to preferred candidates (Currinder 2009; Dwyre et al. 2006; Dwyre and Kolodny 2003; Jacobson 2010).

## EVIDENCE OF PARTY INFLUENCE IN SENATE PRIMARIES

With clear measures of party support for primary candidates we can now move to test the influence of party support in primary elections. The analysis in this chapter and the next focuses on the influence of party support on a candidate's continued participation in the primary. While we will soon get to the effect of party support on a candidate's primary electoral success, we first want to examine how party support shapes the options presented to voters. How does party support affect the likelihood of a candidate's continuing to run for office, even after controlling for other key factors? At the beginning of this chapter, we read several statements by a frustrated candidate, decrying the efforts of party leaders to clear the field. What we want to know is whether or not this effort is actually effective. Can parties clear the field for a preferred candidate? This chapter

---

[10] Also tested were other measures of party support to take into account the relative levels of party support and fundraising of candidates compared to the other candidates in the race (see for example Norrander 2000 and 2006). These are consistent with the results shown here and can be found in the Appendix to this chapter.

[11] This measure of party support is also an excellent proxy for an endorsement. See the Appendix to Chapter 3 for more details.

looks at the effect of party efforts in Senate primaries. The next chapter shows that there are similar results for House primaries as well.

To quantify the effect of party support on the shape of the Senate primary field, the analysis uses the data on candidates described above and estimates a logit model where the dependent variable takes a value of zero if the candidate remained in the race and a value of one if the candidate dropped out during that quarter.[12] After a candidate drops out, all subsequent quarters are then dropped from the sample.[13] For simplicity, the results show the effect in an individual quarter.[14]

These statistical models allow us to estimate the effect of party support on the likelihood of a candidate's remaining in the race after controlling for other factors that might likewise encourage that candidate to drop out of the race. While the vignettes that lead each chapter provide good anecdotal evidence, these statistical models allow us to distinguish whether those examples are evidence of a systematic involvement of parties or are merely unique cases. While many candidates may have individual circumstances that encourage them to drop out, we are looking for influences that stretch across races. While in ordinary least squares regressions the coefficients returned from the regression indicate the marginal impact of a one-unit increase in the dependent variable on the independent variable, the coefficients in logit models are not quite as easy to interpret. Because of this, the effects of party support on the likelihood of a candidate's remaining in the race are also shown graphically. For simplicity, readers can look at the figures provided to understand how increases in party support change the likelihood that a candidate will withdraw from the primary race in a particular quarter.[15] Because of possible concerns

---

[12] In most party primaries, coming in second behind another candidate of the same party means that the candidate does not compete in the general election. With top two primaries, this is not the case. For this reason, the analysis excludes candidates competing in top two primaries in the states of California, Louisiana, and Washington in the years when those primary rules were in place. When those states did not have top two primaries, the candidates running in primaries are included in the analysis.

[13] Following Beck et al. (1998).

[14] Alternative model specifications, using a Cox Proportional Hazard Model, show identical results and can be found in the Appendix to this chapter.

[15] While interviews with party elites identify two resources (campaign staff and financial support) that party networks use to help party-supported candidates in their primaries, this analysis focuses only on party support as measured through party donors. There is no reason to believe, however, that parties would offer one resource but not the other (Kolodny and Logan 1998), and previous work has shown that parties are effectively able to diffuse and coordinate "campaign strategies among a party's candidates" (Nyhan and Montgomery 2015, 292).

about an author-created measure of party support, additional checks and alternative ways of modeling the causal effect are provided in the Appendix to this chapter. These alternative models also provide perhaps a brief insight into the effect of factionalism within the party. Rather than look at an overall level of party support, these models look at a candidate's party support relative to the candidate in the primary with the most support. Regardless of the specifics of the model, however, the relationships between party support and the withdrawal decisions of candidates are consistent.

In addition to estimating the effect of party support, the models also include controls for other key factors that influence the likelihood of a candidate's continuing to compete for the nomination. The first of these is the number of candidates running. More crowded primaries are more likely to cause strategic politicians to withdraw. Candidates running in a crowded primary race recognize that it is difficult to distinguish themselves and to appeal to voters and therefore may choose to run for another office or run at a future date. Because of this, the models include controls for the number of candidates in the race. Although at first it may seem odd not to have excluded races where there is only one candidate running, there are many instances where unopposed candidates have dropped out. To prevent that situation from biasing the effect of party support on the likelihood of dropping out, the models do not exclude races where there was only one candidate. This provides a clearer baseline for the likelihood of dropping out. The inclusion of those races from the analysis, however, does not change the results, and those alternative models, excluding races with only one candidate, can be found in the Appendix.

The other factors for which we must control are fundraising and the past experience of the candidate.[16] Candidates with previous political experience as elected officials are better candidates, have better name recognition, and are more likely to enjoy the campaign success needed to maintain an active and vigorous campaign (Jacobson and Kernell 1981; Lublin 1994). Likewise, without healthy and successful fundraising operations, candidates are not able to keep the lights on in their offices or to

---

[16] The effects of party support and candidate quality shown in the tables here are no different if we use variations of this measure of challenger quality that give higher values to higher office holders (Squire 1992). Because these variations showed no differences in their effects and had no effect on the other variables of interest, for simplicity the analysis presented in this chapter and in subsequent chapters uses the bivariate version of candidate quality.

pay for the mail and other means of communication needed to contact supporters.[17] When the financial stream dries up, it is almost impossible for a candidate to continue to compete.[18]

Table 4.1 shows the result of a logistic regression of the effect of party support on the likelihood that a Senate candidate will withdraw from the primary race. The models also include dummy variables for each quarter of the election cycle to correct for the temporal dependence of the model (Beck and Katz 1995; Beck et al. 1998). The model combines the five election cycles from 2004 to 2014, and standard errors are clustered by primary election race.[19]

The large effect of candidate quality in the first model in Table 4.1 raises a question about possible spurious correlation between party support and the decision of a candidate to drop out of the race. More experienced candidates are less likely to drop out of a primary. Even though party support Granger causes candidate fundraising in Senate races, it is plausible, albeit unlikely because they move at different times, that candidate fundraising and party support are both motivated by a candidate's quality. Candidate quality could motivate both the general public and individuals associated with the party to support the primary candidate and to give to the campaign. To test whether this is the case we can look at Senate primary races where candidates have the same levels of past political experience.

The second model in Table 4.1 looks at races in which candidates had the same level of previous political experience. By looking just at these candidates we are able to eliminate the possibility that candidate quality is driving the effects that both fundraising and party support have on the likelihood that the candidate will remain in the race. As the second model in Table 4.1 shows, in cases where there is no difference in candidate quality in primary elections for a US Senate seat, party support is still a significant predictor of the likelihood that a candidate remains in the race. Likewise, these findings are robust to other specifications of the

---

[17] Speaking about presidential campaigns, Democratic fundraiser Michael Farmer said, "people don't lose campaigns. They run out of money and can't get their planes in the air. That's the reality" (Congressional Quarterly Weekly Report 1992).

[18] Party support and logged fundraising are correlated at 0.44 and have a Variance Inflation Factor of 1.6, well below the normally accepted value of 10 (O'Brien 2007).

[19] There is some variation in the number of observations per year (431 (2004), 451 (2006), 387 (2008), 618 (2010), 562 (2012), and 520 (2014)) and by party (41 percent Democrat).

TABLE 4.1 *Likelihood that a candidate will withdraw from*
*a Senate primary election race*

|  | All primaries | Primaries with candidates with the same level of experience |
|---|---|---|
|  | Withdrawing from primary | Withdrawing from primary |
| Party support (t-1) | −0.025** | −0.024* |
|  | (0.008) | (0.010) |
| Logged fundraising (t-1) | −0.102** | −0.105* |
|  | (0.022) | (0.042) |
| Candidate quality | −0.379* | −0.164 |
|  | (0.212) | (0.337) |
| Number of candidates (t-1) | 0.182** | 0.198* |
|  | (0.044) | (0.080) |
| Constant | −2.545** | −2.790** |
|  | (0.472) | (0.860) |
| Observations | 2969 | 929 |
| Pseudo R-squared | 0.157 | 0.112 |
| Log-likelihood | −602.03 | −234.82 |

Logit coefficients with standard errors clustered by primary race in parentheses.
Quarter dummy variables not shown in results. Asterisks indicate the coefficients are
statistically significant.
**$p < 0.01$, *$p < 0.05$.
*Note*: The second equation includes only candidates in primaries where that candidate
shared the distinction of having the most political experience with at least one other
candidate. More simply, this model looks only at situations where there were not
disparities in political experience.

variable for party support, which can be found in the Appendix to this
chapter.

Figure 4.1 shows the likelihood that a candidate will drop out of
the race in a particular quarter at different levels of party support, while
keeping the total amount of money raised at a constant level (using the
first model from Table 4.1). As a candidate's party support moves from
zero party donors to 100 party donors in the previous quarter (a change
of roughly two standard deviations in party support) the likelihood that a

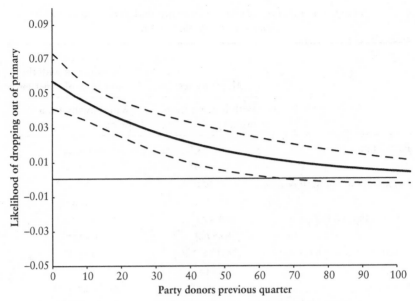

FIGURE 4.1 *Likelihood that a Senate candidate will withdraw*
*from the primary race*
Note: Dashed lines are 95% confidence intervals.

candidate drops out of the race decreases by almost 7 percent in that quarter.[20] A similar two standard deviation increase in fundraising from zero fundraising, however, decreases the likelihood of dropping out of the race by 4 percent.[21] The effects of party support are obviously lower the more money a candidate raises, but even when a candidate raises an amount that is a standard deviation above the amount an average candidate raises, the effect of a two standard deviation change in party support is still 4 percent in that quarter.[22] The cumulative effect over the course of the campaign

[20] The effect is almost 9 percent if you look only at races where the competing candidates have the same level of political experience. In addition, this effect is even greater (upward of 13 percent in each quarter) if you exclude long-shot candidates who run for reasons other than to hold elected office (Boatright 2014; Canon 1993).

[21] This effect of fundraising on a candidate's decision to continue to seek the nomination is even further reduced when we center the change in fundraising on the average fundraising level. If we look at the effect of the change in two standard deviations on fundraising, with the baseline fundraising level being the average fundraising level of a candidate in a quarter, an increase in two standard deviations results in only a 2 percent decrease in the likelihood of dropping out.

[22] The effect of a two standard deviation change in party support when candidate fundraising is one (or two) standard deviations below the mean is 9 (or 11) percent. When

is to increase the likelihood that candidates without party support will drop out during the campaign by over 50 percent.[23] There also does not appear to be any trend over the time period, although the small number of cases per year in the Senate makes that difficult to observe and the estimated effect in each year bounces around due to small sample sizes. On the whole, however, when making decisions about their candidacy, candidates are influenced not only by the quantity of money raised each quarter but also by the level of support they receive from party elites.

It is important to note that, in a time when candidates continue to cite fundraising shortcomings as a reason for dropping out of a race, the results also confirm that fundraising is crucial to a candidate's decision to continue to compete for the nomination. Without the monetary resources required to fund advertising, turnout operations, and other campaign functions, campaigns are ineffective and unlikely to be successful. More important and more specifically to the point for this chapter, the results confirm the importance of the strength of a candidate's connection to party elites.

The graph in Figure 4.1, however, only looks at the direct effect of party support. In addition, because party support Granger causes candidate fundraising, part of the effect of party support is mediated through candidate fundraising. Mediation analysis shows that roughly 6 percent of the total effect of party support is mediated by its influence on the amount that candidates raise. Thus, while the direct effect of increases in party support is to reduce the likelihood that a Senate candidate will drop out of the competition for the nomination in a particular quarter by almost 7 percent, the total effect is even greater.[24] The support of party elites has a significant effect on the willingness of candidates to continue to compete for the party's nomination in a US Senate race. US Senate primary candidates who sense that they do not have the support of party elites are more likely to drop out of the primary race.

Without securing party support, Senate candidates recognize that they will struggle to be competitive. Parties shape the field of Senate primary

---

candidate fundraising is one (or two) standard deviations above the mean, the effect is 4 (or 2.5) percent.

[23] The Cox Proportional Hazard model used in the Appendix to this chapter also pegs the overall effect at about 30 percent.

[24] Mediation analysis was carried out using the *Mediation* package in Stata (Hicks and Tingley 2011) which implements the procedures described by Imai et al. (2011) and Imai et al. (2010) to estimate the causal mechanisms that transmit the effect of a treatment variable on an outcome. Using these path models shows that the total effect of party support is $-0.0022$ and the mediated effect is $-0.00014$ (both statistically significant at the $p < 0.05$ level, two-tailed test).

candidates by ignoring candidates they do not want in the primary field. Ambitious and strategic politicians pick up on these cues and use them in their decisions whether or not to continue to pursue a party's nomination for the US Senate.

## Party Differences in Senate Primaries

While it may be tempting to lump both parties together in analyzing effects, there are fundamental differences between the parties in their structure and norms that warrant an examination of each party individually (Grossmann and Hopkins 2016). These structural differences could lead to different expectations about party unity and the ability of parties to clear the field for their nominee (Herrnson and Gimpel 1995; Schantz 1980). Because Democrats are focused more on group incentives than on an underlying political ideology, the argument could be made that they are less likely to get in line and coordinate their efforts behind a single nominee. Intraparty conflict centered on group identities and interests may make it more difficult for coordination to occur in the Democratic Party. Likewise, candidates without party support may be more willing to buck the party's wishes if they have significant support from other Democratic groups who are not central to the party network.

On the other hand, in recent years commentators have noted that there appears to have been an upswing in the number and strength of anti-establishment challenges to Republican Party candidates in the House and the Senate. While the number of incumbents being challenged in primary elections (being primaried) has actually gone down, the nationalization of these challenges and the formation of new national groups along ideological lines have increased their salience in the public sphere (Boatright 2014). Table 4.2 shows the number of candidates running in each election cycle between 2004 and 2014. The first column under each party shows the number of candidates who announced their candidacies and filed statements with the FEC. The second column shows the number of those candidates that actually appeared on the primary election ballot.

If one looks only at the number of primary candidates on the ballot it appears as if Republicans have faced significant problems in clearing the field for preferred candidates during this period.[25] However, party support is not the only factor which prompts candidates to decide to run for

---

[25] Part of this could be the nature of the seats that were up for election in the Senate. However, during this time period the Senate has been relatively well balanced.

TABLE 4.2 *Number of Senate primary candidates by party*

| | Democrats | | | Republicans | | |
|---|---|---|---|---|---|---|
| | Announced | On ballot | Percent ran (%) | Announced | On ballot | Percent ran (%) |
| 2004 | 62 | 49 | 79.0 | 86 | 71 | 82.6 |
| 2006 | 64 | 53 | 82.8 | 71 | 59 | 83.1 |
| 2008 | 70 | 54 | 77.1 | 61 | 53 | 86.9 |
| 2010 | 86 | 68 | 79.1 | 134 | 93 | 69.4 |
| 2012 | 61 | 44 | 72.1 | 122 | 81 | 66.4 |
| 2014 | 63 | 57 | 90.4 | 143 | 113 | 79.0 |
| Total | 406 | 325 | 78.1 | 617 | 470 | 76.2 |

office. Even if parties are supportive, candidates may choose not to run because of the bad electoral environment, which would likely drag down their electoral fortunes (Jacobson and Kernell 1981). Four out of the six elections studied here took place in electoral environments that favored Republicans, with 2006 and 2008 being the exceptions (and the atrocious 2006 electoral environment for Republicans was not entirely clear until most candidates had already declared their candidacy). The raw number of candidates who announced their candidacy or who appeared on the ballot, or even the number of contested primaries, does not give a clear picture of the ability of parties to clear the field for their preferred candidates.

Looking at the number of candidates on the primary ballot as a percentage of the total number of candidates who declared presents an entirely different story. In this case, while more Republicans were likely to announce their candidacy for Senate, more of them also dropped out of the process. While Republicans had a much larger number of potential candidates in 2010, 2012, and 2014, there was a higher percentage of these Republican candidates dropped out of the race before the primary election day. While these raw numbers provide some indication that there are no major differences between the parties' abilities to get candidates out of the race, we need to control for the variety of other factors that contribute to the decisions of candidates to drop out of primary races.

To look at the independent effect of party support on the likelihood of dropping out, we can model the decision of a candidate to drop out of the race by party. Table 4.3 and Figure 4.2 look at the effect of party support

TABLE 4.3 *Likelihood that a candidate will withdraw from a Senate primary election race by party*

| | Democrats | Republicans |
|---|---|---|
| | Withdrawing from primary | Withdrawing from primary |
| Party support (t-1) | −0.019† | −0.027* |
| | (0.011) | (0.011) |
| Logged fundraising (t-1) | −0.092† | −0.123** |
| | (0.048) | (0.025) |
| Candidate quality | −1.209** | −0.059 |
| | (0.372) | (0.246) |
| Number of candidates (t-1) | 0.281** | 0.175** |
| | (0.097) | (0.046) |
| Constant | −2.498** | −2.589** |
| | (0.771) | (0.607) |
| Observations | 1208 | 1761 |
| Pseudo R-squared | 0.211 | 0.148 |
| Log-likelihood | −199.70 | −390.81 |

Logit coefficients with standard errors clustered by primary race in parentheses. Asterisks indicate the coefficients are statistically significant.
Quarter dummy variables not shown in results.
**$p < 0.01$, *$p < 0.05$, †$p < 0.1$.

on the likelihood that a candidate drops out of the race as a function of party support by party. As before, the models also include controls for candidate fundraising, candidate quality, and the number of candidates currently running in the primary. Figure 4.2 graphs the effect over a two standard deviation change in the number of party donors.

What we actually find are few differences between the parties in their ability to get nonpreferred Senate primary candidates out of the race. The effect of party support on the decision of a candidate to drop out of the race is significant for both Republicans and Democrats. For Republicans, the net effect of a two standard deviation increase in party support in one quarter is to lower the likelihood of a candidate dropping out in the following quarter by six percentage points. For Democrats, a similar increase in party support lowers the likelihood of dropping out by about five percentage points. However, the difference between those two effects is not significant.

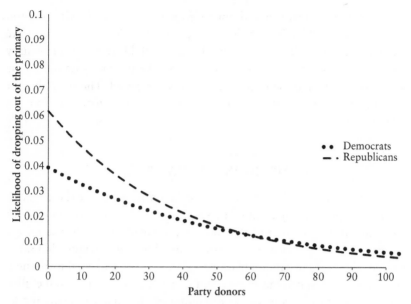

FIGURE 4.2 *Likelihood that a Senate candidate will withdraw from the primary race by party*

## CONCLUSION AND DISCUSSION

The evidence provided here shows that the primary elections for the US Senate do not reflect merely the sum of the candidates' political ambitions and campaigning and fundraising abilities. While the party cannot arbitrarily remove candidates from a primary, strategic candidates are susceptible to the persuasion of party elites. Candidates for federal legislative office weigh the support they receive from the party in their decisions to continue or to conclude their campaign.

Party support matters. It provides access to the competent and experienced campaign staff and financial resources essential to mounting a successful campaign. Without those resources, candidates struggle to compete and confront a more difficult pathway to victory. Recognizing that fact, candidates without party support are more likely to drop out in hopes of securing better odds in the future or of finding a more successful pursuit. Without party support, candidates face an uphill battle to win the nomination. Parties shape the field of candidates by ignoring candidates they do not want in the primary field. Ambitious and strategic politicians pick up on these cues and use them in their decisions whether or not to pursue a party's nomination for a public office.

Rather than indifferent and noncoordinated individuals who respond merely to a candidate's ambition and political abilities, party elites are actively engaged in determining the choices available to voters in primary elections. The question remains, however, of whether this is unique to the Senate or whether these effects are more widespread. The next chapter attempts to examine that question by looking at the influence that parties have in House primaries.

## APPENDIX TO CHAPTER 4

This Appendix provides additional checks on how robust the effect of the party support is on a candidate's decision to continue to compete for the nomination. The text of the chapter presented the models as a logit regression where the outcome measure was a bivariate variable that takes a value of zero if the candidate remained in the race and a value of one if the candidate dropped out during that quarter. That model also included dummy variables to control for the temporal dependence of the model (Beck and Katz 1995; Beck et al. 1998). The result is a model that looks similar to, but is not entirely the same as, a hazard model. A hazard model includes an underlying hazard function plotting how the risk of the event changes over time, eliminating the need to include quarterly dummy variables. Because these models incorporate slightly different assumptions about the influence of each time period, the results of a Cox Proportional Hazard model are presented in this Appendix. Table 4A.1 shows a replication of Table 4.1 using a Cox Proportional Hazard Model, as opposed to the logit model with quarterly dummy variables. Figure 4A.1 graphs that function over the course of the primary election cycle.

As shown in Table 4A.1 and Figure 4A.1, the results are robust to the model specifications used in the analysis. Over the course of the primary election cycle, increasing the number of donors a candidate shares with the national party's senate campaign committee by two standard deviations increases the likelihood of that candidate's remaining in the primary race by over 30 percent.

### ADDITIONAL MODELING RESTRICTIONS AND ASSUMPTIONS

In addition to modeling the likelihood of dropping out of the primary using a hazard model, we can also modify the assumptions about party support and see how it interacts with the likelihood that a candidate will

TABLE 4A.1 *Alternative specification of Table 4.1 (likelihood that a candidate will withdraw from the Senate primary) using a Cox Proportional Hazard Model*

|  | Withdrawing from primary | Hazard ratio |
|---|---|---|
| Party support (t-1) | −0.025** | 0.975 |
|  | (0.008) |  |
| Logged fundraising (t-1) | −0.081** | 0.922 |
|  | (0.017) |  |
| Candidate quality | −0.403* | 0.668 |
|  | (0.185) |  |
| Number of candidates (t-1) | 0.150** | 1.162 |
|  | (0.033) |  |
| Observations | 2964 |  |
| Chi-squared | 130.32** |  |
| Log-likelihood | −1127.35 |  |

Hazard coefficients with standard errors clustered by primary race in parenthesis. Asterisks indicate the coefficients are statistically significant.
**$p < 0.01$, *$p < 0.05$.

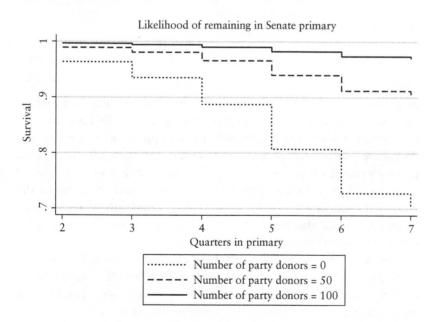

FIGURE 4A.1 *Survival estimates from the Cox Proportional Hazard Model for Senate candidates*

TABLE 4A.2 *Alternative specification of Table 4.1 (likelihood of that a candidate will withdraw from the Senate primary) using only primary quarters with two or more candidates*

|  | Withdrawing from primary |
|---|---|
| Party support (t-1) | −0.021** |
|  | (0.008) |
| Logged fundraising (t-1) | −0.107** |
|  | (0.023) |
| Number of candidates (t-1) | 0.120** |
|  | (0.043) |
| Candidate quality | −0.214 |
|  | (0.203) |
| Constant | −2.148** |
|  | (0.478) |
| Observations | 2,070 |
| Pseudo R-squared | 0.104 |
| Log-likelihood | −570.93 |

Logit coefficients with standard errors clustered by primary race in parentheses. Asterisks indicate the coefficients are statistically significant.
Quarter dummy variables not shown in results.
**$p < 0.01$, *$p < 0.05$.

drop out of a race. One concern might be that including races where there is only a single candidate biases the results. While there are several instances where candidates without any opposition dropped out of the race, either because of health problems or in anticipation of another party-supported candidate's entering the race, including every candidate regardless of the contested nature of the primary could have biased the results by including a number of party-supported candidates with no competition who also had high levels of party support. As Table 4A.2 shows, this is not the case.

Whether or not we include candidates who were running in an uncontested race, party support continues to have a strong effect on the likelihood that a Senate candidate remains in the primary race. These findings show that the results given in the previous chapter are not driven by a small handful of uncontested races, where candidates are less likely to drop out of the race.

ALTERNATIVE MEASURES OF PARTY SUPPORT IN PRIMARIES

Although party donors, on average, were approximately 10 percent of a party-favored Senate candidate's donors each quarter, parties might not invest in all races evenly. Raw counts of party donors might misrepresent what is actually going on in a given state. Candidates in some states may be specially targeted by the party committees, while in other states they may not be a priority and thus may attract only a small number of party donors. What is most important is not the total number of donors a candidate shares with the party committees, but rather the percentage of shared donors a candidate has relative to the party's preferred candidate. Therefore, this Appendix also uses data on a candidate's relative party

TABLE 4A.3 *Alternative specification of Table 4.1 (likelihood of that a candidate will withdraw from the Senate primary) using fundraising and party connectedness as a percentage of the fundraising and party support of the candidate in the primary who raised the most money and received the most party support in that quarter*

|  | Withdrawing from primary |
| --- | --- |
| Percent of most connected candidate's party donors (t-1) | $-0.596^{\dagger}$ |
|  | $(0.328)$ |
| Percent of highest fundraisers' fundraising (t-1) | $-1.503^{**}$ |
|  | $(0.321)$ |
| Number of candidates (t-1) | $0.099^{*}$ |
|  | $(0.042)$ |
| Candidate quality | $-0.315$ |
|  | $(0.214)$ |
| Constant | $-2.735^{**}$ |
|  | $(0.439)$ |
| Observations | 2,896 |
| Pseudo R-squared | 0.166 |
| Log-likelihood | $-580.58$ |

Logit coefficients with standard errors clustered by primary race in parentheses. Asterisks indicate the coefficients are statistically significant.
Quarter dummy variables not shown in results.
$^{**}p < 0.01$, $^{*}p < 0.05$, $^{\dagger}p < 0.1$.

support and fundraising. Rather than a raw number of fundraising and party support, party support and fundraising are calculated as a percentage of that of the candidate in the primary that raised the most money and received the most party support in that quarter in a way that is also consistent with past research (Norrander 2000, 2006). Table 4A.3 shows the results of the same model using this standard alternative way of measuring the relative influence of party support on the campaign process.

As these models show, the results are robust to a variety of alternative specifications. Regardless of how we measure party support or of the exact statistical model specifications that are used, party support has a strong significant influence on the likelihood that a candidate will continue to compete for the party's nomination. Those without party support are simply more likely to drop out of the primary. Party tools, when brought to bear in a primary election, help support a candidate's primary campaign, and candidates without party support realize that they will struggle to compete.

# 5

## Clearing the House Field

*Let me be blunt: You are not going to be able to win this race.*
—Senator Harry Reid (D-NV) pressuring congressional candidate
Jesse Sbaih (D-NV3) to drop out of the primary race[1]

*The DCCC folks and Democratic leaders in the House are pushing Mike*
*[Michaud] (D-ME2) to stay [in the House]*
—Anonymous Democratic Operative[2]

The previous four chapters have each led with an example of party influence in shaping the field of Senate candidates. But party influence in primary elections is not limited just to primaries for the Senate. As Chapter 3 shows, just as in Senate primaries, in certain subsets of House races, party support causes subsequent increases in candidate fundraising. Just as in Senate primaries, party coordination can have a significant effect on primary elections in the House.

In late 2009, Representative Neil Abercrombie (D-HI1) abruptly announced that he would resign his seat as the Representative from Hawaii's 1st Congressional District in order to focus his efforts on his

---

[1] Quoted in Obeidallah (2016). Reid's comments were notable in part because of the reason that he gave for why Sbaih would not win his race. According to Sbaih, the full quote was "Let me be blunt: You are not going to be able to win this race because you're Muslim." Reid's office vehemently denied the accusation. Reid's spokesman said, "Jesse Sbaih is a liar and that's why he is going to lose ... We never said he shouldn't run for elected office. It was that, to run for a congressional seat, your first time, you're going to lose. And you need more experience" (Fahrenthold 2016).
[2] Quoted in Riskind and Bell (2012).

gubernatorial campaign, where he faced a difficult primary against Honolulu mayor, Mufi Hannemann. Although Abercrombie had previously announced he would not run for reelection, his announcement that he would resign his seat prior to the primary, which prompted a special election, was a surprise to many (Rudin 2010).[3]

When Abercrombie announced his resignation in December, several well-qualified candidates had already announced their intentions to seek the seat as his replacement. Former Representative Ed Case, who had previously served as the representative in Hawaii's 2nd Congressional District, before giving up his seat in an attempt to beat Senator Daniel Akaka in the Democratic Primary in 2006, announced his candidacy in March 2009, shortly after Abercrombie announced his intention to run for Governor (DePledge 2009). Later that year, after many months of speculation, Democratic State Senate Majority Leader, Colleen Hanabusa, also announced that she would run for the open congressional seat (Tsai 2009).[4]

Abercrombie's surprise announcement moved up the showdown between Case and Hanabusa by requiring a special election in May of 2010, ahead of the Democratic primary in September that year. The special election, however, would have the added twist of having all candidates on the ballot without separating them by party affiliation. Rather than having to win a majority, the plurality winner of the special election would serve the remaining months of Abercrombie's term.

While many of the policy demanders within the party, most notably the labor unions, strongly supported Hanabusa (Reyes 2010; Strassel 2010), that was not sufficient to drive Case out of the special election. Case had a persuasive argument that his more moderate fiscal ideological positions would make him a better candidate against Honolulu City Council member Charles Djou, the Republican candidate in the race. Moreover, Case was well known for his willingness to push back

---

[3] Hannemann and Abercrombie had had a long and acrimonious relationship in Hawaii Democratic politics, dating back to their run for Congress in 1986, when another member of Congress, this time Representative Cec Heftel (D-HI1), resigned to run for governor. Both the special election, which included all candidates on the ballot, and the Democratic primary were held on the same day. Abercrombie won the special election with 29 percent of the vote, but lost the primary to Hannemann. Hannemann would then subsequently lose to Republican Pat Saiki in the general election (DePledge 2010b).

[4] Hanabusa had served in the state senate since 2002, but had previously lost a congressional special election in 2002 (to Case) and a congressional primary in 2006 (to Mazie Hirono) for Hawaii's 2nd Congressional District seat, before announcing she would run again for the 1st Congressional District seat (Tsai 2009).

against the party establishment to further his own political aspirations. He had previously represented Hawaii's 2nd Congressional District, but had given that seat up in an attempt to unseat long-serving US Senator Daniel Akaka in the Democratic primary in 2006. Those actions had infuriated many of the party elites, especially Senator Akaka's colleague, Hawaii's other US Senator, Daniel Inouye, who had made his displeasure with Case adamantly clear. Case's public spat with Inouye over the 2006 Senate primary had cost Case significant political capital (DePledge 2009).[5]

The party's inability to push Case out of the special election ultimately doomed Democratic chances of winning that election. While party support was enough to help Hanabusa garner more votes than Case, it was not enough to buoy a divided Democratic electorate over a unified Republican electorate. In the end, the presence of both candidates on the ballot did exactly what many Democrats feared, splitting the vote between Hanabusa and Case and letting Republican Charles Djou win with just 39 percent of the vote to Hanabusa's 31 percent and Case's 28 percent (Reyes 2010).

The outcome of the special election only resulted in ratcheting up pressure on Case to withdraw from the primary race to be held later that year. Democrats wanted Case out in order to allow Hanabusa to focus her resources on mounting a better challenge of Djou in what was seen by many as a highly competitive race.[6] Many Democrats adamantly argued that it was important to have a unified party that would allow a candidate to challenge the new incumbent without having to spend resources on a competitive and possibly divisive primary (Miller 2010).

In addition, many within Case's camp suggested to him that continuing to run an uphill battle when party resources were helping his primary opponent would severely limit his political future within the party (DePledge 2010a). Having already challenged one of the party's elder statesmen in 2006, continuing to fight against the party's preferences in the primary would drastically curb his ability to pursue any future

---

[5] When Case challenged Akaka in 2006, party elites expressly vented their frustrations with Case's decision to run for Senate against a sitting senator, indicating that "[Case] is disrespectful, that he should wait his turn, that he should get in line and do what he is told, that he'll never win, and that he will ruin his career" (Zimmerman 2006).

[6] *Cook Political Reports* initially rated the seat as leaning Democrat in January 2010, prior to the special election. Immediately after the special election (but before Case dropped out of the primary), the race was categorized as a toss-up and remained that way through the rest of the election cycle.

political ambitions within the Democratic Party that he might have, especially if he failed to win the primary. Even if he won the primary without party support, failure to win a highly competitive general election after a prolonged and antagonistic primary would likely doom any of his future political aspirations. In short, regardless of the outcome, his actions would reduce party support in the future. In this light, after competing in the special election and only a little more than a week after vowing to compete in the primary immediately following his loss, Case withdrew his candidacy (Pang 2010).

In the end, Ed Case's decision not to run in the primary, delivered strategically at the state Democratic Party Convention to maximize the impact of the decision on party leaders and elites, not only cleared the path for Colleen Hanabusa, but also started to mend some of the fissures between him and Democratic Party elites that had emerged with Case's challenge of Akaka four years previously (DePledge 2010a). Inouye, one of Case's staunchest critics in the special election and Hawaii Democratic Party senior statesman, acknowledged Case's decision with words of high praise. In contrast to his previous biting criticism, Inouye praised Case's decision to withdraw, explaining, "I was happy and deeply moved by Ed Case. He showed he was a Democrat" (Borreca 2010; Honolulu Star-Bulletin 2010). His former opponent, Colleen Hanabusa, called it "an amazing gesture and an amazing gift" (Borreca 2010). Former Congressman Abercrombie similarly expressed admiration: "It took a lot of guts to try to go for the greater good" (DePledge 2010a). Case's decision to withdraw made him a hero within Hawaii Democratic Party circles for the moment, and helped him win back some of the support he would need for future political campaigns that would have been unavailable had he continued to flout the party's preferences.[7] As one analyst described the decision to drop out of the race, "in doing so, he set the stage for something else. He still has the gunpowder of ambition, plus he made nice to Dan Inouye" (Cataluna 2010).

[7] These actions would be enough to placate the perceived party kingmakers. Case would run for Senate in the very next election, in 2012, following the retirement of Senator Daniel Akaka. Case's actions in the 2010 congressional race helped keep Inouye neutral in the race for Senate (Sur 2011) and helped garner support from other key players in Hawaii Democratic politics (Shraine 2011). Although initial polls showed a tight race between Case and Representative Mazie Hirono, who had replaced Case in the 2nd District, Hirono would win the primary and ultimately the Senate seat (Borreca 2011; DePledge 2012).

## CLEARING THE FIELD IN HOUSE PRIMARIES

The anecdotal evidence from the Democratic primary for Hawaii's 1st Congressional District in 2010 suggests that the influence of party elites on candidacy decisions extends beyond the Senate to the House. However, while we have found a strong effect of party support on the decisions of Senate candidates to drop out of the primary election race, there are two factors that should lessen the effect of party support on the candidacy decisions of House primary candidates. The first is that the resources needed to run a successful House campaign are significantly fewer than the resources required to run a successful Senate campaign. Because of this, it is more likely that House candidates might be able to find a small number of good staff or a large enough source of funding outside of the party network for them to be competitive. Because the resources required to run a successful House primary campaign are fewer in number, candidates should be less reliant on the party network to provide those resources. Being able to procure the necessary resources elsewhere, candidates are less dependent on party networks in a decision to continue to compete for the party's nomination.

Second, as detailed earlier, in Chapter 3, the levels of information at House primary level are significantly lower than those in Senate primaries. In House primaries, there is less information about party actions and less information about the strengths and weaknesses of primary contenders. As a result, candidates who are not supported by the party may not get adequate information through the media or the partisan political network to realize that they are not the party's preferred candidate. While party elites may have a preference for a candidate's opponent and may be funneling support to that opponent, the candidate may not be able to gather enough information about the status of the race to realize it. Because House primaries are low information contests, candidates may not accurately gauge the level of support and may miss signals and indicators that would be more readily available and easier to recognize in a Senate race.

The Democratic primary in Hawaii's 1st Congressional District in 2010, for example, was a high-profile race not lacking in communication or information about the candidates. In addition, Case and Hanabusa had already competed against each other once in the special election. Because of the number of House seats up for election each year and other factors that limit the availability of information in House primaries, we should expect the influence of party support on the likelihood of candidates' remaining in the race to be more focused on certain key races for the House than it was for the Senate. That being said, the resources that parties control and can allocate to primary candidates are no different for the House than they are for the Senate. While we might expect that party influence in the House would be reduced, we have no reason to believe that it would disappear entirely. Because we know that party support influences future fundraising, we should expect that, at the minimum, party support would change candidacy decisions through changes in candidate fundraising.

### DATA SOURCES AND PROCEDURES

As with the Senate, to test whether party elites are influential in shaping the field of candidates in House primary elections, this chapter relies on a dataset containing all candidates who declared their candidacy for the US House between 2004 and 2014 and filed a report with the Federal Elections Commission (FEC). As before, these data on House candidates include every candidate who filed with the FEC, even if they withdrew shortly after announcing their candidacy.

Consistent with the analysis in the previous chapter, because we are specifically interested in the ability of parties to clear the House primary field, the data were coded to indicate whether or not the candidate dropped out of the primary race prior to the primary election. For candidates who dropped out before the primary election, the data note the date of each candidate's withdrawal as gathered from local media sources. When no information about a candidate's last date as a candidate was available, either the date a week after the last recorded donation to the campaign, as recorded by the FEC, or the date of the state's candidate filing deadline was entered, whichever was earlier.

To measure party support, this analysis uses the same measure described in previous chapters, counting the number of donors who donated money to both the candidate and the party's Congressional Campaign Committee (in this case, the DCCC for Democrats and the NRCC for Republicans).[8] Just as with the Senate Hill committees, House Campaign committees routinely connect candidates and donors through bundling

---

[8] As before, versions of this measure that eliminate from the count of shared party donors individuals who gave to both major political parties' Hill committees were also examined because of concerns that individuals who give to both parties may not be party elites, but rather merely access seekers. There is no difference in the results.

and cue giving, which provides signals to party elites about which candidates are party favorites (Currinder 2009; Dwyre et al. 2006).

As before, controls for campaign fundraising on a quarterly basis and a measure of candidate quality on the basis of previous elected office experience are also included. *The Cook Political Report*'s measure of general election competitiveness, issued in the first month of the electoral year, is used to identify competitive districts on which the party might be more likely to focus its efforts.

## RESULTS

Table 5.1 shows the results of a logit regression predicting the likelihood that a House candidate will withdraw from the race.[9] As with the Senate primaries shown in the previous chapter, explanatory variables include a candidate's party support, fundraising from the previous quarter, and the quality of the candidate.[10] The model combines six election cycles from 2004 to 2014 and standard errors are clustered by primary election race.[11]

Just as with Senate primaries in Chapter 4, Table 5.1 estimates a statistical model that examines the likelihood of dropping out of the primary race as a function of the support from the party that the candidate receives, while controlling for candidate fundraising and candidate quality. The models show that the influence of party support on the decisions of candidates about continuing to compete for the House nominations is similar to that of the Senate. The direct effect of party support on the likelihood that a candidate will withdraw from the race, as party support increases two standard deviations above having no party support, is also displayed in Figure 5.1.

Before jumping into the effects of party support, it is important to note that in the House, as in the Senate, candidates routinely cite fundraising, or rather the lack thereof, as a reason for quitting a primary race. The results in Table 5.1 confirm that fundraising is an essential component

---

[9] As in Chapter 4, alternative specifications using a Cox Proportional Hazard Model show identical results and can be found in the Appendix to this chapter.
[10] Party support and fundraising are correlated at 0.46 and have a Variance Inflation Factor of 3.4, well below the normally accepted value of 10 (O'Brien 2007).
[11] There are slightly more observations in 2010 (4,452) than there are in 2004 (3,083), 2006 (3,615), 2008 (3,578), 2012 (3,387), or 2014 (3,192). There are also roughly the same numbers of observations by party (47 percent Democrat).

TABLE 5.1 *Likelihood that a candidate will withdraw from a House primary race*

| | All primaries | Competitive district primaries where candidates have the same level of experienc | Competitive district primaries where candidates have the same level of experience |
|---|---|---|---|
| | Withdrawing from primary | Withdrawing from primary | Withdrawing from primary |
| Party support (t-1) | −0.092** | −0.155 | |
| | (0.026) | (0.098) | |
| Relative party donors | | | 1.594** |
| | | | (0.418) |
| Logged fundraising (t-1) | −0.121** | −0.191** | |
| | (0.019) | (0.039) | |
| Relative fundraising | | | 0.892* |
| | | | (0.370) |
| Candidate quality | −0.688** | −0.040 | 0.061 |
| | (0.123) | (0.224) | (0.227) |
| Number of candidates in primary | 0.254** | −0.080 | −0.028 |
| | (0.025) | (0.063) | (0.068) |
| Constant | −3.505** | −1.931* | 2.980** |
| | (0.274) | (0.774) | (0.714) |
| Observations | 18,115 | 1,542 | 1,542 |
| Pseudo R-squared | 0.148 | 0.114 | 0.114 |
| Log-likelihood | −1797.87 | −337.43 | −337.39 |

Logit coefficients with standard errors clustered by primary race in parentheses.
Asterisks indicate the coefficients are statistically significant.
Quarter dummy variables not shown in results.
**$p < 0.01$, *$p < 0.05$.

of the ability of a candidate to continue to compete in a House primary campaign. Candidates who fail to orchestrate a successful fundraising operation find it hard to continue their campaigns. Without the financial resources essential to a campaign, candidates are more likely to drop out of the race to pursue other professional opportunities, whether it may be another political office or a return to the private sector. Deriving from the first model, a two standard deviation increase in fundraising causes

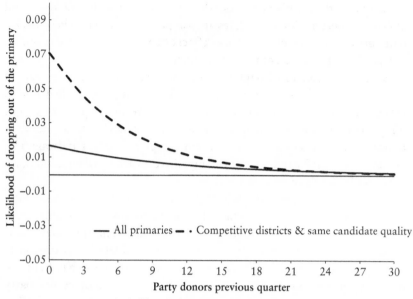

FIGURE 5.1 *Likelihood that a House candidate will drop out of a primary race*

the likelihood of a candidate dropping out to decline by about 1 percent. Estimates from the second model, where candidates are competing in competitive districts against other candidates with the same level of political experience, also place the effect at about 1 percent.

Turning to the effect of party support, this analysis shows that parties have a significant direct influence on the decisions of candidates to continue to pursue the party's nomination or not. Figure 5.1 shows the likelihood that a candidate will drop out of the race in a particular quarter at different levels of party support. For all candidates, as the candidate's party support increases across the full range which is roughly two standard deviations, the likelihood that the candidate drops out of the race in that quarter decreases by 1.6 percentage points in that quarter. For candidates in competitive races where there is no difference in candidate quality, a full increase across the two standard deviation range in party support causes a seven-point drop in the likelihood of the candidate's withdrawal from the race in that quarter.[12] The cumulative effect over

---

[12] If we hold fundraising constant at one (or two) standard deviations below the mean, the effect is slightly larger at 2 (or 3) percent for all primaries and 10 (or 14) percent for

the course of the campaign is more than 10 percent for all candidates and almost 60 percent for candidates in competitive districts where candidates are of the same quality. These effects vary from year to year, but do not display any consistent trend over the period.

Because, as noted in Chapter 3, congressional parties are strategic in their resources, the second model in Table 5.1 (and the dashed line in Figure 5.1) looks exclusively at races where we know parties are not jumping on the bandwagon of already successful candidates. As Chapter 3 indicated, congressional parties are not jumping on the bandwagon of already successful candidates in competitive districts when candidates have similar levels of experience.

In congressional primaries where the choice of candidates makes little difference in the outcome or where differences in candidate quality make it obvious which candidate is stronger, party donors and campaign funds generally move together. In races where one candidate is not obviously more qualified than the other, however, and where the party has an incentive to become involved because of its interest in political outcomes, party support causes increases in other measures of candidate primary election viability. If we look at only these select races in competitive districts with evenly qualified candidates, as shown in the models in columns 2 and 3 of Table 5.1, we again see that party support has a strong influence on the likelihood that a candidate remains in the race. It is in these races that allowing the party's nominee to conserve resources for a competitive general election campaign is most important. Districts where the incentive to coordinate and to clear the field for a preferred candidate is greater are also the districts where parties have a greater effect on the decisions of candidates. While these effects are not quite statistically significant ($p < 0.12$), they closely mirror the results seen in other analyses.

The third model in Table 5.1 is similar to the second, but it also takes into consideration the fact that the need for resources is not the same across districts. Because all candidates are not competing against all other candidates, the total number of party donors or the overall amount of funds raised may not accurately represent the factors that affect the decision-making processes of candidates as they decide whether to continue to compete for the party's nomination or not. Instead, candidates

the subsample of competitive primaries where candidates are equally qualified. Holding fundraising constant at one (or two) standard deviations above the mean decreases the effect to 1.4 (or 1) percent for all primaries and 4 (or 3) percent for the select subsample of primaries.

are likely to compare the fundraising and party support they are receiving relative to the support garnered by their opponents in their assessment of their chance of winning. To control for these aspects, the third model in Table 5.1 uses relative party support and relative fundraising consistent with past practices (see Norrander 2000 and 2006). Party support is calculated as the percentage of donors a candidate has relative to the candidate with the highest number of party donors. Relative fundraising is also calculated as the percentage of funds raised relative to the candidate with the highest fundraising totals. Using these measures, we find a similarly strong effect of party support on the decision of candidates to continue to seek the nomination.

As noted in Figure 5.1, the effects across the full range of House primaries are significantly smaller than those that we find in the Senate (shown in Figure 4.3 in Chapter 4). Yet parties continue to exercise a significant influence on the process, and their ability to convince candidates to drop out of the race appears to have a strong influence on the range of choices available to primary voters. For the small subset of primary elections in competitive districts where there is no substantive difference in the quality of the candidates running, however, party effects on candidate dropout are similar to the effects that we find in the Senate.

While the causal effect of party support on candidate fundraising is not entirely clear for all House primaries, for a select subset of House primaries, leading to competitive general elections where candidates have similar levels of past political experience, party support does have a strong causal effect on future fundraising. Thus, for the second and third models in Table 5.1, which examine the effect of party support in this subset of primaries, the direct effect of party support shown is only a portion of the total effect that party support has on a congressional candidate's decision to withdraw from a congressional primary. Party support influences the likelihood of withdrawing from the House primary in the model both directly and indirectly through the fundraising variable. Mediation analysis shows that 16 percent of the total effect of party support on a candidate's decision to continue to compete for the nomination is mediated through candidate fundraising.[13]

---

[13] Mediation analysis was carried out using the *Mediation* package in Stata (Hicks and Tingley 2011) which implements the procedures described by Imai et al. (2011) and Imai et al. (2010) to estimate the causal mechanisms that transmit the effect of a treatment variable on an outcome.

In summary, just as in the Senate, a party's support in a House primary has a strong influence on the decisions of candidates whether to continue their campaigns, especially in those races that lead to competitive general elections and where candidates have similar levels of past political experience. When making decisions about their candidacy, candidates are influenced not only by the quantity of money raised each quarter but also by the level of support they are receiving from party elites.

### Party Differences in House Primaries

Again, because of structural differences between the parties, it is important to look more closely at the differences between the effects that Democratic Party support and Republican Party support have on candidate decisions. Because of the Senate's phased election cycle, the effect of party networks may be muted or exaggerated because of the set of seats coming up for election. This is not the case for the House. Every election cycle, incumbents and challengers compete for every seat in the House of Representatives.

Despite these differences in the lengths of incumbency terms, the overall trends of candidate emergence and then derecruitment in House primaries look very similar to those in Senate primaries. Table 5.2 shows the number of candidates running in each election cycle under consideration here. As before, the first column under each party header displays the number of candidates who announced their candidacy and filed with the FEC.[14] As in the Senate, on the Republican side we see a sharp increase in 2010, when candidates were confronted with both a highly favorable electoral environment and also an antiestablishment sentiment within the party. In that year, the number of announced candidates almost doubled compared to the previous year. Unlike the situation in the Senate, however, this increase did not spill over into 2012. Perhaps because of the delayed senatorial electoral cycle, individuals frustrated with a certain group of Senate incumbents in 2010 had to wait an additional election cycle before challenging those candidates. On the House side, however, with every seat being up for election, the vulnerability of all incumbents' positions was tested in 2010. There is also a similar

---

[14] These numbers are an underestimation of the total number of declared candidates and candidates on the ballot, because they do not include those candidates who did not raise sufficient funds to necessitate filing their candidacy with the FEC.

TABLE 5.2 *Number of House primary candidates by party*

|  | Democrats | | | Republicans | | |
|---|---|---|---|---|---|---|
|  | Announced | On ballot | Percent ran (%) | Announced | On ballot | Percent ran (%) |
| 2004 | 530 | 489 | 92.3 | 583 | 533 | 91.4 |
| 2006 | 661 | 589 | 89.1 | 513 | 474 | 92.4 |
| 2008 | 664 | 583 | 87.8 | 582 | 509 | 87.5 |
| 2010 | 584 | 535 | 91.6 | 1,135 | 982 | 86.5 |
| 2012 | 609 | 544 | 89.3 | 682 | 603 | 88.4 |
| 2014 | 503 | 449 | 89.3 | 622 | 556 | 89.4 |
| Total | 3,551 | 3,189 | 89.8 | 4,117 | 3,657 | 88.8 |

smaller uptick between 2004 and 2006 for Democrats. In the latter year, Democrats had a favorable election cycle, similar to that of Republicans in 2010. The increase in the number of candidates, however, was not as substantial as it was for Republicans in that later election cycle.

Overall, as with the Senate, just looking at the total number of announced candidates and candidates whose names appeared on the ballot gives a sense that Republicans are less effective at clearing the field for their preferred candidate. The total number of candidates, however, does not take into consideration other factors that might be at play as candidates decide to run for office. On the other hand, if we are only looking at the ability of the party to get candidates out of the race, we might tell a different story. In this case, we find that Republicans have a slight advantage overall, albeit not as substantial as in the Senate, in getting candidates out of the race. Almost 14 percent of candidates dropped out of the race after announcing their candidacy on the Republican side, compared to only 8 percent on the Democratic side. Again, however, these effects do not take into consideration other factors that might influence the decision of candidates to drop out of the race.

Table 5.3 and Figure 5.2 use a logit model to show how party support shapes the decision of individual candidates to continue to compete for the party's nomination in the House. As previously, these models also include controls for candidate fundraising, candidate quality, and the number of candidates running in the primary in that quarter. The models

TABLE 5.3 *Likelihood of that a candidate will withdraw from a House primary election race by party*

| | Democrats Withdrawing from primary | Republicans Withdrawing from primary |
|---|---|---|
| Party support (t-1) | −0.077** | −0.121* |
| | (0.026) | (0.054) |
| Logged fundraising (t-1) | −0.127** | −0.149** |
| | (0.025) | (0.023) |
| Candidate quality | −0.932** | −0.563** |
| | (0.361) | (0.149) |
| Number of candidates (t-1) | 0.280** | 0.252** |
| | (0.049) | (0.027) |
| Constant | −3.537** | −3.455** |
| | (0.393) | (0.356) |
| Observations | 10,065 | 11,242 |
| Pseudo R-squared | 0.161 | 0.155 |
| Log-likelihood | 932.06 | −1,168.42 |

Logit coefficients with standard errors clustered by primary race in parentheses. Asterisks indicate the coefficients are statistically significant.
Quarter dummy variables not shown in results.
**p < 0.01, *p < 0.05.

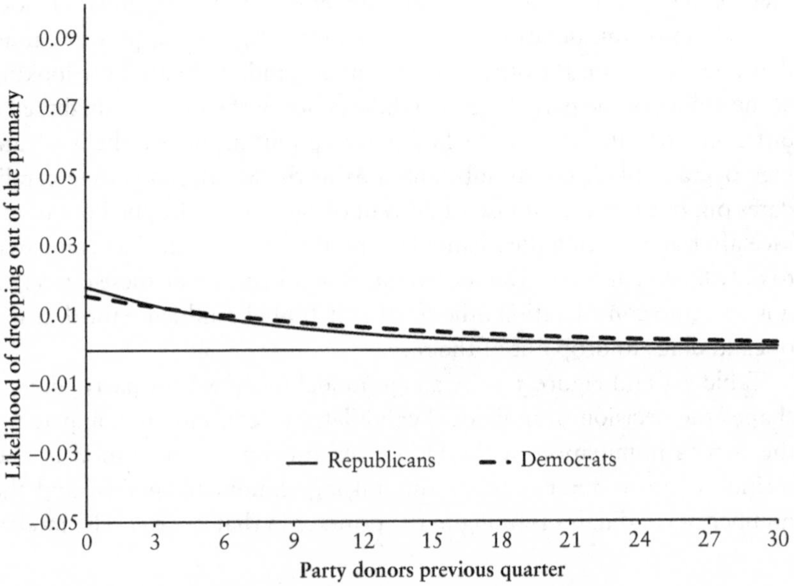

FIGURE 5.2 *Likelihood that a House candidate will drop out of a primary race by party*

presented here are those using all primaries, rather than the smaller subset. However, if we use the smaller subset, the results are similar.

As with the Senate, we find few substantive differences between the abilities of the different parties to encourage candidates to drop out of the primary race. While the effect of an increase in the number of shared party donors on the Republican side by two standard deviations increases the likelihood that a candidate will drop out by three percent, compared to only two percent for the same increase on the Democratic side, these differences are not significantly nor substantively different from each other. These separate party effects are almost identical to the combined effect. For both Democrats and Republicans, the coordination of party elites has the ability to influence the decisions of candidates who are running for the House of Representatives, independent of other factors. When party elites act together in coordination, primary candidates pick up on those signals and are more likely to exit the race if the party is not coordinating to act in support of their candidacy.

## CONCLUSION

The evidence from this chapter and the previous one fundamentally alters the conception of primaries and candidate emergence as being devoid of party influence. Parties are not merely neutral players in the nomination process. Their involvement in the process has a significant and substantial influence on nomination outcomes and also on the choices presented to voters. Such evidence supports a wider view of parties as constituting an extended network which is interested in ensuring the nomination of a preferred candidate.

Party elites clear the field by directing their resources toward a preferred candidate and ignoring those candidates they do not want in the primary field. Aware of their political surroundings, candidates who find themselves without party support will be more likely to drop out of the primary race and forgo the current opportunity to win the party's nomination, in order to pursue other goals. As we will see in the next chapter, part of their reason for dropping out is that candidates not supported by the party are also less likely to succeed in securing the nomination. The lack of party support makes it harder for candidates to compete and thus makes them more likely to get out before suffering an ignominious and potentially career-ending defeat.

## APPENDIX TO CHAPTER 5

Like the Appendix to the previous chapter, this Appendix provides additional checks that examine the effect of party support on a candidate's decision to remain a candidate in the primary. The models, predicting the likelihood that a candidate would withdraw from the race, that were provided in the text of the chapter were logit regressions where the outcome measure takes a value of zero if the candidate was an active candidate for the entire quarter and a value of one if the candidate ceased to contest the nomination. As with the Senate results, those models included dummy variables controlling for the temporal dependence of the model (Beck and Katz 1995; Beck et al. 1998). The result is a model that looks similar to, but is not entirely the same as, a hazard model.

Table 5A.1 and Figure 5A.1 provide hazard model specifications for House candidates. Table 5.1, in this chapter, estimates the probability of a House candidate's withdrawal from the primary race, using a logit model. Table 5A.1 and Figure 5A.1 show the same estimates, but use a Cox Proportional Hazard Model instead.

TABLE 5A.1 *Alternative specification of Table 5.1 (likelihood that a candidate will withdraw from the House primary) using a* Cox Proportional Hazard Model

|  | Withdrawing from primary | Hazard ratio |
|---|---|---|
| Party support (t-1) | −0.099** | 0.905 |
|  | (0.027) |  |
| Logged fundraising (t-1) | −0.122** | 0.885 |
|  | (0.015) |  |
| Candidate quality | −0.726** | 0.484 |
|  | (0.109) |  |
| Number of candidates (t-1) | 0.217** | 1.242 |
|  | (0.021) |  |
| Observations | 21,302 |  |
| Chi-squared | 441.88** |  |
| Log-likelihood | −4194.96 |  |

Hazard coefficients with standard errors clustered by primary race in parenthesis.
Asterisks indicate the coefficients are statistically significant.
**p < 0.01, *p < 0.05.

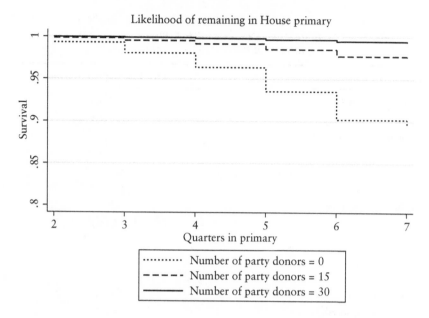

FIGURE 5A.1 *Survival estimates from the Cox Proportional Hazard Model for House candidates*

Table 5A.1 and Figure 5A.1 show an effect similar to the results shown in the chapter. In House primaries party support has a significant influence on the decision of a candidate to soldier on in pursuit of the party's nomination. An increase in the number of donors a House candidate shares with the party's congressional campaign committee from zero to thirty increases the likelihood that a candidate will remain in the primary race by about 10 percent.

## ADDITIONAL MODELING RESTRICTIONS
### AND ASSUMPTIONS

In addition to the choice of models used to document the influence of party support, there are a couple of other assumptions built into the models presented in this chapter. One concern might be that the models in the chapter include races with only one candidate. The inclusion of these races might bias the results, as these candidates are very likely also to be the party's favored candidate. However, there are several instances

TABLE 5A.2 *Alternative specification of Table 5.1 (likelihood that a candidate will withdraw from the House primary) using only primary quarters with two or more candidates*

| | Withdrawing from primary |
|---|---|
| Party support (t-1) | −0.091** |
| | (0.028) |
| Logged fundraising (t-1) | −0.137** |
| | (0.018) |
| Number of candidates (t-1) | 0.108** |
| | (0.027) |
| Candidate quality | −0.227* |
| | (0.104) |
| Constant | −2.860** |
| | (0.279) |
| Observations | 8,955 |
| Pseudo R-squared | 0.077 |
| Log-likelihood | −1764.32 |

Logit coefficients with standard errors clustered by primary race in parentheses. Asterisks indicate the coefficients are statistically significant.
Quarter dummy variables not shown in results.
**$p < 0.01$, *$p < 0.05$.

where candidates without any opposition dropped out of the race, either because of health problems or in anticipation of another party-supported candidate's getting in. The inclusion of candidates without any opposition does not change the results. Table 5A.2 provides the results of a model that excludes these candidates and shows almost identical results.

# 6

## Winning the Nomination

*The NRSC used every weapon at its disposal to defeat me ... In the end, our grassroots effort came close but could not overcome the enormous resources of the national Republican Party.*

—Steve Laffey[1]

On September 9, 2009, former Colorado House Speaker, Democrat Andrew Romanoff, received an email from White House Deputy Chief of Staff Jim Messina. At the time he received the email, Romanoff was a candidate for the US Senate, running in the Democratic primary against recently appointed Senator Michael Bennett. In his email to Romanoff, Messina listed three senior government positions to which the White House would consider appointing Romanoff on the condition that he drop out of the Senate race and clear the field for Bennett (Associated Press 2010). The Obama White House and other major Democratic Party players had rallied around Senator Bennett, who had been the superintendent of Denver schools prior to his appointment to the Senate less than a year earlier, when Ken Salazar had vacated the seat to join the Obama administration.[2] This offer to Romanoff of a presidential appointment

---

[1] Laffey (2007, pages 103 and 152).
[2] Nor was this the first time that a presidential administration had become personally involved in clearing the field for a preferred Senate candidate. In 2002 in Minnesota, the Bush White House had also become involved in the Republican nomination for US Senate. On Tuesday April 17, 2001, just a day before Tim Pawlenty (then the majority leader in the Minnesota House of Representatives) was planning on announcing his official candidacy for the US Senate, President George W. Bush's political advisor Karl Rove called, asking Pawlenty to stay out of the race to allow the former Mayor of

was just a part of the effort to clear the field for Bennett.[3] Eliminating primary competition would allow Senator Bennett to focus his campaign resources on winning the general election rather than having to spend them in defense of a nomination. Republicans had fielded former Colorado Lieutenant Governor Jane Norton to run, and Democrats were concerned that a competitive primary would be harmful to their chances of retaining the seat in what it appeared would be a very competitive general election.[4]

As laid out in Chapter 2, one tool that parties have to assist in their efforts to influence primary elections is the control of access to many of the positions of power within the political profession. This offer by the Obama White House was a blatant attempt by the party to clear the

---

St. Paul, Norm Coleman, to have a clear path to the nomination. Undeterred at that point, Pawlenty continued to organize the resources necessary to make a concerted bid for the party's nomination, with the support of a formidable team. The following day, however, just an hour and a half before the scheduled press conference where he was slated to announce his Senate candidacy, Pawlenty was on his way home from the dentist's office where he had picked up his two daughters. While in the car, with his daughters squabbling in the back seat, he received a phone call from Vice President Dick Cheney, asking him to abandon his interests in the Senate race "for the good of the overall effort." Cheney explained explicitly that he was calling on behalf of President Bush, and that the President was concerned that Coleman and Pawlenty would engage in a primary fight that would "drain the resources and focus away from the main target, which is Paul Wellstone" (Salisbury and Ragsdale 2001). Unlike Romanoff, Pawlenty agreed and bowed to the wishes of party leaders. "For the good of the party, for the good of the effort [against Wellstone] I agreed not to pursue an exploratory campaign," he explained at the time (Smith 2001a). Noticeably, when Pawlenty did announce his candidacy for governor five months later, sitting governor Jesse Ventura joked with reporters about the long delay between announcements and asked rhetorically if Pawlenty had needed to "clear [his candidacy] with anybody?" (Smith 2001b). Both Pawlenty and Coleman would go on to win their elections in 2002 and serve as Minnesota's Governor and Senator, respectively.

[3] The White House had similarly offered positions to Representative Joe Sestak (D-PA7) in July of 2009, to convince him not to run against Senator Arlen Specter in the Senate Democratic primary in Pennsylvania (Rose 2010). Sestak would not drop out. However, Sestak enjoyed more success than Romanoff. Sestak remained in the primary and ultimately beat Senator Specter, who had only recently become a Democrat in hopes of maintaining his seat. Sestak would then go on to lose the general election to Republican Pat Toomey (Gullan 2012). Other administration officials indicated that offering an alternative political job in exchange for a candidate's dropping out of the primary was a practice not restricted to the Obama administration but dated back to at least the George W. Bush administration, if not earlier (Lillis 2011).

[4] The Republican US Senate primary in Colorado was also a failure of party elites to clear the field for their preferred candidate, as Norton would lose the primary to Weld County District Attorney Ken Buck, who was generally considered a Tea Party candidate (Sherry 2010). Buck would then lose the general election by less than two percentage points (Simpson et al. 2010).

field for a preferred candidate by opening another avenue of political influence to Romanoff. But Messina's email and other efforts behind the scenes in this case were not sufficient to clear the field. Romanoff did not get out of the primary race. Instead of agreeing to a deal by which he would withdraw from the race to take one of those positions offered by the White House at a later date, Romanoff chose instead to publicize Messina's email containing the offer, in an attempt to rally public opinion around his campaign and to decry the involvement of the White House in the nomination process.[5]

As this brief example makes abundantly clear, parties are not always successful in their attempts to clear the field for their preferred candidate. The tools that parties have (as documented in Chapter 2) are strong, but they are not always sufficient and parties cannot issue commands that a candidate is required to obey. Many candidates that parties wish would drop out of the primary to clear the path to the nomination other candidates are not responsive to the parties' hints or are resistant to party pressure if they do recognize it. Many candidates do not drop out.

Candidates may choose to soldier onward, in spite of a lack of party support, for a variety of reasons. First, it may be that they are not politically astute and do not pick up the cues that the party gives them, being blinded by the thrill of running for office.[6] Second, candidates may be more interested in the opportunity to run than in the actual holding of office. These non-office-oriented individuals may be more interested in promoting themselves or a particular set of policy positions, and winning office is secondary to motivating a change in the political policy agenda.[7]

Candidates may not be interested in the other political opportunities that might be available to them. Party leaders may suggest and

---

[5] Romanoff indicated that Messina suggested three positions (two with US AID: deputy assistant administrator for Latin America and the Caribbean; director of the Office of Democracy and Governance, and one job as the director of the United States Trade and Development Agency) that might be available were Romanoff not pursuing the Senate race. Romanoff also indicated that in a phone call Messina had "added that he could not guarantee my appointment to any of these positions" (Associated Press 2010; Baker 2010a, 2010b).

[6] Many candidates get caught up in the moment. One candidate with whom I spoke, who was challenging an incumbent, had raised just over $25,000 compared to the incumbent's $1 million, yet was convinced that the election was going to be close. It was not.

[7] Running to promote a set of policies rather than strictly seeking to win may actually be somewhat effective. Once in office, congressional candidates tend to work more on policy areas advocated by their electoral opponents (Sulkin 2009). Candidates may also shape the discussion of issues during the primary campaign and extract promises from the eventual nominee.

encourage these politicians to pursue other political positions, but those positions may not be appealing, for one reason or another, to the candidate the party wants out of the primary race.[8] As one former party chair explained about a competitive gubernatorial primary in his state and the stubbornness of one particular candidate, "There's nothing you can do to get [that candidate] to run for another office. He's already done that. He doesn't want that." Candidates may continue to run because they may not be enticed by the alternative opportunities for political influence that the party offers. They may not be interested in promises of future political office, or for one reason or another, those promises may be severely discounted.

Potential candidates may also buck the party's preferences because they believe they have nothing to lose. Public officials who have been term-limited out of office may see no other political option than to compete for the nomination to higher office. Politicians who are outside the party's graces may feel as if their reputation among party elites cannot be any further degraded and so running against the party will have no serious political consequences.

To run a successful campaign, candidates must procure the necessary campaign resources, namely experienced staff, campaign financing, and media access. Many times it is the party network which provides these resources. However, candidates may also believe that they can procure elsewhere the resources offered by the party that are necessary to run a successful campaign (or may discount the essential nature of those resources to win).[9] Candidates may be independently wealthy or may have the support of a group of donors outside the party network, therefore not needing the fundraising connections that the party has to offer. Candidates may believe that they can find access to the media or good qualified staff without the party's help. In essence, while the party's tools change the considerations that candidates must take into account when

---

[8] At times, this may in part be because party leaders do not have a good grasp of the situation. In one example offered by a campaign staff member, the undesirable candidate was encouraged by national party leaders to run for an office in a district in which the candidate did not reside and had no political connections.

[9] At the presidential level, Donald Trump is the perfect example of the ability of certain candidates to find political resources outside the party network. His celebrity status gave him access to the media that other candidates did not enjoy, and he was able to drive coverage in spite of a lack of professional campaign staff. Over the course of the primary campaign Trump generated more than $2 billion in free media coverage, more than six times the amount of free media coverage of any other Republican competitor (Confessore and Yourish 2016).

deciding to run for office, candidate ambition is shaped by a larger set of institutional and structural considerations, which the candidate also takes into account.

While the party has a strong ability to clear the field, not all candidates are responsive. The question for parties when this happens is whether or not they can effectively defend their champion. Do party support and the resources that parties provide in support of their candidate in the primary race have a significant influence on the outcome of primary elections, above and beyond the normal predictors of electoral success?

Returning to the 2010 Colorado Democratic primary for the US Senate, Andrew Romanoff is a good example of what generally happens to candidates who buck the party and continue to contest the nomination in spite of party opposition: He lost by eight percentage points.

Candidates without party support struggle to win the nomination. In Senate primaries, party-supported candidates win the primary election over 80 percent of the time.[10] In House primaries, party-supported candidates win 67 percent of the time. While these raw data obscure the influence of a number of factors that go into primary outcomes, the overall findings are consistent with the raw numbers. Party-preferred candidates are significantly and substantively more likely to succeed in primaries. These party-supported candidates hold a significant electoral advantage over candidates without party support, even after controlling other factors that routinely affect campaign viability.

## WINNING THE SENATE PRIMARY

To state the obvious, winning a nomination requires receiving more votes in the primary election than the other candidates competing.[11] As documented in Chapter 2, not only do parties have a number of tools to

---

[10] Parties are not always successful in their attempts to coordinate behind a candidate (Dominguez 2005). Party-favored candidates in Senate primaries who lost received, on average, about 50 percent of the donations from party elites (30 percent for party-supported House candidates who lost). Party-supported candidates who won had, on average, 90 percent of the support from party-connected donors in Senate primaries (75 percent in House primaries). When the party is unable to coordinate well or is divided into various factions, the likelihood of the party's succeeding in achieving the preferences of the plurality of the party elite is significantly reduced (for a prime example see the 2016 Republican presidential primary).

[11] The exceptions to this, of course, are states that require that the winning candidate receive 50 percent of the vote to avoid a run-off election between the top two vote-getters. For

encourage candidates to exit a primary race, they also have a significant array of resources available to them that they can use to help candidates win. These tools all are useful in helping candidates run better, more effective campaigns. Party assistance, from campaign funds (Jacobson 1980) to media coverage (Iyengar and Kinder 1987) to knowledgeable and experienced staff (Medvic 2001; Nyhan and Montgomery 2015), enables the candidate to run a better campaign, which maximizes the potential of that candidate in the primary election. Thus, we should expect that candidates who receive higher levels of party support should also be more likely to enjoy primary election success. Just as candidates who do not receive the support of the party are more likely to drop out of a partisan primary, those candidates without party support should also struggle to win the partisan primary.

The measure of party support described in Chapter 3 provides a way to easily examine the effect of party support on primary outcomes in a large number of primaries.[12] This chapter tests the ability of political parties to get their preferred candidates through the nomination process when efforts to persuade other candidates to drop out of the primary race

---

the purpose of maintaining consistency in the electoral environment of primary elections across states, this analysis uses the primary election results, rather than the ultimate outcome, as a basis for all the analysis in this chapter regardless of whether a state had a run-off or not.

[12] It would be remiss to fail to note that the analysis here in this chapter is not the first foray into studying the effect of party support on primary election outcomes. Previous scholarship arguing for a broader understanding of political parties has provided preliminary evidence, tested on a small subsample of primary elections, that party support influences electoral outcomes (Bawn et al. 2012; Cohen et al. 2008; Desmarais et al. 2015; Dominguez 2011; Masket 2009, 2011). These studies, however, have either looked exclusively at presidential nominations which are unique in their long-drawn-out process of multiple primaries and caucuses across multiple months (Cohen et al. 2008), relied on small or nonrepresentative samples of congressional or state legislative races (Dominguez 2011; Masket 2009), or looked at general election outcomes (Desmarais et al. 2015) rather than primary outcomes where the party's nominee is chosen. No research has used a large representative sample of primaries from a wide range of electoral contexts to examine the ability of party elites to control the outcomes of primary elections. Perhaps most relevant to this chapter is the work of Casey Dominguez, who examined the outcomes of 86 open seat congressional primaries from 43 districts in 2002. Dominguez (2011) showed a strong relationship between a candidate's share of partisan endorsements in the primary and the outcome of that primary. These results from a small subset of House primaries from a single election cycle provided some preliminary evidence that party support makes a difference in the primary success of federal candidates. In her study, increasing the share of partisan endorsements from 0 to 100 percent increased the likelihood of winning these open seat House primaries by more than 60 percent, from 21 percent to 87 percent, an effect similar to what is shown here.

fail. Although party-supported candidates are not undefeatable, they are significantly more likely to win than candidates without party support, even after controlling for other factors that contribute to candidate primary success.

This chapter begins by examining the effect of party support on primaries for the Senate. The effect of party support on the likelihood that a candidate wins the senatorial primary election is estimated using a statistical model where the outcome is a dichotomous variable indicating whether or not the candidate was the highest vote-getter in the senatorial primary election in which he or she competed. Because many of these contests are multicandidate affairs, using vote share as the outcome variable would skew the results against candidates who won in primaries with large numbers of candidates. Candidates are also less interested in the percentage of votes that they receive and more interested in whether they receive the most votes in the primary. For what should be obvious reasons (namely that it is nearly impossible for a candidate to lose when that candidate does not have an opponent), these models exclude primaries where there was only a single candidate in the race.[13] As in Chapters 4 and 5, this chapter also provides figures that graph the effects of party support on the likelihood of winning the primary election, derived from the statistical models. These figures show how increasing the level of party support a candidate receives changes the candidate's likelihood of winning the primary. These figures show the effect of party support, while holding constant other key factors that influence primary outcomes.

As in Chapters 4 and 5, these models control for the past political experience of the candidate and the level of candidate fundraising. These controls ensure that we are not overestimating the effect of party support on the primary outcome. Because party support influences future fundraising (as shown in Chapter 3) and fundraising influences electoral outcomes, including a model of primary success without including a measure of fundraising would overestimate the effect of party support. As before, we also want to make sure that it is not candidate quality that is driving both party support and fundraising, as well as primary election outcomes.

---

[13] It is not impossible to lose a primary unopposed. In 2000, Maine State election officials notified a legislative candidate that he had not qualified for the general election ballot because, even though he was unopposed in the primary, he had not received any votes. Maine law states that "the person who receives a plurality of the votes cast for nomination to any office is nominated for that office." Because no votes were cast, the candidate had not received a plurality of the votes and lost the election he was running for unopposed (Quinn 2000).

TABLE 6.1 *Likelihood that a candidate will win the Senate primary*

| | All candidates | Primaries with candidates with same level of experience |
|---|---|---|
| | Primary win | Primary win |
| Party support | 0.007** | 0.008** |
| | (0.002) | (0.002) |
| Logged fundraising | 0.166** | 0.142* |
| | (0.045) | (0.063) |
| Candidate quality | 0.782** | |
| | (0.248) | |
| Candidate (and opponent) quality | | −0.875** |
| | | (0.321) |
| Constant | −3.511** | −2.035** |
| | (0.485) | (0.615) |
| Observations | 730 | 304 |
| Pseudo R-squared | 0.316 | 0.196 |
| Log-likelihood | −310.02 | −164.31 |

Logit coefficients with standard errors clustered by primary race in parentheses. Asterisks indicate the coefficients are statistically significant.
$**p < 0.01$, $*p < 0.05$.

Table 6.1 shows the result of a logit regression model predicting the likelihood of a candidate's victory in Senate primaries between 2004 and 2014 as a function of candidate primary election fundraising, the quality of the candidate, and party support. Just as these aspects have strong effects on the likelihood that a candidate will continue to compete, they also have a strong influence on the candidate's level of success in the primary election. It is important to note that these results are not driven by the fact of incumbents running in primary elections, either. The effects and levels of significance are the same if we exclude incumbents from the analysis.

Figure 6.1 shows the influence of party support on the likelihood of winning the party's nomination, while holding other variables at their means (from the first model in Table 6.1). As a candidate's party support increases two standard deviations from having zero shared donors with the national party organization to having 400 shared donors, the likelihood of his or her winning the nomination increases by more than

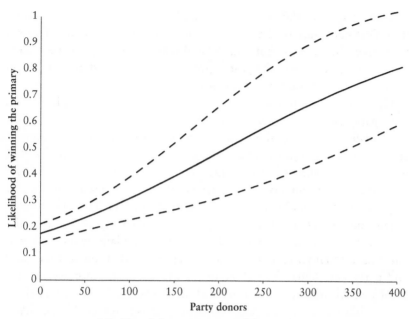

FIGURE 6.1 *Likelihood that a Senate candidate will win the primary*
*Note:* Dashed lines are 95% confidence intervals.

60 percent. Even small increments, for example, increasing the number of donors from zero to fifty, can increase the likelihood of winning by about 7 percent.

Nor are these effects swamped by fundraising. The effect of a two standard deviation change in party support when candidate fundraising is one standard deviation below the mean is 41 percentage points. When candidate fundraising is one standard deviation above the mean, the effect is roughly 55 percentage points. Regardless of the funding levels, party support is vital to the success of a candidate. In comparison, a two standard deviation increase in total fundraising has an effect of increasing the likelihood of the candidate's winning by 40 percentage points.

In the same way that party support has a powerful effect on the likelihood that a candidate will remain a candidate and continuing to compete for the nomination, there is a similarly strong effect of party support on the likelihood of his or her winning the primary election. Senate primary candidates with substantial party support are significantly more likely to win the primary than those who receive little support from the party. When party elites coordinate in support of a candidate, they can have a strong effect on the success of a candidate in securing the nomination. That party support has a strong effect on primary election success is true generally, but more importantly it also holds true in primaries where there is no difference in the past experience of the candidates running in the primary (see Model 2 in Table 6.1).

One concern about the results in Model 1 of Table 6.1 might be that both party elites and voters are picking up on the same cues of candidate quality and using those cues to make a decision about whom to support.[14] Looking just at races where candidates had the same level of past experience allows us to eliminate concerns about the spurious influence of candidate quality on primary electoral outcomes and to look at cases where elites and voters cannot use that shortcut. This allows us to obtain the pure effect of party support without having also to consider the effects of candidate quality. Even when candidate quality is eliminated as a potential underlying motivating factor that might drive voter and party elite behavior, we see that party support continues to have a substantial influence on primary election results. These results show clearly that party elite support significantly affects the likelihood that a candidate will win the primary election for the US Senate.

At the same time, the results also show a strong relationship between the effect of campaign fundraising and candidate success in the primary. These findings do not challenge the well-established relationship between candidate fundraising and electoral success, but show that candidate fundraising is not the sole factor contributing to candidate viability.[15]

## Party Differences in Senate Primaries

Recent research has argued that parties are unified by different sets of underlying motivations (Grossmann and Hopkins 2015). Different party organizations also organize themselves and coordinate party donors

---

[14] As shown in Chapter 3, this does not seem to be the case, at least in the Senate, because while party support predicts future fundraising, current candidate fundraising does not have a significant influence on future party support. In Senate primaries, party elites are not relying on candidate viability cues as a means of determining who to support. In the House this is also the case, but only in competitive districts where there is not a clear distinction in the past experience of the various candidates vying for the nomination.

[15] The findings shown in Table 6.1 and in Figure 6.1 are also robust to other specifications of the variable for party support (see Table 5A.1 in the Appendix to this chapter). Holding candidate quality and fundraising constant, as party support or relative party support increases, candidates are more likely to win the nomination.

TABLE 6.2 *Likelihood that a candidate will win the Senate primary by party*

| | Democrats | Republicans |
|---|---|---|
| | Primary win | Primary win |
| Party support | 0.007* | 0.007** |
| | (0.003) | (0.002) |
| Logged fundraising | 0.115* | 0.247** |
| | (0.054) | (0.087) |
| Candidate quality | 1.210** | 0.485 |
| | (0.389) | (0.315) |
| Constant | −2.854** | −4.525** |
| | (0.494) | (1.047) |
| | | |
| Observations | 272 | 458 |
| Pseudo R-squared | 0.343 | 0.313 |
| Log-likelihood | −116.49 | −188.33 |

Logit coefficients with standard errors clustered by primary race in parentheses. Asterisks indicate the coefficients are statistically significant.
**$p < 0.01$, *$p < 0.05$.

differently (Herrnson 1988). In spite of these structural and organizational differences, however, there is little variation between Republicans and Democrats in the ability of the parties to influence the likelihood that a candidate will win the primary election. Table 6.2 and Figure 6.2 differentiate the effect of party support on the likelihood that a candidate emerges victorious from the primary election by party.

The effect's size and trajectory are similar for Democrats and for Republicans. While the slope of the effect of party support on candidate victory is slightly greater for Democrats, the difference is not statistically significant. In some ways this is a testament to the strength of the Republican Party organizational structure in a time when there has appeared to be a gaping divide between the party's base and its leadership. While commentators have highlighted the apparently significant rifts and disagreements between what they have termed the Republican Party's establishment and its more conservative wing during this time period, the party elite within the Republican Party have continued to exert a significant influence in the primary process. The effect of party support on a candidate's success in the senatorial primary election is driven not just by a more successfully unified Democratic Party. By differentiating the effects of party support on senatorial primary outcomes

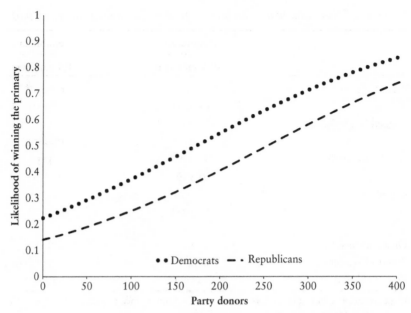

FIGURE 6.2 *Likelihood that a Senate candidate will win the primary by party*

by party we can see that both parties are active and influential in the primary process.

Both parties have a powerful ability to influence the outcomes of senatorial primary elections. An increase of party support by two standard deviations for a Democratic candidate increases the likelihood that that candidate will win the Democratic primary by over 60 percent. For Republicans the effect is almost exactly the same, at a 60 percent. For both Republicans and Democrats, the party support of a candidate during this period increased the likelihood of his or her not only remaining a candidate for public office, as shown in Chapter 5, but also of winning the primary and securing the nomination for Senate.

### WINNING THE HOUSE PRIMARY

These effects are not just limited to primaries for Senate nominations, either. While party-supported House candidates are slightly more vulnerable to defeat than their senatorial counterparts, party support also influences the ability of a candidate to win a House primary. Although party-supported Senate candidates win 80 percent of the primary

TABLE 6.3 *Likelihood that a candidate will win the House primary*

| | All primaries | Competitive district primaries where candidates have the same level of experience | Competitive district primaries where candidates have the same level of experience |
|---|---|---|---|
| | Primary win | Primary win | Primary win |
| Party support | 0.020** | .005 | |
| | (0.004) | (0.004) | |
| Relative party support | | | 0.939* |
| | | | (0.407) |
| Logged fundraising | 0.181** | 0.624** | |
| | (0.018) | (0.137) | |
| Relative fundraising | | | 4.151** |
| | | | (0.529) |
| Candidate quality | 0.826** | | |
| | (0.081) | | |
| Candidate (and opponent) quality | | −0.526** | −0.115 |
| | | (0.151) | (0.137) |
| Constant | −2.997** | −7.702** | −3.665** |
| | (0.179) | (1.616) | (0.375) |
| | | | |
| Observations | 3943 | 541 | 541 |
| Pseudo R-squared | 0.178 | 0.193 | 0.405 |
| Log-likelihood | −2113.83 | −288.63 | −212.78 |

Logit coefficients with standard errors clustered by primary race in parentheses. Asterisks indicate the coefficients are statistically significant.
$^{**}p < 0.01$, $^{*}p < 0.05$.

elections, party-supported House candidates are comparably successful, winning just under 67 percent of primaries (but 81 percent of primaries in competitive districts).

To show the effect of party support on House primary outcomes, this chapter also constructs an identical statistical model predicting the success of US House candidates running in a partisan-contested primary. Table 6.3 shows the results of a logit model looking at the effects of party support, primary fundraising, and candidate quality on the primary electoral success of candidates in House primaries. As before, the outcome variable is a dichotomous variable, indicating whether or not the

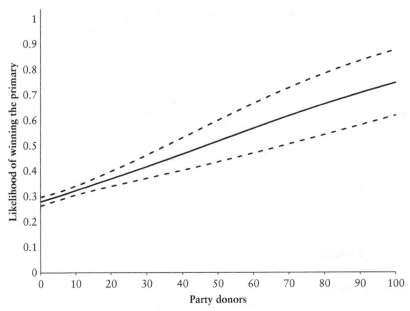

FIGURE 6.3 *Likelihood that a House candidate will win the primary*
*Note:* Dashed lines are 95% confidence intervals.

candidate received the most votes in the primary election. Likewise, this analysis also includes controls for candidate experience and campaign fundraising.

The first model in Table 6.3, using all House primary elections between 2004 and 2014, shows the effect of party support on the likelihood that a candidate will win the primary election. Even after controlling for candidate quality and fundraising, we see that party support has a strong influence on the overall likelihood that a candidate will win the primary. ·

The effect of party support, our key variable of interest, on the likelihood that a candidate will win the primary election, holding other contributing factors constant, is displayed in Figure 6.3. As a House primary candidate's party support increases by two standard deviations, the likelihood of his or her winning the nomination increases by almost 50 percent.[16]

---

[16] An astute reader will notice that the marginal effect of one additional donor has a larger effect than was found for Senate primaries. This is in part because many more House candidates receive only minimal party support. Many do not receive any party support at all, and many of the party-supported candidates in these primaries receive only a small amount of support. On the other hand, in certain circumstances (usually in a

As noted previously, however, there are several key institutional differences between House and Senate primaries that affect the decision-making process of party elites. Because of the vast number of races that the party has to monitor at the House level, party elites are more likely to use many of the same shortcuts that voters do to identify which candidates to support. As a result, party support moves together with candidate fundraising in races where there are clear differences in the political experience of the candidate and also in races where the identity of the nominee has little influence on the outcome of the general election because of lack of competitiveness of the congressional district (as shown in Chapter 3). In these races, the effort required to coordinate on a non-salient candidate (less politically experienced candidate) would require significantly more effort and might not be in the best interests of the party, as candidate quality has a strong effect on the outcome of congressional elections (Jacobson 1989).

In addition, the variation in resources needed to run a successful campaign in each congressional district may affect how much attention the party directs to a particular district. The resources required to run a successful campaign in a rural district are significantly different from those required to run a successful campaign in an urban district. The marginal benefit of additional support declines as campaign support rises, and the decline in marginal benefits is greater in some districts than in others. Political parties are more likely to invest more resources and energy coordinating their support in races that require higher levels of resources to win, rather than flooding a rural district, where the marginal return on the investment declines substantially after a relatively small investment.[17]

The results from the second and third models in Table 6.3 provide a clearer picture of how the institutional dynamics of House primary races affect the ability of party elites to influence primary election outcomes. These models address only primary elections in competitive House

---

primary in a competitive district), a party-supported candidate can receive a substantially large amount of party support. These candidates are usually very successful in primary elections. This explains the difference between the total percentage of party-supported candidates that win the primary election and the marginal effect of one additional party-connected donor to the campaign.

[17] A campaign manager of a congressional challenger in a competitive New England congressional district indicated that additional funding from the party network above a certain level would not provide that candidate with a significant increase in the likelihood of winning. Moreover, too much support from party elites, many of whom lived out of state and were connected through the party Hill committee, would open up the candidate to charges of not being responsive to the district because of support from out of state.

districts where primary candidates have similar levels of political experience. As detailed in Chapter 3, only in these races does party support clearly have a direct causal influence on candidate fundraising. It is in these races that it is clear that party elites are not merely jumping on the bandwagon of the most viable candidate, but rather are identifying their preferred candidates and using the party's resources to assist those candidates in running better campaigns. Other political actors then take their cues from party elite coordination. Because of the clear nature of party coordination in these races, it is important to look at the second and third models in Table 6.3 to understand the effect that party support has on candidate success in these races. By examining primary races that lead to competitive general election races and that have candidates with the same levels of past political experience, we can get a clear view of the effect of party support on partisan primaries for Congress.

Looking only at the select subset of House primary elections where party support has a clear causal relationship with candidate viability provides a slightly different picture of the influence of party elites in House primaries. Because we know that party support in these races increases candidate fundraising (rather than the other way around), we can understand better how party support influences outcomes. In Model 2, we find that the effect of the raw number of shared party donors is mediated through fundraising. Because party support predicts future fundraising, the effect of party support on primary outcomes is mediated by candidate fundraising. Taking candidate fundraising out of the model shows a strong positive relationship between party support and primary outcomes, but including fundraising eliminates the direct effect of party support. Thus, in House primaries, the causal effect of party support on primary outcomes flows through candidate fundraising. Mediation analysis finds that 79 percent of the effect of the total number of shared party donors on primary election outcomes is mediated by candidate fundraising.[18] In short, the more party support received, the more successful the candidate's other fundraising and hence, the more likely that candidate is to win the primary election in which he or she is competing.

---

[18] Mediation effects were calculated using the *Mediation* package in Stata (Hicks and Tingley 2011), which implements the procedures described by Imai et al. (2011) and Imai et al. (2010) to estimate the causal mechanisms that transmit the effect of a treatment variable on an outcome. Using these path models shows that the total effect of party support is 0.003 and the mediated effect is 0.0026 (statistically significant at the $p < 0.05$ level, two-tailed test). While the mediated effects are significant, the direct effects are not.

Model 3 in Table 6.3 takes into account the variation in the volume of resources required to run a successful campaign in different congressional districts. This model uses a candidate's total fundraising and total number of shared donors as a percentage of that of the candidate with the most party support and the highest level of fundraising. This is consistent with previous research, which similarly compares candidates across years and under different electoral and fundraising circumstances (Norrander 2006). When we account for differences in the resources required to run competitive campaigns across districts and years, we find a strong effect of the relative level of party support on primary election outcomes.

Mediation analysis using this model also finds that the effect of relative party support on primary election outcomes is mediated by relative candidate fundraising. Using these specifications, mediation analysis shows that 78 percent of the effect of the relative number of shared party donors on primary election outcomes is mediated by relative candidate fundraising.[19] In House primaries, the effect of party support largely seems to be the result of the increased fundraising that comes with party coordination. Because party support leads to greater fundraising success, party-supported candidates are better able to find the resources necessary to compete and to be successful in the primary election.

Regardless of the specific model specifications, however, we find that party support has an influence on primary election outcomes. Without that party support, candidates face an uphill battle to gain the nomination. Because of the resources that the party has at its disposal to assist its preferred candidates, these candidates have a significant electoral advantage. No matter where we look, the effect of party support significantly influences the success candidates have in House primaries. In competitive districts where primary candidates have similar levels of past elected experience, party support has a significant effect on a candidate's success in the primary. We can also measure this in a variety of different ways. Using both the total number of party donors who gave to the candidate in the primary and a percentage of the most connected candidate's party donors active in that particular primary (a form of the party support variable used in the alternative models to Chapter 4 as shown in the

---

[19] As before, mediation effects were calculated using the *Mediation* package in Stata (Hicks and Tingley 2011). In this instance, path models show that the total effect of relative party support on primary outcomes is 0.590, the mediated effect is 0.496 (statistically significant at the $p < 0.05$ level, two-tailed test), and the direct effect is 0.175. In this case, however, both the mediated and the direct effects are significant at the $p < 0.05$ level.

Appendix of that chapter) shows that party support has a significant positive effect on the likelihood of winning. The likelihood of winning the primary, thus, is affected by party support both in those races where party support moves in tandem with candidate fundraising and also in those races where party support is not the result of previous candidate successes. Put into this context, it is not surprising that candidates who do not have the support of the party are more likely to drop out of the primary race. They do so because without party support their chances of winning are significantly lower, and continuing to run without good chances of winning will only irritate those within the party, thus limiting their future political opportunities.

This large effect of party support decreases significantly when only competitive primaries in which candidates have the same level of political experience are examined. In these cases, an increase in the number of shared party donors by two standard deviations increases the likelihood that the candidate will win by about 10 percent, from 35 percent to 45 percent. Alternatively, using the percentage of party donors who have given to a candidate in the district in these competitive districts with no difference in candidate quality, an increase from having no party donors to having 100 percent of the party donors in the district similarly increases the likelihood of winning by just over 10 percentage points, from 30 percent to 40 percent. While the overall effect of party support is less than it is in the Senate, it still has a strong effect in party primaries for congressional elections.

## Party Differences in House Primaries

While there is some argument about how satisfied each party's base is with its party's elites, this does not seem to affect the ability of parties to influence the outcomes of primary elections. Although there are differences in the size of its effect over the time period, as with the Senate, the effect of party support on a candidate's likelihood of winning the House primary is significant for both major political parties. Table 6.4 and Figure 6.4 differentiate the effect of party support on the likelihood of winning the party's nomination for the US House of Representatives.

For both Democrats and Republicans, the effect of party support is positive and significant. An increase in two standard deviations in the number of party donors on the Democratic side increased the candidate's likelihood of winning the Democratic House primary by 35 percentage points. For Republicans, the effect was to increase the

TABLE 6.4 *Likelihood that a candidate will win the House primary by party*

|  | Democrats | Republicans |
|---|---|---|
|  | Primary win | Primary win |
| Party support | 0.012** | 0.036** |
|  | (0.003) | (0.007) |
| Logged fundraising | 0.162** | 0.202** |
|  | (0.022) | (0.030) |
| Candidate quality | 0.672** | 0.850** |
|  | (0.121) | (0.113) |
| Constant | −2.513** | −3.450** |
|  | (0.207) | (0.301) |
| Observations | 1,604 | 2,339 |
| Pseudo R-squared | 0.145 | 0.216 |
| Log-likelihood | −912.82 | −1175.32 |

Logit coefficients with standard errors clustered by primary race in parentheses. Asterisks indicate the coefficients are statistically significant.
**p < 0.01, *p < 0.05.

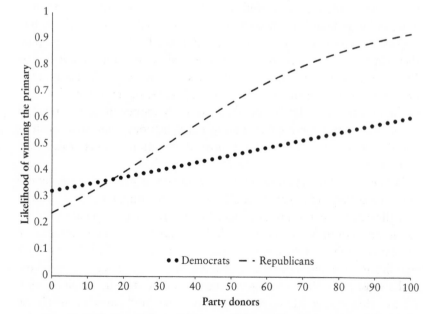

FIGURE 6.4 *Likelihood that a House candidate will win the primary by party*

candidate's chances winning by almost 75 percent. For both Republicans and Democrats, the party support of a candidate during this time period increased the candidate's likelihood not only of remaining a candidate for public office, but also of winning the primary and securing the nomination for the House.

In Chapter 2, we outlined many potential resources that party elites claimed were influential in shaping the outcome of the primary election process. The claims produced there are supported by the empirical evidence showing the effect of party support on primary election outcomes. Party support in a primary election, while not explicitly announced, shapes the process through which the nominee is selected and creates a political competitive environment that strongly favors the party's preferred candidate. While the party's preferred candidates do not always win, they are generally the heavy favorites.

### A QUICK GLANCE AT 2016 AND BEYOND

One might question whether the results from this chapter and the results from Chapters 4 and 5 still hold true in 2016 and beyond. After all, in the 2016 presidential nomination process, Republican elites generally are seen to have failed to successfully coordinate in support of a single candidate, and were unable to clear the field of unwanted candidates, including the one who ultimately became president. Indeed, while not giving up on their claim that the party decides presidential nominations, made in *The Party Decides*, Cohen and his colleagues (2016) have noted a number of factors, including the increased political coverage by the media early in the process, the relative abundance of early money in nominations in recent years, and the conflict among party factions, that have made it more difficult for party elites to control nomination process at the presidential level.

While these factors could ultimately impact primaries for the House and Senate, they are largely absent from primary campaigns for the House and the Senate at the present time. Media coverage of Senate primary candidates continues to be limited. Although Senate nominees receive regular coverage, candidates in the primary are much less likely to receive significant coverage more than a couple of months before the primary, and almost all of that coverage occurs within the state in which the candidates are running. Media coverage of primary candidates for the House is almost entirely nonexistent. This suggests that it remains difficult for candidates to draw any attention or recognition without party support and access to the resources of that political network. Although there have been a couple of notable cases where party-supported candidates have failed to win the primary, these are largely the exception rather than the rule. While some outside groups, such as Club for Growth and the Senate Conservatives Fund, have begun investing money in primaries and attempting to draw attention to conservative challengers, the national prominence of primaries for US Senate nominations is low, and is entirely nonexistent for nominations for House seats, which limits the consequences of factionalism within the party.

In addition, the fundraising changes that have affected the presidential nomination process have not yet reached the Senate or the House. While Super PACs have become more involved in Senate races, these campaign organizations function differently at presidential and senatorial levels. At the presidential level, many candidates have a single-candidate Super PAC associated with the campaign, many of which spent extensively during the primary campaign. In contrast, only a handful of Senate and an even smaller number of House candidates, mostly incumbents in both instances, had a single-candidate Super PAC. Moreover, none of these single-candidate Senate Super PACs spent money in efforts to win primary elections.

Likewise, candidates without party support are unlikely to be able to generate the grassroots support that Bernie Sanders enjoyed. Most potential Senate and House candidates are far too obscure to build a national campaign on small-dollar contributions. While the amount of money raised early in the presidential nomination process has changed significantly in recent years, there does not appear to be similar exponential growth in the amount raised by Senate and House primary campaigns.

Even looking at some of the more salient races in 2016, we see many of the same features and occurrences that have been detailed in this book. Parties attempting to push out candidates to clear the way for their preferred candidate are largely successful. In the following paragraphs, one of these examples, the primary for the Republican senatorial nomination in Indiana, is examined in greater detail.[20]

---

[20] The Democratic senatorial nomination in the same year in Indiana was also marked by party efforts to get a candidate out of the race to clear the field for Evan Bayh, whom the party strongly lobbied to get into the race. However, in this case, the party was not able to do so until after the primary, and only a few months before the general election (Banta 2016).

When Dan Coats announced in late March 2015 that he would not run for re-election the following year, it set up the potential for a crowded and competitive Republican senatorial primary in Indiana in 2016. Although a number of qualified candidates, including State Senators Jim Merritt, Jim Banks, and Mike Delph, and US Representatives Marlin Stutzman and Todd Young (Howey 2015a; Tully 2014). However, it was Eric Holcomb, Coats' chief of staff and the former chair of the state Republican Party, who would announce first, declaring his candidacy just two days after his boss announced his intentions not to seek reelection in 2016 (Joseph 2015).

Yet, despite the strong interest that many individuals had in running for the seat, party leaders had no intention of letting this race go to an extended or competitive primary. Party leaders had seen firsthand what could happen when decisions were left to primary voters. Only four years earlier, in 2012, party leaders had been unable to dissuade State Treasurer and Tea Party favorite, Richard Mourdock, from challenging incumbent moderate Republican Senator, Dick Lugar, in the Republican primary. Lugar (and perhaps many of the party elites) had not taken the primary challenge seriously, confident in his reputation as a "senior statesman" of the Republican Party (Cillizza and Blake 2012). Not only did the party fail to clear the field for the incumbent, but it also failed to defend the incumbent in the primary, which Mourdock won by 21 percentage points.

That lack of action would have serious consequences for Republicans in Indiana.[21] Mourdock's brand of conservatism, and some ill-fated remarks about rape and abortion, when he stated that "life is that gift from God that I think even if life begins in that horrible situation of rape, that it is something that God intended to happen" (Associated Press 2012). Although Mourdock later attempted to clarify his remarks, saying, "God creates life, and that was my point. God does not want rape, and by no means was I suggesting that He does. Rape is a horrible thing," the damage was done and Republicans would lose Lugar's seat by a six-point margin (Raju 2012).

Because of that experience, in 2016 party leaders worked much harder to attempt to ensure that history did not repeat itself. While many potential candidates declined to run, Holcomb, along with US Representatives Todd Young and Marlin Stutzman declared their intention to seek the

---

[21] National Republicans also blamed losses in Indiana and Missouri as the culprits for their inability to win a majority in the Senate in 2012 (Grant 2012).

nomination. Of the three candidates, Marlin Stutzman reminded party elites of Mourdock in many ways. While most party elites felt that Holcomb and Young had similar chances of winning the general election, Stutzman's brand of conservatism worried many members of party elites, who feared that his candidacy would result in a repeat of 2012 (Francisco 2016). The other candidate, Representative Todd Young, however, had similar ideological principles to Holcomb's, and they were both seen as more closely aligned with the party establishment (Fort Wayne News-Sentinel 2015; Slodysko 2015a). While Stutzman raised a significant portion of his money from local grassroots activists, Young and Holcomb were both better connected to the party elites around the country (Francisco 2015). Because of their similar ideologies and political connections, many were concerned that the presences of both Young and Holcomb in the race would prevent voters from coordinating, and would allow the more conservative and controversial Stutzman to win the primary with a plurality (Slodysko 2015b), and Stutzman's original campaign strategy was dependent on such a division (Howey 2016).

Although the party elites respected Holcomb, their clear preference was for Young, and media reports indicated that among the potential candidates "in Republican circles, it has been Reps. Young and Brooks who are seen in close to universal perception as the two emerging members with the most gravitas" (Howey 2015b). As the campaign began to take shape, party leaders began to negotiate with Holcomb to get him out of the race that voters could unite behind Young.

The opportunity to utilize the tools that the party has at its disposal became clear when Governor Mike Pence began to indicate that he would make an effort to push Lieutenant Governor Jill Ellspermann off the gubernatorial ticket. Although the split was framed as allowing Ellspermann to pursue her desire to become the executive of the Ivy Tech Community College system, the rift was largely the by-product of disagreements between the business and social conservative wings of the party (Howey 2016). Even before Ellspermann's resignation was announced, Holcomb dropped out of the race and issued a statement that many recognized as "echo[ing] the same themes as Pence's re-election campaign: transportation, education, jobs and 'record' economic investments" (Slodysko 2016). Two days later, Pence announced he had asked Holcomb to be his running mate. By offering Holcomb a spot on the Pence ticket, the party had solved two problems, getting both candidates an opportunity that would satisfy their political ambitions and also avoiding the chance that Republican primary voters would split their votes between Holcomb and Young, which would allow Stutzman to win the nomination (Associated Press 2016; Osowski 2016).

After getting Holcomb out of the race, Young still faced a challenge from a similarly qualified candidate, but party leaders marshaled their resources to help Young defeat Representative Marlin Stutzman. National party donors rallied to Young and eschewed any significant support of Stutzman, who relied instead on the support of local activists (Francisco 2015). The efforts of party elites in this case were ultimately successful, as Todd Young was able to defeat Stutzman by a two to one margin.

This chapter and previous chapters have shown that party leaders are effective at clearing the field for their preferred candidate, and at helping their preferred candidate win the primary. Evidence from 2016 suggests that things have not changed significantly. Scenarios similar to the one in the Indiana Republican senatorial primary played out in the Democratic senatorial primaries in Pennsylvania, Maryland, and Iowa. At the House level, the same could be said for the Republican Primaries in Nebraska's 2nd Congressional District (Tysver 2015), New York's 3rd Congressional District (Niedzwiadek 2016), and Florida's 2nd Congressional District (Bennett 2015), as well as Democratic primaries in Iowa's 1st Congressional District (Crippes 2015; Iowa Starting Line 2015), Colorado's 6th Congressional District (Pathé 2015a, 2015b), Nevada's 3rd Congressional District (Pathé 2016), and Maine's 2nd Congressional District (Shepherd 2014). In the Democratic primary in Maine's 2nd Congressional District, referring to the power of national party networks, Bangor City Councillor (and the brother of former Maine Governor) Joe Baldacci explicitly said, when announcing his decision to withdraw his candidacy, that, "while I can raise money in Maine—95 percent of our money came from Maine—I don't have the resources to, as other candidates do, to unlimited out-of-state cash" (Sharon 2016).

The parties' efforts and influence in primary elections during the 2016 election cycle were not substantively different than the parties' efforts and influence between 2004 and 2014 which are analyzed in greater detail in this book. Even looking ahead to 2018 and beyond, we can see clear signals of party coordination in support of a favored candidate. Already reports have indicated that the DCCC has been involved in encouraging strong candidates to run, even in races that already have a number of seemingly strong Democratic candidates (Hagen 2017). As in past years, party elites work to coalesce around a preferred candidate, help clear the field for that candidate, and provide the candidate with the resources to win the nomination.

## DISCUSSION AND CONCLUSION

The evidence provided here shows that the primary election outcomes are not merely the product of candidates' campaigning abilities. While the party cannot arbitrarily decide which candidate wins a primary, the party's support of a candidate matters in a primary election. As demonstrated in Chapter 2, the party provides access to resources that are essential to mounting a successful campaign, and as shown here, those resources matter. Without those resources, candidates struggle to compete and confront a more difficult pathway to victory. As a result, those who are not party-favored face an uphill battle for the nomination, while party-supported candidates have fundamental advantages. Those who do compete for the nomination without the party's support are likely to struggle to secure the nomination.

This evidence fundamentally alters our understanding of primaries, candidate emergence, and the roles of parties in these processes. Parties are not merely neutral players in the primary process. Their involvement in the process has a significant and substantial influence on nomination outcomes and also on the choices presented to voters. Such evidence supports a wider view of parties as an extended network of policy demanders who are interested in ensuring the nomination of a sympathetic and electable candidate.

Rather than being disinterested and uncoordinated individuals who merely respond to a candidate's ambition and political abilities, party elites are actively engaged in determining the choices available to voters in primary elections. Party support and the coordinated mobilization of resources strengthen candidates in their quest for the nomination. When those without party support choose not to drop out of the race, they are faced with significant challenges and generally fail to win the nomination.

## APPENDIX TO CHAPTER 6

The models for victory in the House primary include an alternative measure of the party support variable that takes into account the strength of party support relative to other candidates in the race. The logic for the use of that variable in the House nomination process is that the large number of House primaries makes it difficult for the party to focus on every one of those seats equally. In addition, the way that districts are drawn and the number and sizes of television markets that serve those districts make the funds required to compete in different districts vastly

TABLE 6A.1 *Alternative specification of Table 6.3 using fundraising and party connectedness as a percentage of the fundraising and party support of the Senate candidate in the primary who raised the most money and received the most party support in the primary (similar to Model 3 in Table 6.3 for House candidates)*

|  | Primary win |
|---|---|
| Percent of most connected candidate's party donors | 1.023 ** |
|  | (0.374) |
| Percent of highest fundraiser's fundraising | 4.026 ** |
|  | (0.434) |
| Candidate quality | 0.656 * |
|  | (0.269) |
| Constant | −3.806 ** |
|  | (0.263) |
|  |  |
| Observations | 730 |
| Pseudo R-squared | 0.531 |
| Log-likelihood | −212.53 |

Logit coefficients with standard errors clustered by primary race in parentheses. Asterisks indicate the coefficients are statistically significant.
** $p < 0.01$, * $p < 0.05$.

different (Campbell et al. 1984). A similar argument might well be made for the Senate. To show that this decision to use different methodologies for the House and the Senate is not a strategy biased toward to enabling the discovery of statistical significance in both types of race, Table 6A.1 presents the results of a logit model predicting the likelihood of winning the Senate primary using these alternative measures of fundraising and party support.

As Table 6A.1 makes clear, it does not matter how we measure party support or candidate fundraising in Senate primaries. Just as in Table 6.1 in the body of the chapter, the effect of party support on the likelihood of winning the Senate primary is positive and significant. Parties and the support they provide to favored candidates have a strong effect on the likelihood that a candidate for Senate will become the nominee.

# 7

# Influencing the Political System

*I think that is a recipe for winning elections, if we find strong effective can-
didates who can communicate a pro-growth conservative message – with
a smile.*
  —Ted Cruz (R-TX), NRSC Vice-Chairman in charge of recruitment[1]

*There is a broad concern about having blown a significant number of races
because the wrong candidates were selected.*
  —Steven J. Law, President of American Crossroads SuperPAC[2]

To their consternation, parties and party elites do not always get their
way.[3] Despite their efforts, party-supported candidates lose roughly
20 percent of Senate primaries and 33 percent of House primaries. At
times outsider candidates are successful in their efforts to buck the party's wishes in primaries, just as in earlier times outsider candidates were
occasionally able to muster enough grassroots strength to beat the party
in nominations decided at party conventions.

While previous chapters have dealt with the ability of parties to control the nomination process and the mechanisms by which they do so, we
lack a good sense of how party control affects our democracy. Although
there are probably more effects of party influence in primary elections
than an entire book could address by itself, this chapter begins to dig

---

[1] Quoted in Goldmacher (2013).
[2] Quoted in Zeleny (2013).
[3] Nowhere is this clearer than with the Republican presidential nomination of Donald
  J. Trump. However, that is a topic for an entirely different book. This book focuses on
  House and Senate primaries, not the presidential nomination process.

into some of the normative implications. This chapter addresses the preference of parties and party elites for moderate political candidates and considers the possible influence that strengthening parties might have on the polarization that currently plagues the United States.

Having faced a tough reelection campaign in the 2004 election cycle, baseball Hall of Famer and Republican Senator Jim Bunning of Kentucky faced strong pressure from within his own party to retire before the 2010 election. In 2004, Bunning had nearly squandered what had appeared to be a relatively safe Senate seat through his behavior on the campaign trail. In a string of unforced gaffes, Bunning compared the looks of his opponent, State Senator Daniel Mongiardo, to those of Saddam Hussein's sons, accused Mongiardo or one of his staff of roughing up Bunning's wife at a summer event, and canceled scheduled debates at the last minute. In one debate he declined to show up to the television studio as previously agreed and instead had his portion broadcast from the Republican National Committee's TV studio. Bunning's chief of staff (future Congressman David Young of Iowa) later admitted that Bunning had cheated by using a teleprompter to read his opening and closing statements (Farhi 2004). His erratic behavior led the largest newspaper in the state, the Louisville Courier-Journal, to wonder, "is his increasing belligerence an indication of something worse? Has Sen. Bunning drifted into territory that indicates a serious health concern?" (Courier Journal 2010). Instead of a landslide victory, Bunning barely won, by less than 24,000 votes out of the roughly one million ballots cast. At the same time, President Bush won the presidential vote in Kentucky by more than 20 percentage points.

Perceiving him as an electoral liability, party leaders urged Bunning to announce his retirement before the beginning of the election cycle – and urged potential donors not to give to Bunning's reelection campaign – so that the party could recruit a more viable candidate for the seat (Lindenberger 2009; Pershing and Cillizza 2009).[4] These efforts

---

[4] In his announcement that he would not run for reelection, Bunning blatantly accused the party of wrecking his reelection campaign, stating, "over the past year, some of the leaders of the Republican Party in the Senate have done everything in their power to dry up my fundraising. The simple fact is that I have not raised the funds necessary to run an effective campaign for the US Senate." Other political observers, including former Tennessee Senator Wendell Ford, concurred, saying, "The Republican leadership was responsible for drying up his funds. Jim [Bunning] is right about that, but McConnell was focusing on winning or losing. Republicans have lost the last two elections, so McConnell has been losing his taw, as we would say in western Kentucky, and he doesn't want to lose anymore" (Lindenberger 2009).

by party elites had a strong effect on Bunning's ability to raise the funds that he needed to run for reelection. Recognizing the tough upward battle he would face to win reelection in the face of party opposition, he began laying the groundwork to retire.[5] Even before he announced he would not run for reelection, Bunning began to work to find a successor, and he urged Kentucky Secretary of State Trey Grayson to explore the possibility of a Senate run (Abdullah 2009c). Upon his announcement that he was forming an exploratory committee to consider running for the US Senate, party elites quickly gravitated to Grayson's campaign. Less than a month after announcing his interest, Grayson had garnered the support of over 130 major donors and party operatives, including a dozen members of the fifty-four-member Republican State Central Committee, the primary governing board of the state's Republican Party (Musgrave 2009). Grayson also enjoyed the backing of national party elites as well, with support and encouragement from other national party figures, led most prominently by Kentucky's other Senator and Senate Majority Whip Mitch McConnell (Fritze 2010).

Such a unified action on the part of party elites led many in the party to believe that other potential candidates would quickly realize the preferences of the party and decline to run. Many hoped that Grayson's announcement and party support would clear the field for him and enable him to focus his efforts on the general election, where he would likely face a strong challenge from the Democratic nominee. Shortly after his announcement, one prominent state Republican indicated that he was "sure there's not going to be a primary" and said that he thought that "if [Grayson] gets enough money he'll be the candidate and there won't be a primary" (Ellis 2009). Indeed, many well-qualified Republicans who were considering the race ultimately declined to run, including State Senate President, David Williams, and former Bush Ranger and US Ambassador to Latvia, Cathy Bailey (Brammer 2009b; Musgrave 2009).

But party efforts to clear the field were not sufficient, and Grayson would face a challenge from Rand Paul, an ophthalmologist without any political experience, but with a well-known political legacy. Like his libertarian father, Ron Paul, Rand Paul held staunch ideological views that were clearly to the right of Grayson's on many issues. It was these views and some of Paul's uncompromising statements that made some within

---

[5] While Bunning maintained up until the last minute that he planned on running for reelection, he clearly stated that he would not run in an election where he would be at a financial disadvantage (Abdullah 2009a, 2009b).

the party nervous about his electability and his ability to work together with other Republicans to accomplish their policy goals (Brammer 2009a). But it was these same ideologically extreme views that captured the hearts of Kentucky Republican primary voters (Cross 2009).[6]

In the end, despite party elite support, it was the ideologically extreme candidate, riding the wave of antiparty sentiment prominent in the strong ongoing Tea Party movement in 2010, who won the Republican primary. While Republican Party elites were able to force Bunning out of the race and discourage other well-qualified candidates from running, they were not fully able to clear the field for Grayson or even to successfully deliver him the nomination. Despite Grayson's early polling advantage, the eventual encouragement from retiring Senator Jim Bunning, the strong support of Bunning's colleague Mitch McConnell, and the support of many other well-established Republican Party elites as well, it was the more ideologically extreme Rand Paul who won the Kentucky Republican US Senate primary (Brammer 2010).

Recent work has pointed to examples such as the 2010 Kentucky Republican Primary as evidence that strengthening parties would reduce current political polarization. The logic follows that if parties are more likely to support moderate candidates, such as Trey Grayson, because of pragmatic concerns about winning the general election, strengthening parties should boost the fortunes of moderate candidates over more extreme candidates. If the party had been stronger, would it have been able to prevent this more ideologically extreme candidate from taking office? More generally, would increasing party strength consistently reduce the number of ideologues in public office across the board, or is the parties' apparent preference for more moderate candidates a characteristic of the current political situation?

## POLARIZATION IN AMERICAN POLITICS AND THE ARGUMENT FOR STRENGTHENING PARTIES

This chapter will examine only one of the many possible normative implications.[7] This chapter examines what party control of primaries

---

[6] Republican primary voters were not just enamored with Paul, they were also hesitant to support Grayson, who had been a registered Democrat only a few years prior to running for statewide office, and had supported Bill Clinton in 1992 (Stamper 2009).

[7] The ability of parties to influence the selection of nominees, and ultimately representatives, has implications not just for ideological representation or substantive representation, but

means for the ideological preferences of party nominees. In recent decades, the widening ideological gap has garnered significant attention, not just among scholars, but also among the general public, who have become more frustrated with the inability of legislators to reach agreements across the partisan divide. Indeed, as legislators take strong stands on policies, these stances do not accurately represent the preferences of the general public or even of the median voter in the district (Bafumi and Herron 2010).

Nor is polarization necessarily an inherent characteristic of the political process. Congress, in its current ideological state, is the most polarized it has ever been (McCarty et al. 2006). This ideological polarization has fundamentally changed the way that Congress works and reduced its ability to function as a deliberative body (Mann and Ornstein 2012). Increasing polarization has made it harder for policymakers and politicians to take political action, and as a result they are unable to adjust policies to fit a changing economy and changing demographics (McCarty et al. 2006).

The apparent preference of Republican primary voters for ideologically extreme candidates has opened up a clear line of conflict within the party. In early 2013, concerned that far-right conservatives had ruined a Republican opportunity to win a majority in the Senate in 2012, by defeating moderate establishment candidates, a group of large donors came together to form an outside group aimed at promoting Republicans in primary elections. This group, led by Karl Rove, aimed to help coordinate efforts to "pick the most conservative candidate who can win [the general election]" (Zeleny 2013). Many outside the network of the party's elite criticized the efforts of this new group harshly because they (rightly) interpreted "the most conservative candidate who can win" to mean candidates with more moderate ideological views were preferred. "[This effort] is yet another example of the Republican establishment's hostility toward its conservative base," exclaimed Matt Hoskins of the Senate Conservative Fund, which had supported many of the candidates

---

also for descriptive representation in terms of candidate race (Fraga and Hassell 2017; Hennings and Urbatsch 2016; Visalvanich et al. 2017). The party may also prefer certain ethnic candidates, in an attempt to broaden their general election appeal, or alternatively may discriminate against them, because of their lack of political connections (Theilmann and Wilhite 1986). In the same vein, parties also have different preferences for candidate gender. Parties and party elites are more likely to support and nominate female candidates, while the election process and the preferences of primary electorates are more likely to produce male nominees (Hennings and Urbatsch 2016).

with whom party elites were frustrated (Weiner 2013). To conservatives, the formation of this new Super PAC appeared to be an attack by party moderates on the conservative wing of the party and it only highlighted the growing divide between the two party factions.

It is not just party insiders who have worked to strengthen party leaders. Policy reformers concerned about polarization have also pushed policy reforms aimed at strengthening parties in order to reduce polarization. Recent scholarship has argued that changes to campaign finance in recent years that have privileged outside groups over party organizations have strong implications for the ideological makeup of the body of elected officials and for the polarization of American politics.[8] According to this logic, because party organizations have strong incentives to win elections, party leaders are more likely to support and fund moderate candidates, who have a greater chance of winning (Persily 2015; La Raja and Schaffner 2015). While the ideology of donors has not fundamentally shifted in recent years, changes in the campaign finance system have incentivized the mobilization of more ideological donors in recent elections (Barber 2016; La Raja and Wiltse 2011) and encouraged donors to give more money to candidates and to outside ideological groups than to party organizations. By strengthening parties, reformers hope to provide institutional advantages to moderate candidates.

However, the evidence that suggests that strengthening parties would have the intended effect of strengthening the hand of more moderate candidates does not come from directly examining the type of candidates that parties support. Instead, the argument that stronger parties lead to less political polarization has only been tested with either circumstantial evidence (looking at the downstream effects of variance in campaign

---

[8] The original intent of primary elections, as advocated by Progressive Reformers, was fueled by concerns about the inability of public officials to adequately address social and governmental problems because of the corrupting influence of party bosses who were bought out by special interests. This same sentiment has similarly motivated recent battles over campaign finance. As these battles have played out over the past two decades, they have changed the path money follows in politics. These reforms and subsequent Supreme Court decisions have strengthened the hand of interest groups and PACs and at the same time, reforms have actually raised the amount that an individual donor can give to a campaign. The one reform that has been successful is the closure of the "soft money" loophole, which allowed special interests to give unlimited amounts to party organizations. The net effect of these reforms has been to lessen the flow of money through official party organizations and to move campaign dollars away from parties and into other political organizations. These changes have weakened party organizations and limited their ability to manipulate the use of funds (Persily 2015; La Raja and Schaffner 2015).

finance rules on state legislative polarization) or by looking at party support of incumbents in general elections. This presents two problems. First, looking at downstream effects raises the possibility of spurious correlation of campaign finance rules with other unmeasured factors that may also reduce polarization in the state and legislature. States with campaign finance rules that favor parties may also have other characteristics that might moderate polarization. Thus, moderate politics and party-centered politics may move in tandem, rather than having a causal relationship. Parties do not necessarily support moderate candidates. Indeed, party organizations captured by activists often encourage moderates in these states to pursue strategies intended to lessen the strength of the party and promote moderate candidates outside of the party system (Gilbert 1995; Nesmith 1995; Rozell 1995), and there is good reason to "fear ... political capture [of political parties] by the extremes" (Persily 2015). Likewise, limited evidence in primaries for open US House seats suggests that party-associated groups are likely to support champions of their causes who may hold extreme views (Bawn et al. 2015). In short, the argument that parties assist and prefer more moderate ideological candidates rests on the assumption that party elites become pragmatists upon entering the party organizational network. Such a hope may not be realistic. Instead, practical experience suggests that parties are institutions that confer certain electoral nomination advantages to those that control them, and that those in power use them accordingly to support candidates who hold similar ideological preferences to their own.

Second, the limited direct evidence suggesting that parties prefer more moderate politicians has come only from looking at party donations to incumbent politicians in the general election. However, this relationship might be more easily explained by the fact that competitive general election races often tend to feature more moderate candidates anyway. In this case, the relationship between party financial support and moderate candidates may not be the result of a party preference for moderate candidates who can win elections, but rather the result of the party's decision to focus resources in competitive districts (which are inherently more likely to have moderate nominees).

Moreover, looking only at party support of candidates in general elections ignores the important role of parties in primaries. In a general election, parties could funnel money to vulnerable incumbents (who may also happen to be more moderate) but at the same time eschew moderate candidates in favor of more extreme candidates in the nomination process, especially in races where gaining the nomination is tantamount to winning public office. Because, as previous chapters have demonstrated, parties do play a significant role in getting candidates through the legislative primaries, strengthening parties could also strengthen the hands of candidates in primaries whose ideological viewpoints match the preferences of party leaders.

Indeed, scholarship on parties and primary elections has suggested that parties have strong incentives to prefer loyalists who can be trusted to implement their preferred policies after the nomination (Bawn et al. 2012, 2014; Masket 2009). When forced to be responsive to two electoral constituencies, representatives are more responsive to their primary constituency (Brady et al. 2007; Fenno 1978; Hill 2015). In the same vein, primary constituencies have a strong effect on the ideology of the candidates that choose to run for office and who are likely to win (Nielson and Visalvanich 2015). By looking only at party support of incumbents in the general election, arguments that strong parties reduce polarization have ignored the role of primary elections where, as previous chapters have documented, parties are actually most influential in determining their own ideological identity and the ideological identities of the candidates that ultimately win control of public office.

So, in the 2010 Republican US Senate primary in Kentucky it seems clear that the party preferred the more moderate Grayson to the stauncher ideologue Rand Paul, but would this always be the case? Do parties always prefer more moderate candidates, or is the preference for more moderate candidates merely the result of the ideological preferences of individuals that surround the party apparatus? If it is the latter, we should be more cautious about investing more responsibility in parties. If they were given more strength, battles for the direction of the country would become battles waged almost exclusively within the parties, as policy demanders attempt to gain control of the party organizations to use to their advantage. Party organizations are not immune to capture by different groups within the party, who then use them to pursue their policy agendas (Gilbert 1995; Rozell 1995).

More broadly, however, this chapter attempts to illustrate how party control of nominations shapes our politics. The origins of the primary election emanate from the desire to reduce the influence of parties in primary elections. The previous chapters suggest that this has not been the result. Parties and the network of party elites that lead them have a strong influence on the array of options presented to primary voters and also on the outcomes of those voters' choices. Because nominations are the gateway to the election to office, the outcomes of nominations have a significant effect on the nature of our politics. If parties have a strong influence on the outcomes of primary elections, what does this mean for the ideological nature of our political system?

## THE INTENTION OF THE PRIMARY SYSTEM

Having shown that we can directly measure party support of primary candidates and that party support has a significant influence on the outcomes of primaries, this chapter delves into the ramifications of such influence. What are the implications of party influence in primary elections? What effect does party control have on the polarization of American politics? What does the influence of party support tell us about what the effect of further strengthening parties would be? On the one hand, if parties prefer more moderate politicians compared to the preferences of primary electorates for pragmatic reasons, strengthening parties should result in less polarization. On the other hand, if parties are not pragmatic, the effect of strengthening parties on party ideological preferences will vary with the ideological preferences of those who are in control of the party organization.

To examine the effect that party influence in primary elections has on the polarization of American politics, this chapter revisits the explanations that party leaders give about their motivations for supporting candidates in the primary and about the process of coordination. While Chapter 3 looked for and found little evidence that parties were merely jumping on the bandwagon of already viable candidates, this chapter examines the more explicit question of what role ideology plays in encouraging parties to coordinate behind a specific candidate. This chapter also considers how the factors that contribute to party coordination might affect the ideological characteristics of candidates who win party support. Party elites consistently emphasize a preference for candidates they view as being strong candidates in a general election. In spite of pressures from the grassroots activists who are the foot soldiers of the party, party elites acknowledge that they are less concerned about ideological purity. In addition, party elites look to coordinate on candidates within the party network. These two factors constrain the party's ideological choice, but not in a manner consistent with arguments that party elites are entirely pragmatic.

While party elites indicate that they are interested in getting the most viable general election candidate through the nomination process, their search for viability is largely limited to the circle of connections available to them who are more likely to mirror their ideological preferences.

Even when viable alternative candidates are present, partisan elites have a hard time accepting those individuals, because they are not well known within the party network. Because political networks are often populated by similarly minded individuals, this insular search appears to lead to the backing of candidates who conform ideologically with the preferences of those within the party network.

Second, this chapter corroborates these claims by using data that combine information on party-preferred candidates, as shown in previous chapters, with data on candidate ideology estimated from campaign fundraising data. Combining these data sources provides a way to examine explicitly the ideology of candidates with and without party support in a range of primary election contests. These data show that parties do generally support more moderate candidates. However, this preference for moderate candidates does not appear to be the result of pragmatic motivations. While the party does have a preference for more moderate candidates, in those districts where the nomination of a moderate candidate would have the biggest impact on the general election outcome, namely competitive districts, the party does not systematically prefer more moderate candidates. Instead, the bulk of the effect is found in primaries where the candidate's ideology will have little effect on the outcome and where party elites should theoretically be able to express their true ideological preferences.

## PARTY SUPPORT: WHAT THEY SAY

This chapter begins by revisiting findings from interviews and conversations in 2013 and 2014 with 25 party leaders, party staffers, donors, and candidates, some of which were presented in Chapters 2 and 3. Because this information was presented in more detail earlier, this section will summarize those findings here.

First, political elites from both parties indicated that they and other elites were far more willing to accept ideologically moderate candidates than was the party's base. Their preferences, whether pragmatic or sincere, were different from the preferences of the party's base. As one former Democratic state party chairman explained,

Caucus goers are not donors. I mean it's a different group of people. Caucus attendees represent the most ardent supporter of the narrowest issue necessary to win that delegate seat. Because if they narrow the issue narrow enough and they have enough votes to win they never have to compromise ... There absolutely is a disconnect between the elites – party leaders and donors – and party activists. There has been historically. They're focused on different things. They're different types of people.

Party elites genuinely thought of themselves as different from the base of grassroots activists that made up the foot soldiers who were carrying the party and who were passionate and uncompromising about ideological issues.

Party elites' explanations for those differences centered on pragmatic motivations. As a Republican Party official explained,

Higher up the [political] food chain, there's less idealism. It's more about winning. Not to say that there's not idealism, but it becomes pragmatic idealism. Higher level activists, donors, party officials want to back someone who shares their ideals, but who also can win.

While partisan elites maintain that they have many of the same underlying principles, they claim they are ultimately pragmatic idealists with a greater vision that allows them to compromise.

However, party elites' preferences for candidates are largely limited to those individuals they know. Party elites prefer to support candidates that the party has developed and helped to rise through the system. As one staffer explained,

What we're interested in is working with potential candidates long before the election, working with them to get on local offices, to start establishing themselves and positioning themselves to run for higher office down the road.

Whether this motivation comes from the desire to elicit political favors from future public officials, or merely the belief that these candidates are better qualified and better able to run successful campaigns, this preference incentivizes parties to support candidates who are likely to align their preferences with those of leadership.

While party elites indicate that their preferences for more moderate candidates originate in pragmatic concerns, there is some evidence that the preferences of party elites for more moderate candidates may stem from other causes. While the assertion that they are searching for more moderate candidates for pragmatic concerns is more palatable to grassroots organizers, who understand the need to win elections in order to enact preferred policy preferences, party elites also indicate they are drawn toward candidates they know well and with whom they have experience. Party elites admit that their search for candidates centers on individuals who are well connected in their personal and party net-work. Party networks are known to have significantly high levels of homophily, or the tendency of individuals to associate with others who are similar to them. This search within a network containing many other individuals with similar ideological preferences increases the like-lihood of identifying candidates with ideological characteristics that are similar to the preferences of the elites who are making the search (Sinclair 2012).

These interviews with party elites help clarify the relationship between party support and candidate ideology. Yet, they also reveal a tension between the different explanations given by these individuals for their preferences for ideologically moderate candidates. On the one hand, party elites express that they are pragmatic, concerned primarily with nominating a candidate who can win the general election. On the other hand, party elites also reveal that party coordination is easiest when party elites can coordinate on a well-known candidate who has been groomed by party leadership to take the next step up the politi-cal ladder. Because political networks are highly homogeneous in their ideological preferences, even within parties, it is likely that party elites, in their search for prominent candidates in their political network, are biasing their search in favor of finding candidates with similar ideolog-ical profiles.

Party elites also have an incentive to rationalize their decisions in a way that makes those decisions more acceptable to others. Explaining their motivations as pragmatic enables them to promote their own ide-ological preferences without appearing at odds with the party faithful. Preferences for one ideological strain over another are more palatable when they are framed as focused on winning. By explaining their choice to buoy one candidate over another as a matter of electability, party elites are more easily able to mobilize the party's base without having to con-cede to the base entirely on policy preferences.[9]

The parties' preferences for the best general election candidate may also be skewed by their biased perceptions of what makes the most viable general election candidates. In the 1950s and 1960s, conserva-tives and moderates in the GOP both made claims that electoral success

---

[9] While it may be true that extreme candidates do poorly in general elections (Hall 2015), it is not entirely clear whether that effect is due to ideological concerns on the part of the general electorate or to abandonment by party elites as the result of the nomination of a disfavored candidate.

would follow the adoption of their ideological brands of conservatism (Heersink 2016). Likewise, current research on local party leaders finds that Republican county party leaders (not national elites) believe that "extremists are actually much more electable than centrists in general elections" (Broockman et al. 2016, 4–5). The ideological preferences of party elites might bias their perceptions of general election viability.

In short, even though party insiders indicate that they choose who to support on the basis of electability, concerns about the motivations behind these statements, the range of their search, and the process by which they calculate candidate general election viability warrant further investigation into party preferences for ideologically moderate candidates. Even if party elites are searching both for the most electable candidate and for candidates within the party network, these restrictions would limit the set of acceptable candidates to the intersection of these searches. This restriction would also greatly limit claims that parties are pragmatic, the basis on which the argument for strengthening parties rests.

## PARTY SUPPORT: WHAT THEY DO

Because of these somewhat conflicting and unclear motivations, it is important to examine directly the relationship between candidate ideology and party support. To do so, this chapter tests whether or not party-supported candidates are consistently more moderate than are candidates without party support.

The results show that, consistent with party interviews, party elites do routinely support more moderate candidates. These preferences for more moderate candidates, however, do not align with accounts of moderation of candidate ideology in attempts to win marginal districts. While parties do support more moderate candidates, those effects are largely in primary races in noncompetitive districts where candidate ideology has little effect on the outcome of the race. While there is no systematic ideological difference between candidates with and without party support in primary elections that lead to a competitive general election contest, there are significant differences in the ideological preferences of these two types of candidate in noncompetitive districts. The contrast between party support for more moderate candidates and that for their primary competitors is starkest in districts where the moderation of candidate ideology would have little effect on the outcome.

## Data and Procedures

To examine the relationship between candidate ideology and party support this analysis uses the candidates who appeared on the party's primary ballot for US Senate and US House and filed with the Federal Election Commission (FEC). The party's preferred candidate is identified as the candidate in the primary who was most connected to the party, using that measure as described in Chapter 3. The measure identifies the candidate who received the most donations from individuals who also gave money to the party's Senatorial Campaign Committee (the Democratic Senatorial Campaign Committee (DSCC) for Democrats and the National Republican Senatorial Committee (NRSC) for Republicans). Given what we know about the cues that parties send to those connected to the party, that candidate is likely to have received the implicit endorsement of the party organization.[10]

This measure allows us to identify, in each contested primary, the candidate with the highest level of party support and to compare that candidate's ideological placement with the ideology of the candidates that are not supported by the party.

To get an accurate measure of candidate ideology, this analysis relies on the Database on Ideology, Money in Politics, and Elections (DIME). DIME provides ideological ideal point estimates for candidates who received money from at least two unique contributors who gave to at least two candidates. This ideological placement positions candidates on a liberal–conservative scale using data on individual contributions with the assumption that individual donors prefer candidates who are ideologically similar to themselves to candidates who are more distant from them ideologically.[11] Instead of only measuring party support of incumbent politicians, these data enable the ideological placement of every viable candidate who competed in a primary election. While they exclude a number of candidates who did not raise sufficient money, these under-funded candidates are largely long-shot candidates, who run for reasons other than winning (Canon 1993). To standardize the measure of

---

[10] The results are the same if we identify party-supported candidates as only those candidates with stronger support from the party than their opponents have. Increasing the share of party donors who have given to a candidate in the primary race from 50 percent to 65 percent has no significant effect on any of the figures shown here.

[11] This measure includes only donations over $200 which are required to be reported to the FEC and does not include contributions from PACs. Full details on this measure can be found at http://data.stanford.edu/dime and in Bonica (2014).

ideological extremism for both Republicans and Democrats, normally on opposite sides of the ideological spectrum, this analysis uses the absolute value of the candidate's ideological placement. This has the effect that extreme candidates, whether extremely liberal or extremely conservative, have higher values.

## Testing Party Support of Moderate Candidates

For simplicity of interpretation for the reader, the analysis presented here uses simple bivariate comparisons of the ideology of candidates with and without party support in various primary election types. Although they are not provided here, a multivariate regression analysis shows the same results, even after controlling for candidate quality. Figure 7.1 shows the differences in the ideological placement of candidates for US Senate with and without party support for the years 2004 to 2014, and Figure 7.2 does the same for candidates running in a House primary for those same years. Because we are taking the absolute value of candidates' ideological scores, higher values indicate more extreme ideological positions, regardless of whether those extreme ideological positions are liberal or conservative, while smaller numbers indicate more moderate ideological positions. As is evident in Figures 7.1 and 7.2, parties do support more moderate candidates.

The party's preference for moderate candidates is strengthened by the presence of incumbents in the data. Incumbents are more likely to be challenged from the more extreme ideological side of the party (Boatright 2014), and the party organization is designed in part as an incumbent protection system (Boatright 2014; Menefee-Libey 2000). The bottom portions of Figures 7.1 and 7.2 look at the ideological positions of candidates running in primaries without any incumbents. Looking at nonincumbents gives us a better picture of party ideological preferences for candidates.

Even after excluding candidates running in primaries with an incumbent, we continue to find significant differences between the ideological preferences of party-preferred candidates and those of candidates without party support. Senate candidates preferred by the party and running in a primary without an incumbent had an average ideological score of 0.95, compared to 1.06 for candidates who were not preferred by the party. Nonincumbent party-supported House candidates likewise had an average ideological score of 1.04, compared to 1.14 for candidates who were not preferred by the party. These differences are statistically

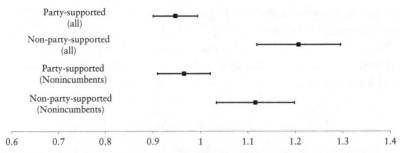

FIGURE 7.1 *Ideological differences between party-supported and non-party-supported Senate primary candidates*

*Note:* Ideological extremism estimates are the absolute value of ideal point estimates calculated from candidate donations taken from the Database on Ideology and Money in Elections (DIME). The bottom portion of the figure excludes all candidates running in a primary where an incumbent was also running. Ninety-five percent confidence intervals included.

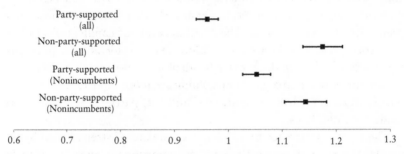

FIGURE 7.2 *Ideological differences between party-supported and non-party-supported House primary candidates*

*Note:* Ideological extremism estimates are the absolute value of ideal point estimates calculated from candidate donations taken from the Database on Ideology and Money in Elections (DIME). The bottom portion of the figure excludes all candidates running in a primary where an incumbent was also running. Ninety-five percent confidence intervals included.

significant at the $p < 0.05$ level for Senate candidates and at the $p < 0.01$ level for House candidates, using a one-tailed test. In general, parties support more moderate primary election candidates, although the strongest moderating force is the party's defense of its own more moderate incumbents from primary challenges.

## Party Differences

Grouping all of these candidates together masks potential important partisan asymmetries. Donors' perceptions of the ideological preferences of candidates and political parties vary by the ideology of the donor. While liberal donors do not distinguish any differences between the ideological preferences of the Democratic Party and Democratic candidates, conservative donors view the Republican Party as significantly more moderate than Republican candidates (La Raja and Schaffner 2015). Thus, the Republican Party might act as a force to reduce ideological extremism by supporting more moderate Republican candidates in a primary because donors differ from party leaders in their perceptions of appropriate candidates. However, the Democratic Party is less likely to reduce the number of ideologically extreme Democratic nominees, because there are few apparent differences between the ideological preferences of the party organization and those of donors. Thus, we should expect there to be differences between the ideological preferences of candidates supported by the Republican Party and candidates not supported by the Republican Party. However, we should be less likely to expect differences between Democratic candidates receiving Democratic Party support and those who are not the Democratic Party's favored candidates.

Figures 7.3 and 7.4 show the differences in ideology between party-preferred candidates and candidates who are not preferred by the party in contested Republican primary elections for the US Senate and US House, respectively, between 2004 and 2012. We see that, consistent with the overall findings, Republican candidates with party support are significantly more moderate, both when all candidates are looked at and when only nonincumbents are. The average ideal point for the full sample of primary candidates supported by the Republican Party was 0.95, compared to 1.12 for candidates who did not have the support of the party, and the average ideal point for Republican Party-supported House candidates was 0.97, compared to 1.15 for House candidates in the primary without party support. These differences are significant at the $p < 0.05$ level for Senate candidates and at the $p < 0.01$ level for House candidates, using a one-tailed test.

If we look at nonincumbent primaries for the US Senate and House, as shown in the bottom halves of Figures 7.3 and 7.4, respectively, we see the same thing. The average party-supported nonincumbent Republican was significantly more moderate than candidates that were not supported by NRSC donors. Nonincumbent Senate candidates supported by the party had an ideological score of 0.97 on the left–right scale, compared to 1.10 for candidates who were not the party's preferred choice. The average ideal point of nonincumbent House candidates supported by the party was 1.03, compared to 1.11 for candidates without party support.

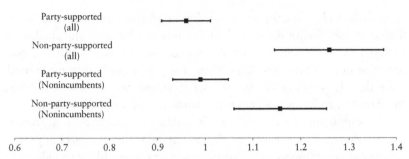

FIGURE 7.3 *Ideological differences between Republican Party-supported and non-party-supported Senate primary candidates*
Note: Ideal point estimates are taken from the Database on Ideology and Money in Elections (DIME). The bottom portion of the figure excludes all candidates running in a primary where an incumbent was also running. Ninety-five percent confidence intervals included.

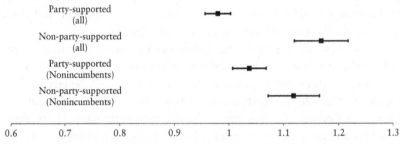

FIGURE 7.4 *Ideological differences between Republican Party-supported and non-party-supported House candidates*
Note: Ideal point estimates are taken from the Database on Ideology and Money in Elections (DIME). The bottom portion of the figure excludes all candidates running in a primary where an incumbent was also running. Ninety-five percent confidence intervals included.

Both of these differences are significant at the $p < 0.05$ level on a one-tailed test.

We do not see a similar party preference for moderate candidates on the Democratic side. Figures 7.5 and 7.6 show the differences between the ideology of candidates with Democratic Party support and those without party support in Senate and House primaries, respectively. While the ideological differences are marked between Republican candidates with and without party support, there are no significant differences between Democratic candidates with and without party support during this period. Simply put, during this period Democratic Party elites did not systematically prefer

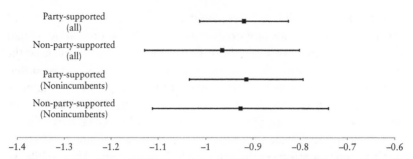

FIGURE 7.5 *Ideological differences between Democratic Party-supported and non-party-supported Senate primary candidates*
Note: Ideal point estimates are taken from the Database on Ideology and Money in Elections (DIME). The bottom portion of the figure excludes all candidates running in a primary where an incumbent was also running. Ninety-five percent confidence intervals included.

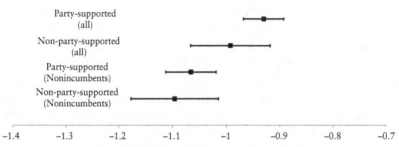

FIGURE 7.6 *Ideological differences between Democratic Party-supported and non-party-supported House primary candidates*
Note: Ideal point estimates are taken from the Database on Ideology and Money in Elections (DIME). The bottom portion of the figure excludes all candidates running in a primary where an incumbent was also running. Ninety-five percent confidence intervals included.

more moderate candidates in primary elections. Thus the preference that the Republican Party shows for primary candidates who are more moderate than the other possible candidates does not appear to be a consistent factor of party politics. Party elites and party organizations do not universally prefer more moderate candidates. Instead, it appears that party preference for moderate candidates is a party-specific phenomenon currently found predominately in the Republican Party.

While this evidence suggests that party elites are sincere in their preferences, it does not necessarily disprove the theory that party elites are pragmatic. While Democratic Party elites do not systematically support more moderate candidates, this could be for a variety of reasons, of which sincere candidate support is only one. What it does show is that while the preferences of Republican Party elites differ from those of the Republican base – for either pragmatic or sincere reasons – those differences do not exist in both parties. Democratic elites could be pragmatic in their preferences, but they have no need to differ significantly from the average Democratic candidate, because most Democratic candidates are sufficiently moderate that more moderation would not be likely to have a significant effect on the general election outcome. Thus, while we can see that Republican elites prefer more moderate candidates, while Democratic elites do not, we cannot easily distinguish the motivations behind these preferences from these tests.

### Yearly Effects

If party support for more moderate candidates is not a consistent factor across parties, it also raises the question of whether or not this preference for more moderate candidates is consistent across time. Over the time of this study, the median voter has remained relatively constant, and in this situation party preferences for a certain type of ideological candidate should also remain relatively constant over time (Fiorina and Abrams 2009). Even if parties can exploit voters' ideological blind spots, we should not expect party preferences to move consistently in one direction, especially in a more extreme direction away from the median voter, that would likely end up outside of the electoral blind spot (Bawn et al. 2012).

On the other hand, party leadership is not constant, and so the sincere preferences of party leaders and the networks that surround them may change. Likewise, the set of available candidates may also shift and present more options that are unsuitable over time. Parties may only exert pressure to nominate more moderate candidates compared to the other candidates running when forces outside the party, but within its voter base, attempt to push the party toward more extreme political positions, which are not shared by party leaders and elites. In recent years the cracks between Republican leadership and the rank-and-file members have grown deeper and wider.

To examine whether these perceived public fissures are actually more apparent in the ideologies of party-supported candidates and candidates without party support we can look at variation of differences between

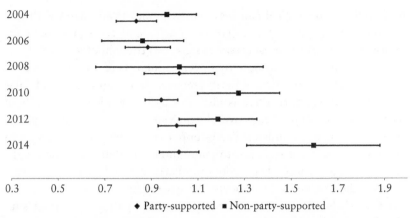

FIGURE 7.7 *Ideological differences between Republican Party-supported and non-party-supported Senate primary candidates by year*
Note: Ideal point estimates are taken from the Database on Ideology and Money in Elections (DIME). Ninety-five percent confidence intervals included.

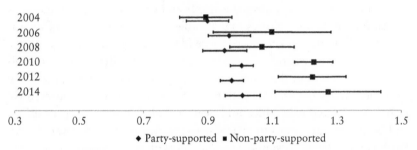

FIGURE 7.8 *Ideological differences between Republican Party-supported and non-party-supported House primary candidates by year*
Note: Ideal point estimates are taken from the Database on Ideology and Money in Elections (DIME). Ninety-five percent confidence intervals included.

Republican Party-preferred candidates and Republicans who did not have the support of the party on a year-to-year basis. Figures 7.7 and 7.8 show that these ideological differences between candidates with and without party support are not consistent.[12] While in most years there is

---

[12] There are no significant variations in the ideological locations of party-supported and unsupported Democratic candidates over time. While Republicans have increased in ideological extremism and in the ideological divergence between party-supported and non-party-supported candidates over the period, there are no significant differences for Democrats, who have remained largely consistent in their ideological preferences both inside and outside the party.

no significant ideological gap between Republican candidates with and without party support, the difference in 2010 and 2014 (and 2012 for House primary candidates) is twice as great as those in other years.[13]

It is also important to note that even though there are differences in the ideological positioning of party-preferred candidates and candidates without party support, there is also an observable ideological shift of party-supported Republicans over the time span, especially among party-supported Senate candidates. Party-supported Republican candidates in 2004 and 2006 were significantly more moderate than were their 2012 and 2014 counterparts. The Republican Party may reduce the extremism of its candidates, but it does not eliminate the rightward movement of the party as a whole. This suggests that perhaps the party is basing its support for candidates not entirely on a desire to win elections, but rather on the ideological preferences of those well connected to the party.

As ideological extremists within the Republican Party have become more integrated into the party and the party leadership structure, their preferences and connections have also been incorporated into the party's search for candidates. Parties may be able to reduce the speed of polarization by limiting the success of more ideologically extreme candidates, but even party elites are susceptible to ideological shifts. When ideological extremists within the party ascend to leadership positions, they take their ideological preferences with them. Over time, as more conservative Republicans have won office and been included in leadership positions and been integrated into the party network, we see that the Republican Party is more likely to support candidates with more staunchly conservative policy views.

However, while this shift suggests that party preferences for more moderate candidates are not a display of ideological pragmatism but rather the expression of true ideological preferences, it again does not explicitly test that theory. The mere fact that the party has moved does not necessarily mean that the party does not act as an ideological moderator. It could be that while the party would prefer more moderate candidates, it is merely picking the best candidates available. As the party faithful have moved rightward, those more moderate candidates could therefore become more extreme in their policy views over time.

---

[13] Even without 2010, party-supported Senate candidates (both excluding and including incumbent primaries) are significantly more moderate than candidates without party support.

## Competitive and Noncompetitive Districts

A better test of the theory that parties are pragmatists that support moderate candidates with the intent of winning elections is to examine the behavior of parties in nomination contests in competitive districts and states and to compare it to the behavior of parties in nominations in noncompetitive districts and states. In unwinnable races or in safe races, parties should have limited motivation to encourage moderate candidates over ideological extremists. In these districts, candidate ideology will likely have little effect on the election outcome. As such, the pragmatic motivation of parties should disappear or be much weaker.

In contrast, in competitive districts candidate ideology is more likely to make a difference in the outcome of the election. It is in these competitive districts that we should see the biggest differences in ideology if parties are pragmatically choosing to support moderate candidates. By comparing the behavior of party elites in those races where ideology is most likely to have an influence on general election outcomes to that in those races where ideology will likely have little influence on election outcomes, we can better understand why parties support more moderate candidates. If parties are interested in moderate candidates because they want to win elections, we should see the biggest differences between the ideologies of party-supported candidates and candidates without party support in competitive districts.

More importantly, as noted in Chapter 3, given the parties' limited resources and the large number of races to monitor in the House, it is only House primaries that lead to general election races that are perceived to be competitive and where party support for primary candidates leads rather than follows candidate fundraising. As such, if the party is acting pragmatically in districts that are competitive, we should see significant differences between party-supported candidates and non-party-supported candidates, while in noncompetitive districts these differences should disappear as parties become less likely to become involved. In safe and unwinnable districts, the party has little incentive to moderate the candidate that it supports for electoral purposes, because moderation will not likely be crucial to victory. Continued differences between candidates with and without party support in noncompetitive districts, or stronger effects in noncompetitive districts, however, would show that social and ideological divisions within the party unrelated to electoral outcome goals are the driving influence of the party's preferences for more moderate candidates.

Figure 7.9 looks at primaries without an incumbent in states identified as competitive and shows the differences in the ideological positions of party-preferred Senate candidates and those without party support. To identify competitive Senate elections, this analysis uses Cook Political Reports' assessment of general-election competitiveness at the beginning of the electoral year.[14] The results are not supportive of a theory of party moderation on the basis of a desire for electoral success. An analysis of the differences in the ideologies of candidates with and without party support in competitive and noncompetitive states shows that parties are not strategically encouraging moderate candidates in those races where moderation matters most. As Figure 7.9 shows, in competitive Senate seats there is no significant difference in the ideological locations of candidates preferred by the party and candidates not preferred by the party. In competitive districts party-supported candidates are no less extreme than candidates without party support. In competitive elections, the elections where moderation might have a significant impact on the outcome of the election, parties are not more likely to support candidates with less extreme ideological views. In primaries leading to competitive general elections, candidates with party backing are just as likely to have extreme ideological views as candidates who are not the party's preferred choice.

Figures 7.9 and 7.10 also show the ideological differences between party-supported candidates and candidates who were not the party's preferred choice in primaries in states and districts that Cook Political Reports did not indicate were competitive. Contrary to the expectations of parties as electorally strategic moderators, it is these primary races where there are significant differences between the ideological placements of party-supported candidates and candidates who do not enjoy the support of the party. In primary elections, parties are more likely to support moderate candidates, but that finding is driven by primaries for seats that are not competitive.[15]

---

[14] Cook Political Reports provide analysis of the competitiveness of the race and the likely winner. For more information see Campbell (2010).

[15] This effect is manifest in both safe seats for Senate (Party-supported: 1.00; Non-Party-supported: 1.16) and unwinnable Senate seats (Party-supported: 0.869; Non-Party-supported: 1.109), although it only reaches statistical significance for unwinnable seats because of the small number of candidates running in nonincumbent safe seats ($n = 34$). For House seats, the effect appears to be only in unwinnable seats (Party-supported: 1.086; Non-Party-supported: 1.339), whereas the differences in safe seats are virtually nonexistent (Party-supported: 0.991; Non-Party-supported: 0.972).

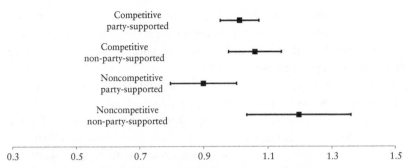

FIGURE 7.9 *Ideological differences between party-supported and non-party-supported Senate primary candidates in competitive and noncompetitive states*
Note: Ideological extremism estimates are the absolute value of ideal point estimates calculated from candidate donations, taken from the Database on Ideology and Money in Elections (DIME). Data exclude candidates running in primaries where there is an incumbent. The top portion of the figure looks at primaries leading to general elections that the Cook Political Report identified as competitive and the bottom portion of the figure looks at primaries leading to general elections that the Cook Political Report identified as uncompetitive. Ninety-five percent confidence intervals included.

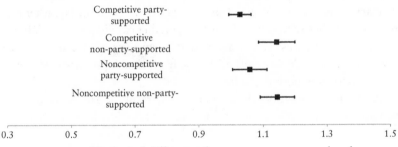

FIGURE 7.10 *Ideological differences between party-supported and non-party-supported House primary candidates in competitive and noncompetitive districts*
Note: Ideological extremism estimates are the absolute value of ideal point estimates calculated from candidate donations, taken from the Database on Ideology and Money in Elections (DIME). The top portion of the figure looks at primaries leading to general elections that the Cook Political Report identified as competitive and the bottom portion of the figure looks at primaries leading to general elections that the Cook Political Report identified as uncompetitive. Ninety-five percent confidence intervals included.

Figure 7.10 tells a slightly different story for party support in House primaries. In both competitive and noncompetitive districts, party-supported candidates running in primaries without incumbents were slightly more moderate than candidates that were not preferred by the party, although, perhaps more consistent with results from the Senate, the effects are only marginally significant in competitive House districts (p < 0.08). Party-supported candidates in competitive seats and noncompetitive seats had ideal points that were significantly less extreme fewer than their unsupported counterparts.

However, if we recall the evidence from Chapter 3, party support for House primary candidates is not independent of candidate viability in all primary races. Because of the large number of congressional districts, party leaders and elites are more likely to use cues about candidate viability and competence in deciding which candidate to support when that information is available. Only in competitive districts, where candidates have the same level of experience and qualifications, does party support Granger-cause candidate fundraising. In this select set of races, party elites are driving the fundraising success of candidates rather than moving in tandem with it.

Figure 7.11 looks at those specific races where we can be sure that party support is substantially affecting candidate success. In this figure, we look at primary races in competitive districts where the candidates competing all had similar levels of experience. It is in this set of House primary races that parties have an influence on the outcomes, rather than moving together with other factors that predict candidate success. In this select group of races we see again that party-supported candidates are not significantly ideologically different from their opponents who were not the party's preferred candidate.

Party moderation does not seem to be the result of parties strategically supporting moderate candidates in races where ideological extremism

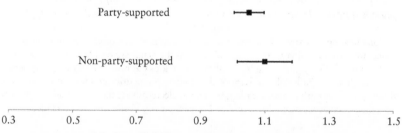

FIGURE 7.11 *Ideological differences between party-supported and non-party-supported House primary candidates in competitive districts with no difference in candidate quality*
Note: Ideological extremism estimates are the absolute value of ideal point estimates calculated from candidate donations, taken from the Database on Ideology and Money in Elections (DIME). Data exclude candidates running in primaries where there is an incumbent. Ninety-five percent confidence intervals included.

could have a significant influence on the outcome of the general election. As mentioned before, these relationships continue to hold even if we use multivariate analysis and control for candidate quality. Party elites and activists appear to have fundamentally different preferences, and it is these preferences that drive the resulting differences in the ideology of party-supported and non-party-supported candidates. In primaries that lead to competitive general election races, where ideological differences might have an influence on the outcome of the election, there are no ideological differences between the party's preferred candidate and the candidate without party support. In short, in these races, parties do not appear to be strategically supporting moderate candidates.

## DISCUSSION

What does all of this tell us about the normative implications of party influence on primaries? While we have examined only one of the many possible normative aspects, we can say something about how party influence on the process affects the ideological preferences of parties in the legislature. First, party elites are ideologically distinct from the party base. Party elites generally express an interest in more moderate candidates. While these individuals indicate that their goal is to recruit and support candidates who, they believe, have the ability to win public office in the general election, other evidence suggests that their view of electability aligns closely with their own preferences. Party elites also indicated that they seek out candidates in their network. Even if they truly are seeking out the best general election candidates, they are searching amidst a pool of candidates whose views are likely to mirror their own.

In addition, there is strong evidence that parties, especially the Republican Party, do support more moderate candidates. Party-supported candidates are significantly more moderate than candidates that are not preferred by the party. With the party organization designed partially to support the defense of incumbent-held seats, this is especially true when including incumbent politicians facing a primary. These primary-challenged incumbents are routinely more moderate than their challengers, and the result is that much of the effect of party moderation on candidate ideology is built into its system of defending incumbents against challengers from within the party, as well as from the opposite party.

Among Democrats, evidence for this tendency is not as strong. While a clear ideological split appears to have emerged among Republicans, largely dividing party elites and those not well connected to the party network, Democrats appear to remain largely unified on their ideological preferences. While party-supported Republicans are more moderate than their unsupported counterparts, there is no significant ideological difference between Democrats with and without party support.

In addition, the differences in ideological positioning between the party's preferred candidates and those candidates who do not enjoy the party's blessing are also most salient in years where the ideological coalition outside the party effectively mobilizes more ideologically extreme candidates to run for office.

Differences appear to be, in part, the result of the increasing conspicuousness of ideological rifts within the Republican Party, rather than the party's incentive to moderate its preferences in order to enable ideological competition. Party elites seem to have different ideological preferences from those of the party's base. If parties had an incentive to moderate their preferences in primary elections in order to win seats in competitive general election races, we should see a clear difference in ideological positioning between candidates with and those without the party's backing in primaries that lead to general elections considered competitive. This is not the case. In fact, we find the opposite. While there is a significant difference between the ideological positioning of party-supported candidates and their opponents in primaries that lead to noncompetitive general elections, there are no ideological differences between these two sets of candidates in primaries that lead to competitive general elections. Quite the contrary, the party's preferred candidates are not fundamentally ideologically different from other candidates running in those primary elections that lead to competitive general elections.

This evidence suggests that party support is more likely to be contingent on the preferences of those well connected to the party structure. At times when politics is polarizing and the parties are moving away from each other ideologically, party leadership may represent yesterday's ideological preferences, which are more moderate. However, as individuals with more extreme views come into the party, party support of candidates in primary elections should also shift. Because a party-supported candidate enjoys an electoral advantage in the primary, moderate candidates currently are at an advantage over their more extreme counterparts. However, this preference for moderate candidates appears to be sincere, rather than strategic, on the part of party leaders, and as such we cannot assume that this preference for more moderate candidates will continue.

While this does not preclude the targeting of moderate candidates in competitive general elections, the strength and influence of the party could also end up advantaging more extreme candidates in primaries for uncompetitive seats over time. Instead of a moderation of preferences to better the chances of winning the general election, the variations in the ideology of candidates supported by the party and of candidates not supported by the party seem to be the result of a rift within the party. While those closely affiliated with the party organization are more willing to support and encourage more moderate candidates, more extreme candidates are less likely to get the support of those affiliated with the party organization, simply because those affiliated with the party are not currently as extreme as those "on the outside."

Thus, in the current environment, strengthening the hand of the party could reduce polarization by giving the upper hand to moderate politicians, but that result would depend on the ability of those individuals to retain control of the party organization. As the year-by-year analysis shows, preferences of party elites for ideological candidates are not stable. Over time, the average ideological position of the Republican Party's preferred candidates has also drifted rightward. Parties are a good means by which to moderate the political ideologies of candidates, but only when those in control of the party hold moderate ideological views. When the ideological preferences of party leaders become more extreme, their support is likewise more likely to go toward candidates who share their more extreme views.

All of this suggests that while the current political system, with its out-of-control polarization, would benefit from the strengthening of political parties, policy reforms that strengthen parties may not necessarily in the long run be the antidote to polarization for which many hope. The evidence presented here suggests that parties prefer moderate candidates just because current party elites sincerely prefer moderate candidates to candidates with extreme ideologies. Parties do not appear to be supporting more moderate candidates for strategic electoral reasons. As party elites change, the party's candidate preferences in terms of particular ideology are also likely to change.

A party is the product of the groups and interests that have a stake in it and are connected to it. As parties come to incorporate these views, or as certain groups and individuals rise to power within the organizations, these organizations can then be mobilized to advance the political and ideological preferences of those very individuals and groups. Empowering a party seems, perhaps unsurprisingly, to empower those who control the institution. Rather than just changing the political system to first empower parties, more thought needs to be given to how to encourage individuals with more moderate views to become more involved in party organizations.[16] That, however, is the topic of another book.

REPRISE

This book has focused on political parties and the network of political elites that surrounds them and how parties work to control the nomination process. While the predominant assumption about primary elections is that they are candidate-centered, it has been my hope that this book has challenged that assumption in a way that helps understand how parties and party elites continue to exert a substantial amount of influence on the process. Although primary elections were originally put forward by Progressive reformers as a means to remove the power of nomination from the hands of party bosses and party elites, the evidence here indicates that these reforms are not as effective as those reformers might have hoped. While the nomination process has fundamentally changed, the power wielded there has not gone away. Party elites and party leaders continue to exert a significant influence on the nomination process.

The implementation of primary elections has merely changed the mechanism of control of the nomination process from that of gently persuading party convention delegates through the use of incentives (whether legal or extralegal) and threats, to taking control of the tools and resources candidates need to run successful campaigns. In order to run a successful primary campaign, a candidate needs a number of critical resources including fundraising, competent and capable staff, and access to the media. While these resources are found abundantly within the party network, they are difficult to procure elsewhere. Party control of primary elections stems from the party's control of these resources. Parties are also able to cajole undesired candidates into pursuing other avenues of political success, through promises of future political influence in other spheres.

These tools are powerful because they change the viability of candidates in the primary election. Party support is not a function of candidate

---

[16] Primaries have not always attracted strict ideological extremists for each party. For more details on how the ideological variation in primary electorates has changed over time see Hill and Tausanovitch (2015).

viability, but rather party support changes the viability of candidates in the primary. Candidates with party support are more likely to remain in the race and more likely to win the nomination if they do stay in the race. About 80 percent of party-supported Senate candidates win their primaries, and over 67 percent of party-supported House candidates win the nomination. While the parties' preferences do not guarantee a nomination victory, they have a strong influence on the likelihood of winning.

Most importantly, the influence of parties on primary election outcomes has an effect of shaping the ideological nature of politics. Because of the divides between populist activists and party elites, party influence in the nomination process has the effect of moderating the ideological profiles of those candidates that are nominated for office. While this gives some hope to those who advocate the strengthening of parties as a means of reducing the extreme polarization evident in politics today, we should be careful that we do not move the balance of power so far that candidates become even more responsive to party elites than to the general public.

# References

Abdullah, Halimah. 2009a. "Bunning Raises Less Money than Mongiardo in First Quarter." *Lexington Herald-Leader*, April 16.

2009b. "Bunning Raises Less than Half of Grayson's Haul." *Lexington Herald-Leader*, July 16.

2009c. "Grayson: Bunning Blessed Plan to Test Senate Waters – But Incumbent Shows No Sign He's Leaving." *Lexington Herald*, May 2.

Abramson, Paul R., John H. Aldrich, and David W. Rohde. 1987. "Progressive Ambition among United States Senators: 1972–1988." *Journal of Politics* 49(1):3–35.

Aldrich, John H. 1995. *Why Parties?: The Origin and Transformation of Political Parties*. Chicago: University of Chicago Press.

Alvarez, R. Michael, David T. Canon, and Patrick Sellers. 1995. "The Impact of Primaries on General Election Outcomes in the U.S. House and Senate." California Institute of Technology Working Paper.

Ansolabehere, Stephen, John M. de Figueiredo, and James M. Snyder. 2003. "Why Is There So Little Money in U.S. Politics?" *Journal of Economic Perspectives* 17(1):105–30.

Ansolabehere, Stephen and Shanto Iyengar. 1994. "Of Horseshoes and Horse Races: Experimental Studies of the Impact of Poll Results on Electoral Behavior." *Political Communication* 11(4):413–30.

Associated Press. 2005. "Vermont Lt. Gov. Dubie Drops Senate Exploratory Bid, Says He'll Seek Re-Election." *Associated Press*, October 26.

Associated Press. 2010. "Sen. Candidate Says White House Discussed 3 Jobs." *CBS News*, June 2.

Associated Press. 2012. "Mourdock Talks Rape, Pregnancy, and God's Plan." *Associated Press*, October 23.

Associated Press. 2016. "The Latest: Top Indiana Lawmakers Backing Holcomb Selection." *Associated Press*, February 9.

Auster, Elizabeth. 2005a. "Do We Have a Blue-Talker for a Red State?" *Plain Dealer*, December 18, H1.

2005b. "Primary Challenge to Brown Excites, Irks Democrats." *Plain Dealer*, December 12, A1.

Auster, Elizabeth and Stephen Koff. 2005. "Iraq-Vet Democrat Hackett Plans to Challenge DeWine Avon's Rep. Brown Weighing Race, Too." *Plain Dealer*, October 4, A7.

Bade, Rachel and John Bresnahan. 2016. "Trump Will Meet with Rank-and-File Republicans before FBI Director Comey Testifies about Why He Decided against Charges for Clinton." *Politico*, July 7.

Bafumi, Joseph and Michael C. Herron. 2010. "Leapfrog Representation and Extremism: A Study of American Voters and Their Members in Congress." *American Political Science Review* 104(3):519–42.

Baker, Peter. 2010a. "White House's Role in Primaries Spurs Sharp Debate." *New York Times*, June 4.

2010b. "White House Confirms Discussing Jobs with Candidate." *New York Times*, June 3, 4–6.

Banta, Megan. 2016. "Poll Released by Democrats Shows Bayh Leading Young." *Herald-Times*, July 19.

Barber, Michael J. 2016. "Ideological Donors, Contribution Limits, and the Polarization of American Legislatures." *Journal of Politics* 78(1):296–310.

Barton, Albert Olaus. 1922. *La Follette's Winning of Wisconsin (1894–1904)*. Des Moines: Homestead Company.

Bawn, Kathleen et al. 2012. "A Theory of Political Parties: Groups, Policy Demands and Nominations in American Politics." *Perspectives on Politics* 10(3):571–97.

et al. 2014. "Parties on the Ground: A Preliminary Report on Open Seat House Nominations in 2014." *Meetings of the American Political Science Association*.

et al. 2015. "Social Choice and Coordination Problems in Open House Primaries." *Meetings of the American Political Science Association*.

Beck, Nathaniel and Jonathan N. Katz. 1995. "What to Do (and Not to Do) with Time-Series Cross-Section Data." *American Political Science Review* 89(3):634–47.

Beck, Nathaniel, Jonathan N. Katz, and Richard Tucker. 1998. "Taking Time Seriously: Time-Series-Cross-Section Analysis with a Binary Dependent Variable." *American Journal of Political Science* 42(4):1260–88.

Bennett, Lanetra. 2015. "Neal Dunn Announces Candidacy for Florida Congressional District 2." *WCTV*, August 10.

Bernstein, Robert A. 1977. "Divisive Primaries Do Hurt: U.S. Senate Races, 1956–1972." *American Political Science Review* 71(2):540–45.

Black, Eric. 2005. "Kennedy Is Off and Running." *Star Tribune*, February 12.

Bleich, Erik and Robert Pekkanen. 2013. "How to Report Interview Data." Pp. 84–105 in *Interview Research in Political Science*, edited by Layna Mosley. Ithaca, NY: Cornell University Press.

Boatright, Robert G. 2014. *Getting Primaried: The Changing Politics of Congressional Primary Challenges*. Ann Arbor, MI: University of Michigan Press.

Bonica, Adam. 2014. "Mapping the Ideological Marketplace." *American Journal of Political Science* 58(2):367–86.

Born, Richard. 1981. "The Influence of House Primary Election Divisiveness on General Election Margins, 1962–76." *Journal of Politics* 43(3): 640–61.

Borreca, Richard. 2010. "Case Bows Out – The Candidate Terminates His Run for Congress, Leaving Hanabusa as the Democrats Top Pick." *Honolulu Star-Bulletin*, May 31.

2011. "Case Just Can't Seem to Get a Break from Fellow Dems." *Honolulu Star-Advertiser*, August 5.

Bowser, Jennie Drage, Tim Storey, Wendy Underhill, and Susan Frederick. 2011. *The Canvass: States and Election Reform*. Denver, CO: National Conference of State Legislatures.

Brace, Paul. 1984. "Progressive Ambition in the House: A Probabilistic Approach." *Journal of Politics* 46(2):556–71.

Brady, David W., Hahrie C. Han, and Jeremy C. Pope. 2007. "Primary Elections and Candidate Ideology: Out of Step with the Primary Electorate?" *Legislative Studies Quarterly* 32(1):79–105.

Brammer, Jack. 2009a. "SurveyUSA: Grayson and Mongiardo Lead in U.S. Senate Primaries." *Lexington Herald-Leader*, August 18.

2009b. "Williams Won't Run for U.S. Senate; Predicts Bunning Will Stay in." *Lexington Herald-Leader*, June 15.

2010. "Paul Thumps Grayson; Conway Edges Mongiardo." *Lexington Herald-Leader*, May 19.

Broockman, David E. 2014. "Mobilizing Candidates: Political Actors Strategically Shape the Candidate Pool with Personal Appeals." *Journal of Experimental Political Science* 1(2):104–19.

Broockman, David E., Nicholas Carnes, Melody Crowder-Meyer, and Christopher Skovron. 2016. "Having Their Cake and Eating It, Too: (Why) Local Party Leaders Prefer Nominating Extreme Candidates." *Stanford University Working Paper*.

Brown, Adam R. 2013. "Does Money Buy Votes? The Case of Self-Financed Gubernatorial Candidates." *Political Behavior* 35(1):21–41.

Brunell, Thomas L. 2005. "The Relationship between Political Parties and Interest Groups: Explaining Patterns of PAC Contributions to Candidates for Congress." *Political Research Quarterly* 58(4):681–88.

Budd, Lawrence. 2005. "Hackett Hopes Duty in Iraq Gives Him Edge in Contest – Democrat Seeks Seat That Was Held by Rob Portman." *Dayton Daily News*, July 25, B4.

Burke, Edmund. 1770. *Thoughts on the Causes of the Present Discontents*. London: J.Dodsley.

Burnham, Walter Dean. 1970. *Critical Elections and the Mainsprings of American Politics*. New York: W.W. Norton and Company Inc.

Butler, Daniel M. and Adam M. Dynes. 2016. "How Politicians Discount the Opinions of Constituents with Whom They Disagree." *American Journal of Political Science* 60(4):975–89.

Butler, Daniel M. and Jessica Robinson Preece. 2016. "Recruitment and Perceptions of Gender Bias in Party Leader Support." *Political Research Quarterly* 69(4):842–51.

BuzzFeed. 2012. "Audio Exclusive: In 1996 Phone Call, Gingrich Sought To Ease Out Wisconsin Challenger." *BuzzFeed Politics*, January 26.

Campbell, James E. 2010. "The Seats in Trouble Forecast of the 2010 Elections to the U.S. House." *PS: Political Science & Politics* 43(4):627–30.

Campbell, James E., John R. Alford, and Keith Henry. 1984. "Television Markets and Congressional Elections." *Legislative Studies Quarterly* 9(4):665–78.

Campbell, Angus, Philip E. Converse, Warren E. Miller, and Donald E. Stokes. 1960. *The American Voter*. Chicago: University of Chicago Press.

Canon, David T. 1990. *Actors, Athletes, and Astronauts: Political Amateurs in the United States Congress*. Chicago: University of Chicago Press.

1993. "Sacrificial Lambs or Strategic Politicians? Political Amateurs in US House Elections." *American Journal of Political Science* 37(4):1119–141.

Cantor, Eric, Paul Ryan, and Kevin McCarthy. 2010. *Young Guns: A New Generation of Conservative Leaders*. New York: Simon and Schuster.

Cassata, Donna. 2014. "Tea Party Ready for Fight with GOP Establishment." *Associated Press*, March 1.

Cataluna, Lee. 2010. "Case Out for Now, but Far From Pau." *Honolulu Advertiser*, June 1.

Chancellor, Carl. 2006. "Hackett Ends Bid for Seat in Senate – Letter Says Iraq Veteran Reluctantly Drops Out after Requests by Party Leaders." *Akron Beacon Journal*, February 15, B1.

Cillizza, Chris and Aaron Blake. 2012. "Why Dick Lugar Lost." *Washington Post*, May 9.

Clarke, Peter and Susan H. Evans. 1983. *Covering Campaigns: Journalism in Congressional Elections*. Palo Alto, CA: Stanford University Press.

Cohen, Marty, David Karol, Hans Noel, and John Zaller. 2008. *The Party Decides: Presidential Nominations Before and After Reform*. Chicago: University of Chicago Press.

2016. "Party Versus Faction in the Reformed Presidential Nominating System." *PS: Political Science & Politics* 43(4):701–8.

Collins, Michael. 2005a. "Hackett in Talks with Dean." *Cincinnati Post*, September 10, A10.

2005b. "This Man Keeps His Word." *Cincinnati Post*, November 12, A12.

Confessore, Nicholas and Karen Yourish. 2016. "$2 Billion Worth of Free Media for Donald Trump." *New York Times*, March 17, A3.

Congressional Quarterly Weekly Report. 1992. "Tsongas Suspends Campaign." *Congressional Quarterly Weekly Report*, March 21, 749.

Converse, Philip E. 1964. "The Nature of Belief Systems in Mass Publics." Pp. 206–61 in *Ideology and Its Discontents*, edited by David E. Apter. New York: Free Press of Glencoe.

Courier Journal. 2010. "Bunning's Fitness." *Courier Journal*, October 10.

Crippes, Christinia. 2015. "Vernon Secures Another Congressional Endorsement." *Waterloo Courier*, June 25.

Cross, Al. 2009. "Fancy Farm Picnic Can Be a Minefield for Front-Runners." *Owensboro Messenger-Inquirer*, August 11, A9.

Currinder, Marian L. 2009. *Money in the House: Campaign Funds and Congressional Party Politics*. Boulder, CO: Westview Press.

Daily Kos. 2005. "Paul Hackett, Daily Kos & The New Republic." *Daily Kos*, August 4.

Dao, James. 2005. "A Veteran of Iraq, Running in Ohio, Is Harsh on Bush." *New York Times*, July 22, A1.

DePledge, Derrick. 2009. "Case Sets His Sights on Returning to Congress." *Honolulu Advertiser*, March 29.

2010a. "Case Stuns with Withdrawal from Hawaii Congressional Primary." *Honolulu Advertiser*, May 31.

2010b. "Hannemann, Abercrombie Sum It Up." *Honolulu Advertiser*, May 30.

2012. "Hirono Beats Case." *Honolulu Star-Advertiser*, August 12.

Desmarais, Bruce A., Raymond J. La Raja, and Michael S. Kowal. 2015. "The Fates of Challengers in U.S. House Elections: The Role of Extended Party Networks in Supporting Candidates and Shaping Electoral Outcomes." *American Journal of Political Science* 59(1):194–211.

Diaz, Kevin. 2005. "Gutknecht Says He Won't Play 'Kingmaker' for Kennedy." *Star Tribune*, March 5, 1B.

Diaz, Kevin and Pat Doyle. 2010. "Dayton Has a Record of Going It Alone: The Former U.S. Senator Has Always Been Liberal, but Not Always Predictable." *Star Tribune*, October 18.

Djupe, Paul A. and David A. M. Peterson. 2002. "The Impact of Negative Campaigning: Evidence from the 1998 Senatorial Primaries." *Political Research Quarterly* 55(4):845–60.

Dominguez, Casey B. K. 2005. *Before the Primary: Party Participation in Congressional Nominating Processes*. Ph.D Dissertation, Berkeley, CA: University of California.

2011. "Does the Party Matter? Endorsements in Congressional Primaries." *Political Research Quarterly* 64(3):534–44.

Dowdle, Andrew J., Scott Limbocker, Song Yang, Karen Sebold, and Patrick A. Stewart. 2013. "Why Contested Primaries May Not Be Divisive Primaries." Pp. 1–15 in *The Invisible Hands of Political Parties in Presidential Elections*, edited by Andrew J. Dowdle, Scott Limbocker, Song Yan, Karen Sebold, and Patrick A. Stewart. New York: Palgrave Macmillan US.

Downs, Anthony. 1957. *An Economic Theory of Democracy*. New York: Harper and Row.

Doyle, Pat. 2008. "Ciresi in Parting: Choose Wisely – The DFLer Leaves the U.S. Senate Race, Saying the Real Opponent Is GOP Incumbent Coleman." *Star Tribune*, March 11.

Dwyre, Diana, Eric S. Heberlig, Robin Kolodny, and Bruce Larson. 2006. "Committees and Candidates: National Party Finance after BCRA." Pp. 95–112 in *The State of the Parties*, edited by John C. Green and Daniel Coffey. Lanham, MD: Rowman and Littlefield.

Dwyre, Diana and Robin Kolodny. 2003. "The Committee Shuffle: Major Party Spending in Congressional Elections." Pp. 115–31 in *The State of the Parties*, edited by John C. Green and Richard Farmer. Lanham, MD: Rowman and Littlefield.

Dynes, Adam M., Hans J. G. Hassell, and Matthew R. Miles. 2016. "Personality Traits, Candidate Emergence, and Political Ambition: How Personality

Affects Who Represents Us." *Meetings of the American Political Science Association.*

Ellis, Ronnie. 2009. "Prominent Republicans Named to Grayson's Finance Committee." *Sentinel Echo*, May 28, 5747.

Ensley, Michael J. 2012. "Incumbent Positioning, Ideological Heterogeneity and Mobilization in U.S. House Elections." *Public Choice* 151(1–2):43–61.

Ezra, Marni. 1996. *The Benefits and Burdens of Congressional Primary Elections.* Washington, DC: American University Press.

Fahrenthold, David A. 2016. "Nev. Candidate Says Reid Urged Him to Quit, Because 'A Muslim Cannot Win This Race.'" *Washington Post*, March 29.

Farber, Dan. 2010. "Christine O'Donnell TV Ad: 'I'm Not a Witch … I'm You.'" *CBS News*, October 5.

Farhi, Paul. 2004. "Bunning's Wild Pitches Tighten Kentucky Senate Race." *Washington Post*, October 15.

Fenno, Richard F. 1978. *Home Style: House Members in Their Districts.* Boston, MA: Little, Brown.

Fiorina, Morris P. 1977. "The Case of the Vanishing Marginals: The Bureaucracy Did It." *American Political Science Review* 71(1):177–81.

Fiorina, Morris P. and Samuel J. Abrams. 2009. *Disconnect: The Breakdown of Representation in American Politics.* Norman, OK: University of Oklahoma Press.

La Follette, Robert. 1898. *Primary Elections for the Nomination of All Candidates by Australian Ballot Address Delivered Before.* Ann Arbor, MI: University of Michigan (March 12).

 1913. *La Follette's Autobiography: A Personal Narrative of Political Experiences.* Madison, WI: Robert M. La Follette Company.

Forliti, Amy. 2005. "Grams Drops Out of 2006 Senate Race: Former Senator Says He'll Back GOP Nominee." *Pioneer Press*, April 25.

Fort Wayne, News-Sentinal. 2015. "'Tea Party-Backed Rival' Would Not Just Go Along: How Has that 'Republican Establishment' Been Working Out for You?" *Fort Wayne News-Sentinal*, October 16, 6A.

Fox, Richard L. and Jennifer L. Lawless. 2010. "If Only They'd Ask: Gender, Recruitment, and Political Ambition." *Journal of Politics* 72(2):310–26.

Fraga, Bernard L. and Hans J. G. Hassell. 2017. "Are Minority Candidates Penalized by Party Politics?" *Meetings of the American Political Science Association.*

Francisco, Brian. 2015. "Senate Candidates Raise Funds Far from Home." *Journal Gazette (Fort Wayne, IN)*, October 31, 1A.

 2016. "2 Left in GOP Senate Race – Holcomb Quits; Could Be Next Lieutenant Governor." *Journal Gazette (Fort Wayne, IN)*, February 9, 1C.

Fritze, John. 2010. "Giuliani Backs Grayson in Kentucky GOP Primary." *USA Today*, April 19.

Frommer, Frederic J. 2006. "Gutknecht Contemplates Life After Congress." *Post Bulletin*, December 9.

Galderisi, Peter F., Marni Ezra, and Michael Lyons. 1982. "Is the Direct Primary a Threat to Party Maintenance? The Divisive Primary Revisited, Again." Meetings of the Midwest Political Science Association.

Garrett, R. Sam. 2014. *Increased Campaign Contribution Limits in the FY2015 Omnibus Appropriations Law: Frequently Asked Questions*, R43825. Washington, DC: Congressional Research Service 7–5700.

Gilbert, Christopher P. 1995. "Christians and Quistians in Minnesota." *PS: Political Science & Politics* 28(1):20–23.

Goldmacher, Shane. 2013. "Why Would Anyone Ever Want to Run for Congress?" *The Atlantic*, April 19.

Goodliffe, Jay and David B. Magleby. 2001. "Campaign Finance in U.S. House Primary and General Elections." Pp. 62–76 in *Congressional Primaries and the Politics of Representation*, edited by Peter Galderisi, Marni Ezra, and Michael Lyons. Lanham: Rowman and Littlefield.

Gram, David. 2005. "Dubie Seeks Donations for Possible Senate Bid." *Times Argus*, August 23.

Grant, David. 2012. "If GOP Misfires on Bid for Senate Takeover, Is Tea Party to Blame." *Christian Science Monitor*, November 6.

Greenfield, Daniel. 2015. "Move to the Right to Win Minority Votes." *Frontpage Mag*, October 23.

Grossmann, Matt and Casey B. K. Dominguez. 2009. "Party Coalitions and Interest Group Networks." *American Politics Research* 37(5):767–800.

Grossmann, Matt and David A. Hopkins. 2015. "Ideological Republicans and Group Interest Democrats: The Asymmetry of American Party Politics." *Perspectives on Politics* 13(1):119–39.

    2016. *Asymmetric Politics: Ideological Republicans and Group Interest Democrats*. New York: Oxford University Press.

Grow, Doug. 2011. "Mark Dayton's Turnaround: How Can a 'Failing' Senator Seem to Have the Makings of a Star Governor." *MinnPost*, April 25.

Gullan, Harold I. 2012. *Toomey's Triumph: Inside a Key Senate Campaign*. Philadelphia, PA: Temple University Press.

Hacker, Andrew. 1965. "Does a 'Divisive' Primary Harm a Candidate's Election Chances." *American Political Science Review* 59(1):105–10.

Hagen, Lisa. 2017. "Dems Crowd Primaries to Challenge GOP Reps." *The Hill*, May 26, 4–7.

Hall, Andrew B. 2015. "What Happens When Extremists Win Primaries?" *American Political Science Review* 109(1):1–46.

Hammer, David. 2005. "Hackett Sticks to Bid for Senate." *Cincinnati Post*, December 6, A1.

    2006. "Dems to Hackett: Run for House." *Cincinnati Post*, February 13, A2.

Harvey, Anna and Bumba Mukherjee. 2006. "Electoral Institutions and the Evolution of Partisan Conventions, 1880–1940." *American Politics Research* 34(3):368–98.

Hasen, Richard L. 2008. "Political Equality, the Internet, and Campaign Finance Regulation." *The Forum* 6(1):Article 7.

Hassell, Hans J. G. 2007. "Managing Conflict: The Preliminary Phases of the 2006 Minnesota Senate Race." *Meetings of the Midwest Political Science Association*.

    2012. "*The Party's Primary: The Influence of the Party Hill Committees in Primary Elections for the House and Senate*." San Diego, CA: University of California.

2016. "Party Control of Party Primaries: Party Influence in Nominations for the U.S. Senate." *Journal of Politics* 78(1):75–87.

Hassell, Hans J. G. and Nicholas Marn. 2015. "Message Bias: Campaign Strategy As Seen Through TV, Mail, Print, and Electronic Communications." *Meetings of the Midwest Political Science Association.*

Hassell, Hans J. G. and Kelly R. Oeltjenbruns. 2016. "When to Attack: The Trajectory of Congressional Campaign Negativity." *American Politics Research* 44(2):222–46.

Haynes, John Earl. 1984. *Dubious Alliance: The Making of Minnesota's DFL Party.* Minneapolis, MN: University of Minnesota Press.

Heersink, Boris. 2016. "Party Brands and the Democratic and Republican National Committees." *Meetings of the American Political Science Association.*

Hennings, Valerie M. and R. Urbatsch. 2016. "Gender, Partisanship, and Candidate-Selection Mechanisms." *State Politics & Policy Quarterly* 16(3):290–312.

Herrnson, Paul S. 1986. "Do Parties Make a Difference? The Role of Party Organizations in Congressional Elections." *Journal of Politics* 48(3):589–615.

1988. *Party Campaigning in the 1980s.* Cambridge: Harvard University Press.

2005. "National Party Organizations at the Dawn of the Twenty-First Centruy." Pp. 47–78 in *The Parties Respond: Changes in American Parties and Campaigns,* edited by L. Sandy Maisel. Cambridge: Westview Press.

2009. "The Roles of Party Organizations, Party-Connected Committees, and Party Allies in Elections." *Journal of Politics* 71(4):1207–24.

Herrnson, Paul S. and James G. Gimpel. 1995. "District Conditions and Primary Divisiveness in Congressional Elections." *Political Research Quarterly* 48(1):117–34.

Hershey, William. 2005. "Candidates Stake Positions for '06 Elections – Hackett May Seek U.S. Senate Seat." *Dayton Daily News*, September 20, B2.

Hicks, Raymond and Dustin Tingley. 2011. "Causal Mediation Analysis." *The Stata Journal* 11(4):609–15.

Hill, Seth J. 2015. "Two-Step To Win: Balancing Representation of Primary and General Electorates in Congress." *Meetings of the Midwest Political Science Association.*

Hill, Seth J. and Chris Tausanovitch. 2015. "A Disconnect in Representation? Comparison of Trends in Congressional and Public Polarization." *Journal of Politics* 77(4):1058–75.

Hinckley, Katherine A. and John C. Green. 1996. "Fund-Raising in Presidential Nomination Campaigns: The Primary Lessons of 1988." *Political Research Quarterly* 49(4):693–718.

Hirano, Shigeo, James M. Snyder, Stephen Ansolabehere, and John Mark Hansen. 2010. "Primary Elections and Partisan Polarization in the US Congress." *Quarterly Journal of Political Science* 5(2):169–91.

Hofstadter, Richard. 1955. *The Age of Reform.* New York: Vintage Books.

1969. *The Idea of a Party System: The Rise of Legitimate Opposition in the United States, 1780–1840.* Berkeley, CA: University of California Press.

Homans, Charles. 2005. "Grams Runs Against Odds His Profile Is Low, His Party Unsupportive." *Pioneer Press*, March 28, B1.

Honolulu Star-Bulletin. 2010. "Case Pulls Out of Congressional Race." May 30.

Horstman, Barry M. 2005. "A Race of a Different Sort – Iraq War Veteran Makes Run for Rob Portman's Seat Interesting." *Cincinnati Post*, July 30, A1.

Hotakainen, Rob, Dane Smith, and Paul Sand. 2005. "Filling Dayton's Seat – Senate Race: The Ins, Outs, Maybes – Grams Will Run; Franken Won't; Kennedy Readies." *Star Tribune*, February 11.

Howey, Brian. 2015a. "Howey: A Fascinating U.S. Senate Race Is Setting Up." *News and Tribune*, May.

2015b. "If Sen. Coats Doesn't Run, Who Does?" *Hendricks County Flyer*, January 22.

2016. "Holcomb In, Ellspermann Out, in Indianapolis Drama." *Elkhart Truth*, February 13, A4.

Imai, Kosuke, Luke Keele, and Dustin Tingley. 2010. "A General Approach to Causal Mediation Analysis." *Psychological Methods* 15(4):309–34.

Imai, Kosuke, Luke Keele, Dustin Tingley, and Teppei Yamamoto. 2011. "Unpacking the Black Box of Causality: Learning About Causal Mechanisms from Experimental and Observational Studies." *American Political Science Review* 105(4):765–89.

Iowa Starting Line. 2015. "Shocker: Ravi Patel Withdraws from 1st District Race." *Iowa Starting Line*, June 23.

Iyengar, Shanto and Donald R. Kinder. 1987. *News That Matters*. Chicago, IL: University of Chicago Press.

Jacobson, Gary C. 1978. "The Effects of Campaign Spending in Congressional Elections." *American Political Science Review* 72(2):469–91.

1980. *Money in Congressional Elections*. New Haven, CT: Yale University Press.

1989. "Strategic Politicians and the Dynamics of U.S. House Elections, 1946–86." *American Political Science Review* 83(3):773–93.

2010. "A Collective Dilemma Solved: The Distribution of Party Campaign Resources in the 2006 and 2008 Congressional Elections." *Election Law Journal* 9(4):46–49.

Jacobson, Gary C. and Samuel Kernell. 1981. *Strategy and Choice in Congressional Elections*. New Haven, CT: Yale University Press.

Jewell, Malcolm E. and Sarah M. Morehouse. 2001. *Political Parties and Elections in American States*. 4th ed. Washington, DC: CQ Press.

Jewitt, Caitlin E. and Sarah A. Treul. 2014. "Competitive Primaries and Party Division in Congressional Elections." *Electoral Studies* 35:140–49.

Johnson, Dennis W. 2007. *No Place of Amateurs: How Political Consultants Are Reshaping American Democracy*. 2nd ed. New York: Routledge.

Johnson, Donald Bruce and James R. Gibson. 1974. "The Divisive Primary Revisited: Party Activists in Iowa." *American Political Science Review* 68(1):67–77.

Johnson, Gregg B., Meredith-Joy Petersheim, and Jesse T. Wasson. 2010. "Divisive Primaries and Incumbent General Election Performance: Prospects and Costs in U.S. House Races." *American Politics Research* 38(5):931–55.

Joseph, Cameron. 2015. "Chief of Staff Launches Senate Bid for Coats's Seat." *The Hill*, March 26.

Kaplan, Rebecca. 2014. "Why Outgoing Presidents Stay Off the Campaign Trail." *CBS News*, November 24.

Karon, Tony. 2001. "How Jim Jeffords Changed the World." *Time*, May 29.

Kazee, Thomas A. and Mary C. Thornberry. 1990. "Where's the Party? Congressional Candidate Recruitment and American Party Organizations." *Western Political Quarterly* 43(1):61–80.

Kenney, Patrick J. and Tom W. Rice. 1984. "The Effect of Primary Divisiveness in Gubernatorial and Senatorial Elections." *Journal of Politics* 46(3):904–15.

   1987. "The Relationship between Divisive Primaries and General Election Outcomes." *American Journal of Political Science* 31(1):31–44.

Key, V. O. 1949. *Southern Politics in State and Nation*. Knoxville, TN: University of Tennessee Press.

   1964. *Politics, Parties, and Pressure Groups*. New York: Crowell.

Koger, Gregory, Seth E. Masket, and Hans Noel. 2009. "Cooperative Party Factions in American Politics." *American Politics Research* 38(1):33–53.

Kolodny, Robin. 1998. *Pursuing Majorities: Congressional Campaign Committees in American Politics*. Norman, OK: University of Oklahoma Press.

Kolodny, Robin and David A. Dulio. 2003. "Political Party Adaptation in US Congressional Campaigns: Why Political Parties Use Coordinated Expenditures to Hire Political Consultants." *Party Politics* 9(6):729–46.

Kolodny, Robin and Angela Logan. 1998. "Political Consultants and the Extension of Party Goals." *PS: Political Science & Politics* 31(2):155–9.

Kousser, Thad, Scott Lucas, Seth E. Masket, and Eric McGhee. 2015. "Kingmakers or Cheerleaders? Party Power and the Causal Effects of Endorsements." *Political Research Quarterly* 68(3):443–56.

Krawzak, Paul M. 2006. "Ryan, Brown Consider Challenging DeWine for His Senate Seat." *The Repository*, July 26.

Laffey, Steve. 2007. *Primary Mistake: How the Washington Establishment Lost Everything in 2006 (and Sabotaged My Senatorial Campaign)*. New York: Sentinel.

Lasswell, Harold D. 1948. *Power and Personality*. New York: Norton.

Lawrence, Eric, Todd Donovan, and Shaun Bowler. 2011. "The Adoption of Direct Primaries in the United States." *Party Politics* 19(1):3–18.

Lazarus, Jeffrey. 2005. "Unintended Consequences: Anticipation of General Election Outcomes and Primary Election Divisiveness." *Legislative Studies Quarterly* 30(3):435–61.

Lewis, David. 1969. *Convention: A Philosophical Study*. Cambridge, MA: Harvard University Press.

Lillis, Mike. 2011. "Issa Says He Won't Investigate White House Job Offer to Rep. Sestak." *The Hill*, January 2.

Lindenberger, Michael A. 2009. "How Mitch McConnell Ended Jim Bunning's Career." *Time Magazine*, July.

Lopez, Patricia. 2006a. "Is Wetterling About to Leave Senate Race? – The DFL Candidate Has Scheduled a News Conference Today Amid Speculation That She Will Be Ending Her Campaign." *Star Tribune*, January 20.

   2006b. "Senate Race Puts State in Spotlight; Minnesota's Contest Has Defined Itself Quickly, a Sign of Intense National Interest." *Star Tribune*, February 12, 1A.

*Los Angeles Herald*. 1908. "Great Welcome Is Given Heney." *Los Angeles Herald*, May 3, 3–4.

Lublin, David Ian. 1994. "Quality, Not Quantity: Strategic Politicians in U.S. Senate Elections, 1952–1990." *Journal of Politics* 56(1):228–41.

Lynch, Julia F. 2013. "Aligning Sampling Strategies with Analytical Goals." Pp. 31–44 in *Interview Research in Political Science*. Ithaca, NY: Cornell University Press.

Maestas, Cherie D., Sarah Fulton, L. Sandy Maisel, and Walter J. Stone. 2006. "When to Risk It? Institutions, Ambitions, and the Decision to Run for the U.S. House." *American Political Science Review* 100(2):195–208.

Maestas, Cherie D., L. Sandy Maisel, and Walter J. Stone. 2005. "National Party Efforts to Recruit State Legislators to Run for the U.S. House." *Legislative Studies Quarterly* 30(2):277–300.

Maisel, L. Sandy. 1982. *From Obscurity to Oblivion: Running in the Congressional Primary*. Knoxville, TN: University of Tennessee Press.

Maisel, L. Sandy and Walter J. Stone. 1997. "Determinants of Candidate Emergence in U. S. House Elections: An Exploratory Study." *Legislative Studies Quarterly* 22(1):79–96.

Mann, Thomas E. and Norman J. Ornstein. 2012. *It's Even Worse Than It Looks: How the American Constitutional System Collided with the New Politics of Extremism*. New York: Basic Books.

Martin, Jonathan. 2010. "DCCC to Highlight 'Palin's Primaries'." *Politico*, February, 23.

Marx, Claude R. 2004. "Parke Targets Sanders, Then Pulls the Ad." *Times Argus*, October 30.

Masket, Seth E. 2009. *No Middle Ground: How Informal Party Organizations Control Nominations and Polarize Legislatures*. Ann Arbor, MI: University of Michigan Press.

2011. "The Circus That Wasn't: The Republican Party's Quest for Order in California's 2003 Gubernatorial Recall Election." *State Politics & Policy Quarterly* 11(2):123–47.

2016. *The Inevitable Party: Why Attempts to Kill the Party System Fail and How They Weaken Democracy*. New York: Oxford University Press.

Masket, Seth E., Michael T. Heaney, Joanne M. Miller, and Dara Z. Strolovich. 2012. "Polarized Networks: The Organizational Affiliations of National Party Convention Delegates." *American Behavioral Scientist* 56(12):1654–76.

Matthews, Donald R. 1984. "Legislative Recruitment and Legislative Careers." *Legislative Studies Quarterly* 9(4):547–85.

Mayhew, David R. 1974. *Congress: The Electoral Connection*. 1st ed. New Haven, CT: Yale University Press.

McCallum, Laura. 2000. "Senate Candidate Profile: Mike Ciresi." *Minnesota Public Radio*, August 14.

McCarty, Nolan M., Keith T. Poole, and Howard Rosenthal. 2006. *Polarized America: The Dance of Ideology and Unequal Riches*. Cambridge, MA: The MIT Press.

McCarty, Nolan M., Jonathan Rodden, Boris Shor, Chris Tausanovitch, and Christopher Warshaw. 2014. "Geography, Uncertainty, and Polarization." *Meetings of the European Political Science Association*.

Medvic, Stephen K. 2001. *Political Consultants in U.S. Congressional Elections.* Ohio State University Press.

Menefee-Libey, David. 2000. *The Triumph of Campaign-Centered Politics.* New York: Chatham House Publishers.

Merriam, Charles E. 1923. "Nominating Systems." *Annals of the American Academy of Political and Social Science* 106(1):1–10.

Merriam, Charles E. and Louise Overacker. 1928. *Primary Elections.* Chicago, IL: University of Chicago Press.

Miller, Sean J. 2010. "Ed Case Ends His Campaign for Hawaii House Seat." *The Hill,* May 30.

Miller, Penny M., Malcolm E. Jewell, and Lee Sigelman. 1988. "Divisive Primaries and Party Activists: Kentucky, 1979 and 1983." *Journal of Politics* 50(2):459–70.

Morehouse, Sarah M. 1990. "Money versus Party Effort: Nominating for Governor." *American Journal of Political Science* 34(3):706–24.

Mosley, Layna. 2013. "Just Talk to People? Interviews in Contemporary Political Science." Pp. 1–28 in *Interview Research in Political Science,* edited by Layna Mosley. Ithaca, NY: Cornell University Press.

Musgrave, Beth. 2009. "Grayson Signing Up Influential Republicans." *Lexington Herald-Leader,* May 22, C2.

Mutz, Diana C. 1995. "Effects of Horse-Race Coverage on Campaign Coffers: Strategic Contributing in Presidential Primaries." *Journal of Politics* 57(4):1015–42.

National Public Radio. 2002. "Sen. Paul Wellstone, 1944–2002." *NPR,* October 25.

Nesmith, Bruce. 1995. "Rosy Scenario: The Republican-White Evangelical Alliance Holds in Iowa." *PS: Political Science & Politics* 28(1):18–20.

Neustadt, Richard. 1960. *Presidential Power.* New York: Macmillan.

*New York Times.* 2005. "Senator Mark Dayton Will Not Run for Re-Election." *New York Times,* February 9.

Niedzwiadek, Nick. 2016. "Appellate Court Cancels Special GOP Primary in 3rd Congressional District." *Politico,* September 14.

Nielson, Lindsay and Neil Visalvanich. 2015. "Primaries and Candidates: Examining the Influence of Primary Electorates on Candidate Ideology." *Political Science Research and Methods* 5(2):397–408.

Niven, David. 2006. "Throwing Your Hat Out of the Ring: Negative Recruitment and the Gender Imbalance in State Legislative Candidacy." *Politics & Gender* 2(4):473–89.

Noel, Hans. 2013. *Political Ideologies and Political Parties in America.* New York: Cambridge University Press.

2016. "Sanders Needs Open Primaries Because He's Not Winning Democrats." *Vox,* April 25.

Norrander, Barbara. 2000. "The End Game in Post-Reform Presidential Nominations." *Journal of Politics* 62(4):999–1013.

2006. "The Attrition Game: Initial Resources, Initial Contests and the Exit of Candidates during the US Presidential Primary Season." *British Journal of Political Science* 36(3):487–507.

Norris, George W. 1923. "Why I Believe in the Direct Primary." *The Annals of the American Academy of Political and Social Science* 106(1):22–30.

North Star Politics. 2006. "Breaking News." northstarpolitics.blogspot.com. Retrieved January 1, 2016 (http://northstarpolitics.blogspot.com/2006/02/breaking-news.html).

Nyhan, Brendan and Jacob M. Montgomery. 2015. "Connecting the Candidates: Consultant Networks and the Diffusion of Campaign Strategy in American Congressional Elections." *American Journal of Political Science* 59(2):292–308.

O'Brien, Robert M. 2007. "A Caution Regarding Rules of Thumb for Variance Inflation Factors." *Quality and Quantity* 41(5):673–90.

O'Keefe, Ed. 2016. "This Is the Last Stand for the 'Never Trump' Movement. Here's What Might Happen." *Washington Post*, July 13.

Obeidallah, Dean. 2016. "Harry Reid Tells Muslim Congressional Candidate: Get Out of the Race." *The Daily Beast*, April 5.

Osowski, Zach. 2016. "'An Orderly Transition' – Pence Selects Eric Holcomb as His Next Running Mate." *Courier & Press*, February 10, 1A.

Pang, Gordon Y. K. 2010. "Democrats Shift Focus to Primary." *Honolulu Advertiser*, May 23.

Parker, Chris. 2005. "Shepard, Dubie Test State GOP Waters." *Bennington Banner*, September 17.

Pathé, Simone. 2015a. "Colorado Candidate 'Immediately Serious' with $1M Loan." *Roll Call*, July 20.

2015b. "Democrats Land Mike Coffman Challenger in Colorado." *Roll Call*, July 7.

2016. "Democrats Land Reid Recruit in Competitive Nevada District." *Roll Call*, January 26.

Peoples, Steve. 2016. "Many Experienced GOP Strategists Unwilling to Work for Trump." *PBS Newshour*, June 25.

Pershing, Ben and Chris Cillizza. 2009. "Under Pressure to Retire, Bunning Announces Plans to Quit Senate." *Washington Post*, July 28.

Persily, Nathaniel. 2015. "Stronger Parties as a Solution to Polarization." Pp. 123–36 in *Solutions to Political Polarization in America*, edited by Nathanial Persily. New York: Cambridge University Press.

Phillip, E. L. 1909. "The Revolution of the Primary Under Leadership of La Follette." *Milwaukee Sentinal*, October 10.

Piereson, James E. and Terry B. Smith. 1975. "Primary Divisiveness and General Election Success: A Re-Examination." *Journal of Politics* 37(2):555–62.

Pore, Robert. 2007. "Immigrant Issues to Go Before Senate Next Week – Hagel Says Congress Must Act Quickly; Nelson Contends That Border Must Be Secured First." *Grand Island Independent*, May 11.

Porter, Louis. 2005a. "Dubie Off to School for Senate Candidates." *Times Argus*, June 3.

2005b. "Dubie Opts Out of U.S. Senate Race." *Times Argus*, October 27.

Preece, Jessica Robinson and Olga Stoddard. 2015. "Does the Message Matter? A Field Experiment on Political Party Recruitment." *Journal of Experimental Political Science* 2(1):26–35.

Prewitt, Kenneth. 1970. "Political Ambitions, Volunteerism, and Electoral Accountability." *American Political Science Review* 64(1):5–17.

Provance, Jim. 2005. "Sherrod Brown's Advocates Saddened Polls Can't Convince Him to Seek Senate." *The Blade*, August 19, A3.

Quinn, Francis X. 2000. "Unopposed Green Party Candidate Loses Race with Zero Votes." *Bangor Daily News*, July 14.

La Raja, Raymond J. 2008. *Small Change: Money, Political Parties, and Campaign Finance Reform*. Ann Arbor, MI: University of Michigan Press.

La Raja, Raymond J. and Brian F. Schaffner. 2015. *Campaign Finance and Political Polarization: When Purists Prevail*. Ann Arbor, MI: University of Michigan Press.

La Raja, Raymond J. and David L. Wiltse. 2011. "Don't Blame Donors for Ideological Polarization of Political Parties: Ideological Change and Stability Among Political Contributors, 1972-2008." *American Politics Research* 40(3):501–30.

Raju, Manu. 2012. "Richard Mourdock Under Fire for Rape Remarks." *Politico*, October 23.

Rakove, Milton. 1975. *Don't Make No Waves, Don't Back No Losers: An Insider's Account of the Daley Machine*. Bloomington, IN: Indiana University Press.

Ranney, Austin. 1975. *Curing the Mischiefs of Faction: Party Reform in America*. Berkeley, CA: University of California Press.

Reeve, Elspeth. 2012. "Meet Chuck Hagel, Your 'Likely' New Secretary of Defense." *The Wire*, December 12.

Republican Minnesota. 2006. "Ciresi Pushed Out?" RepublicanMinnesota .blogspot.com. Retrieved January 1, 2016 (http://republicanminnesota .blogspot.com/2006/02/ciresi-pushed-out.html).

Reuters. 2006. "Democrats Lose House Race in Ohio, But Celebrate the Margin." *New York Times*, August 3, A1.

Reyes, B. J. 2010. "Djou Wins U.S. House Seat – The GOP Trumpets a Victory on Obama's Home Turf, While Dems Promise to Regroup." *Honolulu Star-Bulletin*, May 23.

Riley, Brendan. 2009. "Congressman Hedges on Senate Bid." *Associated Press*, April 17.

Riskind, Jonathan and Tom Bell. 2012. "Under Pressure, Michaud Skips Race for Senate." *Press Herald*, March 1.

Rohde, David W. 1979. "Risk-Bearing and Progressive Ambition: The Case of Members of the United States House of Representatives." *American Journal of Political Science* 23(1):1–26.

Rose, Alex. 2010. "Sestak, White House Still Mum on Alleged Job Offer." *Delaware County Daily Times*, May 25.

Rozell, Mark J. 1995. *God at the Grass Roots: The Christian Right in the 1994 Elections*. Lanham, MD: Rowman & Littlefield.

Rudin, Ken. 2010. "Hawaii's Abercrombie to Resign House Seat Next Month to Focus on Gov Race." *NPR*, January 5.

Salisbury, Bill and Jim Ragsdale. 2001. "Pawlenty Abandons Senate Run: Cheney Asks Him to Defer to Coleman; He'll Ponder Options." *Pioneer Press*, April 19, 1A.

Schantz, Harvey L. 1980. "Contested and Uncontested Primaries for the U. S. House." *Legislative Studies Quarterly* 5(4):545–62.

Schelling, Thomas C. 1960. *The Strategy of Conflict*. Cambridge, MA: Harvard University Press.

Schlesinger, Joseph A. 1966. *Ambition and Politics: Political Careers in the United States*. Chicago, IL: Rand McNally.

1991. *Political Parties and the Winning of Office*. Ann Arbor, MI: University of Michigan Press.

Schumer, Charles E. 2014. "End Partisan Primaries, Save America." *New York Times*, July 21, A21.

Sclar, Jason, Alexander Hertel-Fernandez, Theda Skocpol, and Vanessa Williamson. 2016. "Donor Consortia on the Left and Right: Comparing the Membership, Activities, and Impact of the Democracy Alliance and Koch Seminars." *Meetings of the Midwest Political Science Association*.

Scott, Janny. 2007. "Different Paths From Vietnam to War in Iraq." *New York Times*, March 18, A1.

Seligman, Lester G. 1961. "Political Recruitment and Party Structure: A Case Study." *American Political Science Review* 55(1):77–86.

Seligman, Lester G., Michael R. King, Chong Lim Kim, and Roland E. Smith. 1974. *Patterns of Recruitment: A State Chooses Its Lawmakers*. Chicago, IL: Rand McNally College Publishing Company.

Sewell, Dan. 2005a. "Iraq War Vet to Face Brown in Senate Bid – 'Citizen Legislator,' 7-Term Congressman Compete to Unseat Republican DeWine." *Akron Beacon Journal*, October 25, B1.

2005b. "Losing Ohio Congressional Candidate Still Drawing National Attention." *Associated Press*, August 29.

2005c. "The Loser's a Winner – 'Media-Genic' Hackett Being Hailed for Future Offices." *Cincinnati Post*, August 27, A1.

Sharon, Susan. 2016. "Joe Baldacci Drops Out of Congressional Race." *Maine Public Radio*, February 5.

Shaw, Charley. 2005. "MN's GOP Faithful Should Embrace New Leader, Blogger Urges." *Legal Ledger*, June 16.

Shear, Michael D. and Matthew Rosenberg. 2016. "Released Emails Suggest the D.N.C. Derided the Sanders Campaign." *New York Times*, July 22, A10.

Shepherd, Michael. 2014. "Democrats Push for Cain vs. Poliquin 2016 Rematch in Maine's 2nd District." *Kennebec Journal*, November 14.

Sherry, Allison. 2010. "Buck Defeats Norton in Bruising GOP Primary for Senate Seat." *Denver Post*, August 10, A1.

Shraine, Brendan. 2011. "Ed Makes Case for Senate." *West Hawaii Today*, August 24.

Simpson, Kevin, Michael Booth, and Allison Sherry. 2010. "Bennet Wins in Senate Race." *Denver Post*, November 2, A1.

Sinclair, Betsy. 2012. *The Social Citizen*. Chicago, IL: University of Chicago Press.

Skinner, Richard M., Seth E. Masket, and David A. Dulio. 2013. "527 Committees, Formal Parties, and the Political Party Network." *The Forum* 11(2):137–56.

Skocpol, Theda. 2016. "When Wealthy Contributors Join Forces: New Research on Donor Consortia in U.S. Politics." *Ford Foundation Conference*.

Slodysko, Brian. 2015a. "GOP Campaigns to Succeed Sen. Coats Report Fundraising." *Associated Press*, October 14.

2015b. "Republican Field Appears Set in Race for Open US Senate Seat." *Associated Press*, September 15.

2016. "Ex-Indiana GOP Chairman Holcomb Drop US Senate Campaign." *Associated Press*, February 8.

Smith, Dane. 2001a. "Cheney Advises Pawlenty Not to Run for Senate; Majority Leader Bows to Request from White House." *Star Tribune*, April 19, 1A.

2001b. "Pawlenty Dons Running Shoes for Governor's Race – The House Majority Leader Has One Chief Rival so Far for the GOP Endorsement." *Star Tribune*, September 6, 1B.

2005. "GOP's Ron Eibensteiner Faces Challenge to Lead – Some in Party Say His Tenure Has Been a Failure." *Star Tribune*, June 8, 1A.

2006. "Will Summer Tiffs Hurt the DFL in This Fall's Elections? – A Bout of Infighting and Party Dissension Has Beset the DFL, Giving Great Glee to Political Foes." *Star Tribune*, July 13.

Sniderman, Paul M. and Michael Tomz. 2005. "Brand Names and the Organization of Mass Belief Systems." *Stanford University Working Paper*.

Squire, Peverill. 1992. "Challenger Quality and Voting Behavior in U.S. Senate Elections." *Legislative Studies Quarterly* 17(2):247–63.

Stamper, John. 2009. "Grayson: 'Some People in College Tried Pot. I Tried Clinton.'" *Lexington Herald-Leader*, August 1.

Stassen-Berger, Rachel E. 2005a. "Kennedy First Out of Gate to Chase U.S. Senate Seat – High-Profile Republicans Are Backing Congressman." *Pioneer Press*, February 12.

2005b. "Minnesota Politics – Gutknecht Will Seek Re-Election." *Pioneer Press*, March 5, B3.

2006a. "Ciresi Won't Run for Senate – He Cites Frustration with Inertia in D.C." *Pioneer Press*, February 9, B5.

2006b. "Wetterling Jumps Back in the Race – This Time for U.S. House, Again." *Pioneer Press*, February 4.

Stassen-Berger, Rachel E. and Bill Salisbury. 2005. "Kennedy Gets Nod From Pawlenty – McCollum Won't Run for Open Senate Seat." *Pioneer Press*, March 8.

Steen, Jennifer A. 2006. *Self-Financed Candidates in Congressional Elections*. Ann Arbor, MI: University of Michigan Press.

Steinhauer, Jennifer. 2015. "Through It All, Pelosi Keeps House Democrats Moving in One Direction." *The New York Times*, March 6.

von Sternberg, Bob. 2002. "Minnesota's Second District – GOP's Kline Defeats Four-Term Rep. Luther – The Third Time Was the Charm for John Kline, Whose Victory over Bill Luther Marks the First Time in 20 Years That Minnesota's Eight-Member House Delegation Does Not Have a Democratic Majority." *Star Tribune*, November 6, 20A.

Strassel, Kimberly. 2010. "WSJ: A Case of Hanabusa." *Hawaii Reporter*, June 4.

Sulkin, Tracy. 2009. "Campaign Appeals and Legislative Action." *Journal of Politics* 71(3):1093.

Sur, Peter. 2011. "Case, Inouye Cleared the Air." *Hawaii Tribune-Herald*, April 12.

SurveyUSA. 2006. *SurveyUSA News Poll #9977*. Clifton, NJ: SurveyUSA.

Tankersley, Jim. 2005a. "Brown's Jump into Senate Race Makes It a 3-Way Contest – Hackett's Run Still On, Aide Says." *The Blade*, October 7, A1.

2005b. "Brown Plans to Challenge DeWine for Senate Seat." *The Blade*, October 6, A1.

2005c. "Hackett Agrees to Challenge DeWine – U.S. Rep. Sherrod Brown Is Reconsidering His Decision Not to Run." *The Blade*, October 4, A3.

2005d. "Will DeWine Be Challenged? – $10M Campaign Frightens Off Opponents." *The Blade*, August 21, B1.

The Blade. 2005. "Sherrod Brown's Timidity." *The Blade*, August 21, B6.

The Green Papers. 2016. "Election Years in Which the DIRECT PRIMARY Has Been Specifically Authorized." Retrieved November 7, 2016 (www.thegreenpapers.com/Hx/DirectPrimaryElectionYears.phtml).

Theilmann, John and Allen Wilhite. 1986. "Differences in Campaign Funds: A Racial Explanation." *The Review of Black Political Economy* 15(1):45–58.

Thompson, Jake. 2007. "Closer to Joining the Fray – President Says Johanns Would Be Great Senator – Bush Sends His Ag Chief Home, Where He Likely Faces a Costly Primary." *World-Herald*, September 20.

Time. 2006. "Mark Dayton: The Blunderer." *Time*, May.

Times Argus. 2005. "Dubie's Prospects." *Times Argus*, September 26.

Tsai, Michael. 2009. "Hanabusa Enters Race for Congress." *Honolulu Advertiser*, October 1.

Tully, Matthew. 2014. "Tully: Dan Coats Weighing Another Term in Senate." *Indianapolis Star*, March 4.

Tysver, Robynn. 2007a. "Bruning Says Choice to End Bid Was His – The Attorney General Says He Acted to Avoid a Divisive Primary Against Mike Johanns, Not Because of GOP Pressure." *World-Herald*, November 21, 1A.

2007b. "Daub Give His Support to Johanns – Omaha's Ex-Mayor Leaves the Senate Race and Says He May Seek Office Again." *World-Herald*, September 28, 1A.

2007c. "Daub Says He'll Raise Funds for Senate Bid." *World-Herald*, May 15.

2015. "Citing Military and Foreign Policy as Priorities, Retired Brig. Gen. Don Bacon Announces Bid for Congress." *World-Herald*, March 25.

Tysver, Robynn and Leslie Reed. 2007. "Bruning Expected to End Bid for Senate – Fearing an Ugly Primary Battle, GOP Officials Are Said to Have Pressued the Attorney General Not to Challenge Mike Johanns." *World-Herald*, November 21, 1A.

Urbina, Ian. 2006. "Popular Ohio Democrat Drops Out of Race, and Perhaps Politics." *New York Times*, February 14.

Visalvanich, Neil, Keith E. Schnakenberg, and Hans J. G. Hassell. 2017. "Race, Representation, and Campaign Finance Networks: The Effect of Party Support on Minority Candidates." *Meetings of the Midwest Political Science Association*.

Walton, Don. 2007a. "Bruning Poll Shows Lead over Hagel." *Lincoln Journal Star*, April 24, B1.

2007b. "Daub Might Challenge Hagel: Ex-Omaha Mayor Now Raising Funds for a Possible Senate Bid." *Lincoln Journal Star*, B2.

2007c. "Don't Make Too Much of GOP Poll." *Lincoln Journal Star*, October 1.

2007d. "Kerrey, Johanns Stir Follows Hagel's Exit." *Lincoln Journal Star*, September 9.

Ware, Alan. 2002. *The American Direct Primary*. New York: Cambridge University Press.

Weiner, Rachel. 2013. "Karl Rove's New 'Conservative Victory Project' Earns Conservative Ire." *Washington Post*, February 4.

White, William Allen. 1910. *The Old Order Changeth: A View of American Democracy*. New York: Macmillan.

Whitlock, Craig. 2012. "Vietnam Scars Shape Hagel's Outlook." *Washington Post*, December 20.

Zdechlik, Mark. 2006. "DFLers Set To Endorse Klobuchar For Senate." *Minnesota Public Radio*, June 8.

Zeleny, Jeff. 2013. "Top Donors to Republicans Seek More Say in Senate Races." *New York Times*, February 3, A1.

Zimmerman, Malia. 2006. "Bucking the Old Boys – Ed Case Says Chance 'Em, Makes a Run for Congress Despite Threats from Some of Hawaii's Most Senior Politicians." *Hawaii Reporter*, January 20.

# Index